D0944542

Not Just Any Land

st Any Land Not Just Any Land Not Just Any Land Not Just Any Land Not Just Any Land Not Just Any Land Not

Any Land Not Just Any Land **Not Just Any Land** Not Just Any Land Not Just Any Land Not Just Any Land N

A Personal and Literary Journey into the American Grasslands

JOHN PRICE

University of Nebraska Press : Lincoln & London

Acknowledgments for previously published material
appear on pages x–xi.

Library of Congress Cataloging-in-Publication Data
Price, John, 1966–
Not just any land : a personal and literary journey
into the American grasslands / John Price.
p. cm. Includes bibliographical references.
ISBN 0-8032-3707-3 (cloth : alkaline paper)
1. American prose literature – Great Plains – History
and criticism. 2. Price, John, 1966 – Homes and
haunts – Great Plains. 3. Authors, American – Homes
and haunts – Great Plains. 4. Great Plains –
Biography – History and criticism. 5. Great Plains –
Intellectual life – 20th century. 6. Great Plains –
Description and travel. 7. Heat Moon, William Least –
Interviews. 8. O'Brien, Dan, 1947 – Interviews.
9. Hasselstrom, Linda M. – Interviews. 10. Swander,
Mary – Interviews. 11. Grasslands – West (U.S.)
I. Title.
PS274 .P75 2004   810.9′978 – dc22   2003016610

For my parents

And Stephanie

Contents

Acknowledgments

This is a memoir. It recalls a time, nearly a decade ago, when I embarked on a personal and literary journey to better understand my relationship to home. The narrator is also of that time, and though my life has moved forward and my thinking about the issues has expanded—thanks to, among other things, the growing number of authors and scholars in the field—I have done my best to stay close to that earlier self, however limited. To do otherwise would be to violate the original intention of the book, which is to bear witness to the beginning of one writer's conscious commitment to place. So much of contemporary environmental writing focuses on those who are already inside commitment and not enough on those who are struggling to find the door. Finding that door is often an awkward, contradictory, and painful process—but also humorous, inspiring, and transformative. To these readers, I hope this book is of some help.

The memoir form has posed additional challenges with regard to the authors I interviewed. Their lives and careers, like mine, have moved forward. I've tried to provide brief updates in the notes, but I encourage those interested in catching up with the lives of these writers to read their more recent nonfiction, some of which I've listed in the bibliography. What hasn't changed, however, is my debt of gratitude to Dan, Linda, William, and Mary—for their books and their personal generosity. It began when they answered the inquiries of an unknown graduate student, agreeing to lengthy interviews and, in some cases, inviting him into their lives. They have continued to be generous, providing honest and constructive suggestions during the revision process. I cannot express in words my appreciation —without their example, I would not have found my way home as a writer.

There are many others who made this book possible. In addition to those mentioned in the chapters, I'd like to thank those who read and commented on earlier drafts, those who assisted me in my research by providing essential information and insights, and those who offered encouragement during the writing process. These include Marilyn Abildskov, Karla Armbruster, Thomas Fox Averill, Jenn Backer, Julene Bair, Isabel Barros, Frank Bramlett, Tracy Bridgeford, Christopher Cokinos, Diane Comer, Carol de Saint Victor, Paul Diehl, Kathleen Diffley, Elizabeth Dodd, Ellen Fagg, Ed Folsom, Patricia Hampl, Jim Hoy, Wes Jackson, Charles Johanningsmeier, Elizabeth Kaplan, Joni Kinsey, Carl Klaus, Joan Latchaw, Harvey Leavitt, Tom Lutz, Susan McCollum, John McKenna, Michele Morano, Andy Nesler, David Peterson, Joseph Price, Diane Quantic, Dale Rigby, Barbara Robins, Dan Roche, Loberta Runge, Kent Ryden, Gregory Sadlek, Robert Sayre, Michael Skau, Phil Smith, Lloyd Strine, Ned Stuckey-French, Mary Trachsel, Kathy Wallace, and my students. Special thanks go to Thomas Simmons at the University of Iowa, whose vision and guidance made it possible to begin; Susan Maher at the University of Nebraska at Omaha, whose wisdom and encouragement made it possible to finish; and Elmar Lueth, whose friendship sustained me throughout.

Completing this book was facilitated by a UCR Summer Grant awarded by the University of Nebraska at Omaha and by a Prairie Lights/Sherman Paul Scholarship awarded by the University of Iowa English Department. I am also indebted to the English Department at the University of Nebraska at Omaha for granting me a course release during the final stages of revision.

Thanks as well to those who allowed me to use previously published material. Chapter 3 was originally published as "Not Just Any Land: Linda Hasselstrom at Home on the American Grasslands," in *Breaking Boundaries: New Perspectives on Women's Regional Writings,* ed. Shari A. Inness and Diana Royer (Iowa City: University of Iowa Press, 1997), 237–58. Reprinted with permission. Chapter 6 originally appeared as "What This Prairie Will Awaken," *Organization and Environment* 11 (September 1998): 356–62. Copyright © 1998 by Sage Publications, Inc. Reprinted by permission of Sage Publications, Inc. Lines from "The Heaven of Animals," *James Dickey: The Selected Poems,* ed. Robert Kirschten (Hanover NH: Wesleyan University Press, 1998), 32, are reprinted by permission of Wesleyan University Press. Lines from Mary Swander, *Heaven-and-Earth House* (New York: Knopf, 1994), copyright © 1994 by Mary Swander, are used by permission of Alfred A. Knopf, a division of Random House, Inc.

My deepest gratitude is to my family. To my parents, Tom and Sondra Price; my sisters, Carrie Anne Whittaker, Susan Saylor, and Allyson Rushford; and my grandmother Kathryn Anderson — long before this journey, you all taught me the importance of home. Thanks also to my "western" family, especially Gary and Helen Strine. Most of all I am grateful to my wife, Stephanie, and to our boys, Benjamin and Spencer. Your unwavering love and innumerable acts of grace have made it possible not only to write but to live.

Finally, this book is dedicated to the memory of Mildred Wagner Price — loving grandmother, faithful daughter of the prairie.

We can be ethical only in relation to
something we can see, feel, understand,
love, or otherwise have faith in.
                    —Aldo Leopold

Faith is the substance of things hoped for,
the evidence of things not seen.
                    —Hebrews 11:1

CHAPTER 1

The First Miracle of the Prairie *Buffalo Gap, South Dakota*

During my first hour on the Dakota grasslands it was dark and cold and the walls of my tent were puffing, the top lifting. Waves of drizzle spattered against the nylon. I was sitting inside, legs crossed, hands clutching both drapes of the tent flap, peering out of the mosquito netting. Out there, I reminded myself, is Buffalo Gap National Grassland, nearly six hundred thousand acres of mixed-grass prairie. But I could see nothing through the dark and the mist, not one blade of grass, not one star. In an effort to "feel" the open space, to absorb its character, its magnitude, I closed my eyes. I wanted something special to mark this as an arrival, something spiritual, mystical—God. Instead, I felt cold gusts working the collar of my sweatshirt, the itch of fly bites, the painful throb in my right palm where I had stuck myself on a prickly pear. I opened my eyes and stared, once again, into the dark. What did I expect to find? A new connection to my home landscape, I thought, a grasslands bioregion I'd lived in all my life but never seen, never known. I sought some new notion of myself as well, a twenty-seven-year-old Iowan who had never camped alone in any vast natural place like that, ever.

What was most obvious at the moment, though, was this: I was no camper. I felt vulnerable, exposed. Too easily, out there on the prairie, I saw my situation from a murderer's perspective: a bright white Toyota parked alongside a gravel road; a lone pup tent perched nearby; a solitary occupant unable to hear approaching footsteps because his tent walls are shaking and snapping. The perfect prey. I reached into my backpack, retrieved the collapsible fire shovel and lay it next to me. Then I sat and stared. As my eyes adjusted and the mist lifted a little, I began to see tiny, distant lights moving just above the earth. Running, like wild eyes in the moonlight.

This, I think, was what Margie had called "dispersed recreation." Margie was the forester in charge of the National Grasslands Visitor Center when I dropped by earlier that afternoon. The center is located in Wall, South Dakota, just a few miles north of Buffalo Gap. It's the only visitor center in the nation dedicated to the national grasslands, and on that day in June 1994 it was celebrating its one-year anniversary. I pulled into the parking lot after many hours traveling from Iowa on Interstate 90, hoping to get camping information. I was pleasantly surprised by the building, set low and wide like the prairie itself. The doorway opened into a large bright room where, engraved along the top edges of the walls, were the names of all twenty national grasslands—lyrical, evocative names like Oglala, Thunder Butte, Crooked River, Curlew, Comanche, Rita Blanca. Hanging just above these were green-and-white sketches of various grasses: little bluestem, buffalograss, prairie sandreed, sand love-grass, needle and thread. Some of these grasses, from a short bunch of rice grass to six-foot stems of Indian grass, could be seen in vases and clay pots throughout the room. Coming from a place where grasses are often considered weeds or worse, I felt a little disoriented standing in a building created entirely to celebrate them.

"Be sure to sign our guest book," Margie said. She was sitting behind a wide counter, dressed in the tan uniform of the U.S. Forest Service.

"Great place you have here," I said as I scribbled my signature beneath those of a couple from Germany.

"Thanks," she replied. "We've only been here a short while. Where're you from and what brings you to the visitor center?"

"I'm from Iowa, and I want to camp on the prairie."

That was the simple answer. In truth, the journey to this place had been much longer and circuitous than the straight-arrow shot of Interstate 90. For me it had begun the summer before, during the 1993 floods when the familiar, corn-stalked Iowa landscape suddenly became wild. Born and raised in Fort Dodge, a mid-sized city in west-central Iowa, I had spent eight years attending university in Iowa City, on the eastern side of the state. After getting married my wife, Stephanie, and I decided to move to the nearby small, rural town of Belle Plaine, closer to her new teaching job. We considered it our first real home together but knew it would only be temporary. The plan was for me to finish my graduate studies in literature and creative writing and then for us to move on, probably out of the region. Still, having both grown up in cities, Steph and I were excited about living close to the country. That first evening in Belle Plaine, our moving van rumbled into town during a thundershower and stopped in front of a tall, run-down Victorian house, the top floor of which we were renting. Unloading the van turned out to be an exhausting, disastrous process that resulted in our couch becoming lodged, shoulder-high, between two inside doorways. After pushing and pounding and cursing we finally decided to leave it there, aloft. We collapsed on the musty carpet and slept to the familiar sound of rain.

The next morning we got up and peeked around the doorway: the couch was still there, elevated as if by magic. Delaying the inevitable confrontation, we stepped under it and went for a walk. Outside, the cloud-dimmed surroundings were soaked in moisture. The maples and oaks that lined our street seemed about to collapse from their own verdancy, their branches nearly touching the deep curbside pools. The air was too rich to breathe. Along the sidewalks and in the streets, the bodies of hundreds of frogs lay scattered and broken as if they had fallen from the sky. After stepping around more puddles and dead frogs, we paused to observe a small lake in a cornfield, created by a flooding creek. Standing in the middle was the slender, calligraphic figure of a blue heron. We admired it for a while and talked about the strange chain of miracles we had just witnessed, from the floating couch to the frogs to the newborn lake with its heron. Portents, we hoped, of good things to come.

That was early July and we still did not fully grasp the disaster occurring around us. During the next month, we watched the small lake swell until it nearly engulfed the entire field—a flooding far gentler than what was happening a hundred miles east on the Mississippi River, where cars and homes and people were being swept away by what some in the national press called "nature gone mad." That summer Iowans were confronting unexpected and often overwhelming natural forces. The capital city of Des Moines was without water for weeks, while just a few miles west of us the small town of Chelsea, almost totally destroyed, sought federal funds to move itself, brick by brick, to higher ground. Even the dead weren't safe. As cemeteries became saturated, our neighbor Dave, a mortician, traveled to Missouri to help people recover and identify the bodies of long-buried relatives sent adrift in the waters.

The Iowa I saw that summer was one of awesome destruction yet also one of surprising natural beauty. Commuting between Belle Plaine and Iowa City to take classes, I became transfixed by a wild Iowa landscape I had never known. Cornfields and bean fields became inaccessible wetlands where snowy egrets stood piercing frogs in the shallows. There were swirling tornadoes of white pelicans; bald eagles snatching fish out of floodwaters; large, freckled hawks peering from the top of what seemed every fence post, every sign. I witnessed the flight of thousands of birds, the play of river otters, the sun-drenched sleep of turtles at a nearby marsh, suddenly lush and swollen. When the floodwaters began to retreat, the ditches near our home erupted into wildflowers and grasses, some of them six feet tall. I bought a field guide and searched hungrily for their names: tiger lily and horsemint and primrose, big bluestem and switchgrass. For a few months the wild prairies seemed to awaken, and so did I. Along every country road, around every bend, there was some new wild thing for me to discover: rattlesnake master, compass plant, shooting star.

I thought a lot about the biblical Noah that summer, about those final days on the ark between the release of the raven and the return of the dove, between the knowledge of a decimated, flooded landscape and the faith in one that was recovering, becoming born anew. I often felt that way, suspended between hope and despair, as I watched the floodwaters swell then recede, as I watched wetlands become cornfields again, the sudden wilderness become tame, the unknown become known, the miraculous become mundane. I had seen in a few short months a little of the wildness that had been lost to the years of cultivation and drainage and poisoning here in the "heartland." And yet I had also become aware of what still remained, pushed to the margins, surviving. As I continued to explore those small patches of native wildflowers and grasses, I began to feel, for the first time, a sense of longing for the lost land. I began to won- der what a thousand acres of prairie, with its attendant wetlands and oak savannahs, might look like, feel like. How might living near or within such a wild place have changed me and my relationship to home? Like many born in the Midwest, I had given little thought to committing to the place where I grew up—had, in fact, always wanted to leave. Sometimes it felt as if I were already gone, a ghost in my own house. What was the source of that inner exile? Was it related in any way to my exile from the land? If so, how might I overcome it? Where might I seek the reasons to commit myself to this damaged place, help it to heal? And would seeking those reasons, in the end, make any difference in my life or in the life of the land? Perhaps we were both too far gone.

"Camping?" Margie said, raising her eyebrows.

She paused as if she were getting ready to hand me a pink slip.

"I should tell you, John, we don't really have any developed camp- sites in Buffalo Gap. We have what we call 'dispersed recreation.' It's more of an exploring-on-your-own type of experience. You're free to camp anywhere—that's not a problem—but there just aren't many services."

I told her that was fine. She smiled and said she'd dig out one of their new maps. After rustling around beneath the counter, she popped her head up and said it might take a while. She recom- mended I check out the new display room.

"Great," I said. "I'll do that."

How do you begin to tell the story of the land? The exhibit revealed just how difficult it was to shape the history of the grasslands into a cohesive narrative.[1] It was a difficulty I'd already experienced when, after reading one book or another, I'd tried to picture the prairies in my mind, the way they used to be. It was impossible, but book knowledge was all I had—the actual prairies had all but disappeared. As I stood in front of a map at the visitor center, staring at the great green blob in the middle of North America that represented the original grasslands, I ran through the technical stuff. Of the four major biomes of North America—desert, tundra, forest, and grassland—grassland is the largest. It once covered 40 percent of the contiguous United States, containing several different grassland communities: tallgrass, mixed, shortgrass, desert, intermountain or sagebrush, California, and eastern. I was interested in the central grasslands, which contain the more abstract regions referred to as the Midwest and Great Plains. Where the Midwest ends and the Great Plains begin is a subject of debate, but many draw the line somewhere around the 100th meridian, the rough borderline between humid and semi-arid country. So, for example, Iowa and eastern Nebraska are in the Midwest, while western Nebraska and eastern Colorado are in the Plains. Regardless of where we locate the boundary, one thing is clear: before Euro-American settlement, the Midwest and Plains were both engulfed by one of the largest unbroken grasslands in the world, stretching from the Appalachians to the Rockies, from southern Canada to Texas. This included Buffalo Gap, a mixed prairie sandwiched between tallgrass and shortgrass.

I had tried to envision the original immensity of the grasslands by organizing its details along horizontal and vertical lines, like a cross. Traveling horizontally across the rolling surface of the presettlement prairies, an explorer would have seen a vast, mostly treeless landscape dominated by a myriad of perennial grasses and flowering plants, millions of different species. Moving east to west, from humid to semi-arid country, the grass would slowly shorten, from the eight-foot big bluestem of the tallgrass region, to the two-foot little bluestem of the mixed-grass region, to the four-inch buffalograss of the shortgrass region. Breaking up the expanses of grass would have been wetlands, prairie potholes, woody draws, and oak savannahs. There

would have been color, waves of color, created by millions of different flowering plants moving through the seasons: the white, pink,
and lavender of spring; the yellow-gold of summer; the crimson and
bronze of autumn; the slate of winter. Traveling over and within
all of this would have been the richest population of animal life
in North America, including — numbering in the tens of millions
— the largest migrating community of mammals in the world: the
bison.

Thinking vertically, moving up and down, into sky and earth, the
grasslands would have revealed a distinguishing balance of extremes.
The region lay within the collision zone of three major air masses:
the cold, dry mass from the Northwest; the warm, wet mass from
the Gulf of Mexico; and the westerly mass, left dry and hot by the
rain shadow of the Rockies. This creates volatile weather that moves
quickly from sub-zero to one hundred degrees, from downpour to
drought, from calm, crystalline blue skies to cyclonic winds. The
wet months might bring sweeping floods in the east, while the dry
months might bring roaring walls of flame in the west. Native prairie plants and animals have adapted themselves to these extremes by
occupying, at once, the contrary inclinations of migration and entrenchment. Many birds and waterfowl nest here in the fair seasons
then ride either side of winter to warmer skies; bison and pronghorn and elk remain all year but move from spot to spot, the bison snuffing through snowdrifts in search of forage. Gray wolf and
grizzly bear and mountain lion hunt here — or used to — in all seasons, while others, like prairie dogs and badgers, retreat beneath
the surface of the earth, migrating down then up. Grass, too, survives here by simultaneously reaching out and digging in, its tiny
seeds riding the wind while beneath the earth, safe from the scouring forces of fire and ice and tooth, its reproductive stems branch,
sending up new shoots.

The native human population also lived successfully within these
extremes, drawing off abundant supplies of forage and game, exist-
ing in various states of migration and settlement. There were several
nomadic tribes who followed and lived off the herds of bison: the
Blackfeet, Crow, Sarsi, Arapaho, Cheyenne, Kiowa, Kiowa-Apache,
Assiniboin, Teton Sioux, Gros Ventre, and Comanche. There were

seminomadic tribes that hunted bison in conjunction with cultivating vegetables like squash and maize: the Hidatsa, Arikara, Kansa, Omaha, Oto, Missouri, Ponca, Osage, Mandan, Pawnee, Wichita, Santee Sioux, Yankton Sioux, and Iowa. Others lived in permanent settlements in the upper Midwest, hunting bison only occasionally: the Caddo, Plains Cree, Quapaw, Plains Ojibwa, and Shoshone.[2] European expeditions into the region came in trickles starting with the Spanish in the 1500s, but settlement didn't begin in earnest until the 1800s, a century that included the Removal Act of 1830, which forcibly relocated eastern tribes onto the Plains, creating new environmental and social stresses. Euro-American settlement was further encouraged by western expansion of the railroads and the federal Homestead Act of 1862 that promised cheap land to anyone willing to settle in the central Plains. Other settlers were enticed by misleading, utopian descriptions of the territory and pseudo-scientific jargon such as "rain follows the plow."

Euro-American settlement brought massive destruction to native plant, animal, and human populations in the grasslands. Cultivation wreaked havoc on prairie plants, shredding their root systems, eroding topsoil, and introducing invasive species—a process that culminated in the worst environmental disaster in American history, the dust bowl of the 1920s and 30s. Today native grasslands that once covered 40 percent of the nation have been reduced to a splotchy 10 percent.[3] In Iowa, my home state, only one-tenth of 1 percent of the native tallgrass prairie still exists.[4] Animal life has been similarly devastated. Bison, numbering between 50 and 60 million in 1800, were reduced to around 13 million by 1870 and fewer than a thousand by the turn of the century. Prairie dog towns, one of the most important Plains ecosystems, once occupied up to 700 million acres of western grasslands in the early 1900s but now occupy around 2 million acres.[5] The black-footed ferret, which feeds on prairie dogs, is one of the most endangered mammals in North America. As for the human residents, the historian Elliott West notes that during the four hundred years after 1500, the aboriginal population of North America may have dropped 95 percent as a result of disease, warfare, and famine. This is, according to West, "the greatest die-off in the human record."[6] Great Plains tribes suffered especially severe losses

during the smallpox epidemics of the early nineteenth century—
in one year alone (1815–16), the Comanche population fell from ten
thousand to six thousand.[7] Many of those who survived were forcibly
removed from their ancestral homelands and placed on distant reser-
vations. And then there was the massacre at Wounded Knee, a mere
fifty miles south of the Grasslands Visitor Center.

Altogether, no other American biome has suffered such an enormous loss of life with so little protest. In fact, the presence of Wall
Drug just down the street with its severed buffalo heads, cigar-store
Indians, and quick-draw video games confirmed that the demise of
the grassland ecosystems—its human, plant, and animal interrela-
tionships—was and still is the occasion for some grand celebrating.

Of course these disembodied facts do not even begin to tell the
full story of the land, and the exhibits at the visitor center weren't
much better. Like all museums, what is meant to draw us in ultimately keeps us out. There were, for example, several glassed-in displays representing Buffalo Gap's major habitats: Upland Grasslands,
Prairie Dog Town, Woody Draw, and Prairie Pothole or Wetland.
Within each were the stuffed bodies of various wildlife—coyote,
sharp-tailed grouse, swift fox, wood duck, rattlesnake—placed before a painted backdrop. On another wall a panel describing Plains
Indian life was mounted near one describing the heroic struggle of
prairie pioneers. One display offered an electronic multiple-choice
quiz on the science of grasses. Another challenged visitors to identify prairie birds from drawings of their wings, while another invited
them to stroke the pelts of badgers, skunks, and raccoons. There were
some interesting omissions—there were very few images of bison,
for instance. The painted backdrop for the Upland Grasslands ecosystem featured an Angus bull.

For me these displays created an accurate and disheartening im-
pression: here was a beautiful and complex landscape yet also a nego-
tiated, piecemeal landscape, one without fear or mystery. Something
soft and dead to run your fingers through.

When I emerged from the display room, Margie was leaning over
a map of Buffalo Gap.

"I was just thinking about good places you might camp," she said.

At the center of the map was a brown, oblong space representing

Badlands National Park, surrounded by a ring of green-and-white checkered squares. Margie explained that the green was the national grasslands, public land, and the white was private. I could camp anywhere on the green but should stay out of the white.

"I don't think the ranchers will shoot you if you make a mistake," she added, "but you might wake up next to a grazing cow."

"Any chance that could be a bison cow?"

"No, just a regular cow."

Margie said that if I wanted to see bison, I'd have to camp in Badlands National Park; bison weren't allowed in Buffalo Gap. It's too small for them, she explained, and local ranchers don't want them mixing with their herds. Brucellosis, you know. She said that unlike the Badlands, Buffalo Gap—like most national grasslands—represented an attempt to balance environmental and agricultural interests, demonstrating, as their brochure explained, "how lands classified as unsuitable for cultivation may be managed for forage, wildlife habitat, prairie woodlands, energy/minerals, water and outdoor recreation to the benefit of both land and people." It's all about calculated use, but the beginning of the national grasslands was about accident, about rediscovering the value of the broken, forgotten places. In the 1930s during the dust bowl, the Department of Agriculture agreed to buy and restore millions of submarginal or highly eroded acres from struggling ranchers and farmers in the Great Plains. For several decades these lands were considered part of the national forests and did not receive their distinct status as national grasslands until 1961. Currently, national grasslands encompass around four million acres, mostly in the Great Plains.

"In a way, the national grasslands are the orphan child of the forest service," Margie continued. "There was really no cohesive vision behind their creation, just a series of circumstances. It's taken a while for it to catch on as something distinct, something special, but now every time I hear the top people in the forest service give a talk, it's 'national grasslands' this and 'national grasslands' that. So I think enthusiasm is growing."

Margie explained that the idea for the visitor center began in late 1987, and the building was finally completed in 1993. The permanent exhibits had been there only a few months before my arrival. Buffalo Gap was selected as the site for the center because of its large size (591,000 acres), central location, and close proximity to Badlands and Black Hills National Parks. It has also been unusually successful in exchanging acres with local landowners, creating the most consolidated public grasslands in the system. Though it has taken a lot of work, Margie believes they've created a relatively successful balance at Buffalo Gap: ranchers can still purchase grazing rights if they agree to rotate their herds and maintain protective fences around delicate ecosystems such as stream beds and woody draws. Hunting is also allowed. Meanwhile, the U.S. Forest Service is cooperating with Badlands National Park and the U.S. Fish and Wildlife Service to reintroduce black-footed ferrets to prairie dog areas in Buffalo Gap. The new visitor center is meant to open the grasslands to another, relatively recent kind of use: tourism.

"Last year, from June to December, we had around 14,000 visitors come through," Margie said. "That's really incredible, considering. This year we have signs on the interstate and the South Dakota Department of Tourism has included us in their vacation guide. The Wall chamber of commerce has been incredibly supportive. So we expect even more visitors."

I asked her how she explains the recent enthusiasm.

"Well, I think people are beginning to change their perceptions of this area. Traditionally, Badlands National Park has not been a destination park—it's hot, it's open, and it's part of the Midwest, a place most people see as drive-through country. Now I think people are seeking experiences in nature where they aren't so contained and crowded. Plus, grasslands are a mystery to a lot of people. They were to me. I'm a forester by education and background, but I've learned to appreciate and love the prairies. That surprised me. I can't really explain how that happened, learning to love the prairies. I've tried to explain it to others, but it's impossible. There're just so many interesting things about it. Did you know that grasslands aren't that different from forests? They both take a long time to go from a disturbed state to a climaxed state, and one single grass plant can live as long as any tree. It's really amazing. I think so, anyway."

"If there's so much public interest," I asked, "how come there aren't more federally protected areas?"

"Well, there are restoration projects going on in places like Illinois, Wisconsin, Minnesota, and Missouri, but they're pretty small. The problem with the Midwest is that so many acres here are cultivated. Even if we wanted to buy up enough land to create a bunch of grasslands national parks, where would we find it? It just isn't here anymore. We can't even really expand Buffalo Gap. There aren't the resources or the land base. All we can do is keep exchanging pieces and try to keep everyone happy."

Margie looked down at the map, at its green-and-white checkerboard pattern, and for a moment her face seemed to reflect my own longing.

"We just hope, someday, to put all the pieces together."

Heading east on Interstate 90, I turned on the wipers to clean the heavy mist off the windshield. I could see rain-distorted herds of cattle, new hay fields, and the empty backsides of Wall Drug signs. The view continued to remind me of the Grasslands Visitor Center, the glassed-in pieces of the ecosystem, the displays meant to show a place capable of sustaining many uses, many individual desires. That's one kind of story about the land. Then I thought about Margie, her momentary slip into the personal, her stumbling to find the language to express her surprising affinity, as a forest person, for grass. That's another, more elusive story.

Annie Dillard once wrote that seeing is a matter of verbalization, of language. During the floods of 1993, I had indeed felt blinded by my inability to describe the wild beauty erupting around me. Searching bookstores and libraries, I discovered texts like John Madson's *Where the Sky Began* (1982) that introduced me to the cycles of ecology, to the magnificent interconnections among the life, weather, and soil of the prairie. But I also discovered that memorizing natural history and botanical information was not the best place for me to begin; I did not know what to do with this knowledge or if I truly cared about it. What I needed before all that, before blind activism, was knowledge — verbalization — of what was going on inside of me, the elation and grief of that initial discovery, how it had lifted me, compromised me. I wanted to see my life in this land, the past and potential of that life, in a new way. That meant learning to articulate my own confused and contradictory relationship to my home region, my own tenuous reach, as a resident and writer, toward commitment, responsibility, and love.

This required piecing together a different kind of map than the topographical. What I needed was a map of words, of firsthand accounts and stories that portrayed how this land has taken shape over time in the human imagination. The Grasslands Visitor Center, whatever its other limitations, seemed to appreciate this kind of mapping. They had a bookshelf full of literary titles, including James Fenimore Cooper's *The Prairie* (1827), Dee Brown's *Bury My Heart at Wounded Knee* (1971), and Aldo Leopold's *A Sand County Almanac* (1949). While there I picked up the copy of *The Prairie*, one of the first serious books I'd read that used the central grasslands for a setting. On the cover was a painting of the prairie wilderness, an endless expanse of tall, windblown grass, melting toward the bloodline of dusk — the kind of place I hoped to find on my journey. I opened the cover and read the epigraph:

> *I pray thee, shepherd, if that love, or gold*
> *Can in this desert place buy entertainment,*
> *Bring us where we may rest ourselves and feed.*

Though taken from Shakespeare, the "desert" implied here is the "Great American Prairies" of the eighteenth and nineteenth centuries, what Cooper called "those broad plains which extend with so little diversity of character to the bases of the Rocky Mountains."[8] The trans-Missouri Plains. Cooper had never visited them, relying instead on published firsthand accounts. Yet they were out there, those prairies, and Cooper clearly saw them as a wilderness, which is to say a place of danger and mystery, a place in which to get lost, even die — *if that love, or gold.*

And he was right. In the fall of 1832, five years after Cooper published *The Prairie*, Washington Irving, the creator of the Headless Horseman and Rip Van Winkle, made a journey to the grasslands of what is now Oklahoma. Despite the relative wealth and comfort of his traveling party, they suffered from hunger, cold, and disorientation. Following a violent thunderstorm, Irving observed that "our scattered cavalcade looked like a tempest-tost fleet, driven hither and thither, at the mercy of wind and wave." Later he remarked that there was "something inexpressibly lonely in the solitude of a prairie: the loneliness of a forest seems nothing to it." In 1846 the historian Francis Parkman traveled to the prairies of what is now Nebraska and the Dakotas and described the wretched condition of an escaped slave who had wandered, lost, for thirty-three days on the open Plains, surviving only by eating crickets and lizards: "Utterly bewildered in the boundless, hopeless desert that stretched around him, offering to his inexperienced eye no mark by which to direct his course, he had walked on in despair, till he could walk no longer, and then crawled on his knees, until the bone was laid bare."[9] Parkman himself, while traveling across the prairies, would suffer from severe dysentery, fever, and an aggravated blindness that would remain with him for the rest of his life.

Circling around these historic voices, for me, were other first encounters with the wild prairies, moments when a vast, unknown land first imposed itself on the individual imagination. Together these accounts created a complex portrait of fear and awe, wonder and disdain. Albert Pike in his *Journeys in the Prairie* (1831–32) proclaimed: "The sea, the woods, the mountains, all suffer in comparison with the prairie. . . . The prairie has a stronger hold upon the senses. Its sublimity arises from its unbounded extent, its barren monotony and desolation, its still, unmoved, calm, stern, almost self-confident grandeur, its strange power of deception, its want of echo, and, in fine, its power of throwing a man back upon himself."

Sam Butler, an Irish explorer, wrote this in the 1870s: "The great ocean itself does not present more infinite variety than does this prairie-ocean of which we speak. In winter, a dazzling surface of the purest snow; in early summer, a vast expanse of grass and pale pink roses; in autumn too often a wild sea of raging fire. No ocean of water in the world can vie with its gorgeous sunsets; no solitude can equal the loneliness of night shadowed prairie."

Other, more overtly negative responses seem to confirm a European preference for the romantic enclosures of forest, mountain, and vale. Charles Dickens, for instance, while visiting Looking-Glass Prairie in Illinois in 1842, called it "the great blank," a landscape not to be remembered "with much pleasure, or to covet the looking-on again in after life." James Fenimore Cooper, though he never visited the trans-Missouri grasslands, also imagined them less as an ecosystem with its own integrity than as a testing ground for his social theories. To Cooper and many others the prairie seemed stark, hostile to civilized culture, destined only for the plow. "I often think," exclaims his Natty Bumpo, "the Lord has placed this barren belt of prairie behind the States to warn men to what their folly may yet bring the land!"[10]

Of course what was denigration on Cooper's part proved to be prescience — the prairies did indeed become a warning for what our folly might accomplish. Little more than a century later Aldo Leopold, whose *Sand County Almanac* was displayed next to *The Prairie* in the Grasslands Visitor Center, would remark while observing a small, graveyard patch of what had once been the vast Wisconsin prairie: "Few grieved when the last buffalo left Wisconsin, and few will grieve when the last Silphium [native compass plant] follows him to the lush prairies of the never-never land."[11]

While reading these literary accounts, I had wondered what took us in such a short time from one prairie chorus to the other, from voices filled with awe and wonder and fear to those filled with anger and mourning and, for some of us living in the Midwest and Plains, indifference. How might we return to that other perspective, facing in the grasslands that thing which humbles us, inspires us, throws us back upon our selves? This is, according to some, the responsibility of the nature writer, to call attention to what is unique and worth saving in our environment, to write places into our collective consciousness. Think of Barry Lopez in the Arctic Circle, Terry Tempest Williams in the Utah deserts, or Rick Bass in the Montana forests. These writers have the power through their words to place us inside the landscapes they describe, inside particular ecological relationships, and perhaps most important inside a mind that sees in these relationships the intimate, the beautiful, the worthy. They move us to care and to act.

The prairie has had few such writers. Part of the problem, as Margie pointed out, is that there isn't much native prairie left to write about. Yet the prairie, even when plentiful, has had little success in inspiring the commitment of its literary sons and daughters — especially Euro-Americans like me who were born here. In grasslands literary history, a settled, committed life for such a writer is unconventional, even radical. Wallace Stegner, who was raised on the prairies of Iowa and Saskatchewan, observed that the migratory lives of western writers had resulted in a regional "literature of motion, not of place." Likewise, many of the authors most associated with the Great Plains and Midwest—among them Willa Cather, Hamlin Garland, Wright Morris—spent their childhood in the rural grasslands but eventually wrote about home from a distant, usually coastal city. Though the difficulty for these writers of living in the region can be ascribed in part to practicalities—distance from editors, research libraries—Robert Thacker argues that it was also due to a rural culture that "schooled" young prairie writers to worship the cosmopolitan East. The Indiana essayist Scott Russell Sanders suggests the exodus of writers from the region may also be owing to a residual Puritanism that works to control and repress the "promiscuous, sensual, earthy" qualities of the human imagination. In contrast, the environmental writer Richard Manning claims that the nature of grasslands life itself, both human and animal, has always been "nomadic, uncivilized, and therefore hostile to literature," making the literature of absentee Plains writers more, not less, credible.[12] Whatever the reasons, the fact that so many writers left the rural Midwest and Plains to write about them from a distance has made any discussion of a "regional" literary tradition decidedly ironic: absence, in such a tradition, is presence.

However, the ecological and social crisis facing the grasslands—whether in the Great Plains, the Midwest, or the West—has led some to call for a more reciprocal relationship between resident and region. "Neither the country nor the society we built out of it can be healthy," writes Stegner, "until we stop raiding and running, and learn to be quiet part of the time, and acquire the sense not of ownership but of belonging." The environmental historian and Kansan Donald Worster argues that we need to "discover a new regional identity and set of loyalties, more inclusive and open to diversity than we have known, more compatible with a planet-wide sense of ecological responsibility." The Kentucky author and farmer Wendell Berry offers a definition of literary regionalism that is, simply, "*local life aware of itself*. It would tend to substitute for the myths and stereotypes of a region a particular knowledge of the life of the *place* one lives in and intends to *continue* to live in. It pertains to living as much as to writing, and it pertains to living *before* it pertains to writing."[13] What is needed, these writers seem to be saying, is a different story, one that guides us by example through the challenges of living responsibly in place. Indeed, having grown up in Iowa where nearly all of the native habitats have been destroyed and where the rich topsoil continues to pour into the Gulf of Mexico, it has become increasingly difficult for me to take comfort in the words of fictional characters like Cather's Alexandra Bergson in *O Pioneers!* who proclaims: "We come and go, but the land is always here."

Yet even if writers want to live responsibly in the grasslands, how do they define that responsibility, how do they choose it, how do they, in William Kittredge's words, "make it come to be"? This is not a new question for prairie writers—Hamlin Garland asked it over a century ago. Raised on the prairies of Wisconsin and Iowa, Garland at age thirty-three delivered a paper titled "Local Color in Fiction" at the 1893 Chicago World's Columbian Exposition. There he called out for a new story in American literature, one written by and about the children of the middle border, the prairies of the nation's interior. Later in *Crumbling Idols* (1894) he raged against an educational system that privileged the teaching of European and eastern authors and turned the western American youth "away from the very material which he could best handle, which he knows most about, and which he really loves most,—material which would make him individual, and fill him with hope and energy." That material, according to Garland, could be found near at hand in the communities and landscape of home—what he called "local color." Local color, he claimed, has "such quality of texture and back-ground that it could not have been written in any other place or by any one else than a native. It means a statement of life as indigenous as the plant growth." Such a statement does not arise from calculated literary choices but rather from a perspective so intrinsic that "the writer naturally carries it with him half-consciously, or conscious only of its significance, its interest to him." It is a way of writing as natural as living, and if followed you will be, according to Garland, "'true to yourself, true to your locality, and true to your time.'"[14]

Garland did his best to live up to that responsibility. After graduating from Iowa's Cedar Valley Seminary in 1881, he left home for the first time for an extended trip through the East, including Boston. He worked odd jobs and briefly taught at a country schoolhouse in Illinois. By that time his restless father had once again moved the family west, this time to South Dakota where Hamlin himself would stake a claim in 1883. The severe drought and winter that followed quickly ended Garland's homesteading ambitions, and against his father's will he returned east. Nevertheless, while studying literature and supporting himself as a lecturer in Boston, Garland continued to feel a deep "homesickness" for his family and region. Perhaps in search of comfort, he wrote his first sketches about prairie life. In 1887 at age twenty-six, Garland once again journeyed west, stopping in Chicago to meet with the author Joseph Kirkland who encouraged him to continue writing about his farming background. But as he traveled on through Iowa to South Dakota, Garland found little comfort in the landscapes of home. He observed instead a growing regional tragedy, a population that seemed perpetually ravaged by harsh natural and economic forces. The living conditions of his own family had also worsened, and though he wanted to help he rationalized that the only way to do so as a writer was to earn money back east.

In 1891 while living in Boston, Garland published *Main Travelled Roads*, a collection of semi-autobiographical stories written during a time of "deep personal sorrow" over the death of his sister, whom he had left back on the Plains. He considered it the first western book to seriously address the region's problems: low crop prices, absentee landlords, miserable living conditions (especially for women), and the flight of bright young people from the region. Though Garland had found his niche as a writer, he continued to believe his work insignificant compared to the suffering of his family and region. "I was disturbed," he wrote, "by the feeling that in some way my own career was disloyal, something built upon the privations of my sister as well as upon those of my mother. I began definitely to plan their rescue." Soon after, he turned down a teaching job in Boston to begin a reformation campaign in Iowa, speaking for the Farmer's Alliance and for the populist People's Party. It was during this time that he delivered his speech on local color at the 1893 exposition and decided to reside in Chicago. He also finally succeeded in "rescuing" his pioneering family, using his own money to move them back to Wisconsin, a place where they might "catch and cling" after a lifetime of toil and transience.[15]

But Garland's journey was only beginning. He remained resentful that Main Travelled Roads, meant to shed light on the struggles of the western farmer, had received scathing reviews by some western critics who challenged the accuracy of his brutal descriptions. Even harder to accept were the opinions of family members. Garland's father responded to the book with silence, while his mother, whose physical hardships Garland had sought to expose and alleviate, suggested he should not reveal too many unpleasant truths in his writing. "Farmer's wives have enough to bear as it is," she told him. Garland's political causes also fell short. The defeat of the Populists in 1896, for whom Garland had left Boston to campaign, drained him of any remaining desire to promote economic reform in the rural Midwest. Soon after Garland shifted the scene for his fiction to the less personal Rocky Mountain West. He studied Native American cultures and wrote a biography of Ulysses S. Grant and a few novels on psychic phenomena in which, as the scholar Joseph B. McCullough puts it, Garland was mostly interested in "developing the theme of bondage to a cause"—a burden that led some to madness.[16] Meanwhile, as advances in mass transportation and communication softened regional differences, the Midwest failed to become the glowing nucleus of indigenous culture and art that Garland had hoped it would.

Given these disappointments, it's perhaps understandable why Garland would want to leave the region, which he did in 1916, moving to New York and eventually to Los Angeles where he died in 1940. He felt he had done the right thing as an artist, had been true to himself and to his locality, and still nothing had changed. And since he could not "change the condition" of his midwesterners, Garland decided to "live away from them." In New York, however, Garland became emotionally exhausted and physically ill. During those difficult years he once again wrote about the Midwest, this time in a series of autobiographical books. In these "Middle Border" narra-

tives, he not only sought to record pioneer life for posterity, the hardships faced by his family, but also to revise the very pioneer myths he
blamed for those hardships. Garland's new "backtrailer" myth had
as its hero the western writer who overcomes the difficulties of rural
life to eventually conquer the eastern literary establishment. His own
success, Garland wrote, showed that the "pen had proved itself to be
mightier than the plow. Going east has proved more profitable than
going west!"[17]

Writing had indeed proved profitable for Garland, but it had also
been costly. His Middle Border series got him elected to the American Academy of Arts and Letters, and he was awarded a Pulitzer Prize
in 1921. The writer who had once called for a new democratic, regional literary tradition now proclaimed himself to be "an intellectual aristocrat" who had "no confidence in a democratic art" or the
opinions of the common reader. The man who was celebrated by
William Dean Howells and others as a brave new voice in American literature became one of its most talked about disappointments.
"The glamour of success and of association with the successful was
dazzling to him," writes Henry B. Fuller in his 1901 satirical story
about his friend Hamlin, "The Downfall of Abner Joyce." "Yes, Abner
had made his compromise with the world. He had conformed. . . .
He—a great, original genius—had become just like other people.
His downfall was complete."[18]

But what interested me most about Garland, more than his "fall"
from realism to romanticism, from populism to elitism, was his relationship to the land, especially the prairies of his childhood. In this
relationship, I thought, might be found another, less articulate reason why Garland felt alienated from his home: grief over the lost
prairies. Great Plains and midwestern authors have rarely expressed
such grief—I had certainly never experienced it myself. Garland,
however, recalls an Iowa boyhood saturated with the life of the un-
plowed grasslands, wild and beautiful places where "the warm sun,
falling on radiant slopes of grass, lit the meadow phlox and tall tiger
lilies into flaming torches of color." As those same grasslands were
transformed into fields, Garland claims to have witnessed "something sweet and splendid" leave the land, later acknowledging his
own role in those changes: "The prairies are gone. I held one of the

ripping, snarling, breaking plows that rolled the hazel bushes and wild sunflowers under. I saw the wild steers come into pasture and the wild colts under harness. I saw the wild fowl scatter and turn aside; I saw the black sod burst into gold and lavender harvests of wheat and corn—and so there comes into my reminiscences an unmistakable note of sadness. I do not excuse it or conceal it. I set it down as it comes to me." For Garland this "sadness" was, in part, ecological (though he never used the term), the destruction of the land's deep and distinguishing past: "[T]he garden that had bloomed and fruited for millions of years, waiting for man, lay torn and ravaged. The tender plants, the sweet flowers, the fragrant fruits, the busy insects, all the swarming lives which had been native here for untold centuries were utterly destroyed." The prairie "had vanished as if it had all been dreamed," he exclaims. "The pigeons, the plover, the chickens, the vultures, the cranes, the wolves—all gone—all gone!"[19]

The loss was also personal. Though Garland often saw the plowing of the prairie as something heroic or epic, the finality of its destruction ultimately became associated with the finality of his own aging process, his ever-lengthening exile from home. In fact his lost childhood seems to have become synonymous for him with the lost prairies, both irrecoverable, "till the coulee meadows bloom again unscarred of spade or plow." Pedro de Castañeda, a member of Coronado's expedition into the central grasslands over four hundred and fifty years ago, once described "the great pain in the heart" that is felt when we lose what was once commonplace in our lives; suddenly "we are all the time imagining and trying to find ways and means by which to get it back again." So it was with Garland and the prairies, together losing something essential, longing to find it again:

> "We'll meet them yet, they are not lost forever;
> They lie somewhere, those splendid prairie lands,
> Far in the West, untouched of plough and harrow
> Unmarked by man's all-desolating hands."[20]

Though nearly a century old, Garland's story is one that I return to repeatedly for inspiration and warning. What he put down on the page—the regional identity he proclaimed, the causes he served, the wild land he fought and ultimately eulogized—drew him into public contradiction, judgment, and sorrow. His life asks important questions about what it means for writers to attach themselves to specific landscapes and communities. Wendell Berry claims that "[w]ithout a complex knowledge of one's place, and without the faithfulness to one's place on which such knowledge depends, it is inevitable that the place will be used carelessly and eventually destroyed." For Berry this means seeing the land not just as literary subject but also as someplace to live, as home. By doing so "[o]ne's relation to one's subject ceases to be merely emotional or esthetical, or even merely critical, and becomes problematical, practical, and responsible as well. Because it must. It is like marrying your sweetheart."[21]

Yet what does that commitment cost the writer at the daily, most intimate levels? That's the question Garland's life seems to ask, the story rarely told. What does it mean for our relationships to family and neighbors and for our careers? What does it mean for the land? And what, ultimately, does it mean for our selves, the persons we become in those commitments? "When people give some of their allegiance to a place," Donald Worster claims, "they become more complex minds than they were before, more filled with contradictions, more unpredictable, more capable of learning. They may still persist in taking the wild risks of the uncommitted; on the other hand they may seek to discipline their desires and nurture that relationship. . . . [W]e have not always given those stickers and nurturers their due."[22]

Perhaps we have not given them their due because, in grasslands literature, it is hard to find writers who are willing to take these personal and professional risks, to commit to a place in such social and ecological peril, a bioregion where writing about nature is as much about faith in the unseen as knowledge of what remains. The risk of writing yourself into a commitment to such an endangered place is that you may spend the rest of your life, like Garland, trying to write yourself out of it.

And yet they're out there, those stickers and nurturers. While perusing libraries and bookstores I had found several contemporary authors whose work focused on their daily lives in the grasslands. There were those such as Kathleen Norris and Gretel Ehrlich who—reversing the trend established by past prairie writers—had moved to the Plains from coastal cities. There were Native Americans, such as Mary Crow Dog in South Dakota and Ray Young Bear in Iowa, who spoke from within tribal cultures that—for centuries before and after the first Europeans arrived—honored the ecological and spiritual connection between humans and the earth. The work of these authors provided me with necessary, immensely helpful perspectives. But because mine was a personal as well as literary journey, I was especially drawn to authors who represented a cultural perspective closer to my own—a Euro-American born and raised in the central grasslands—and thus faced similar challenges of belonging and responsibility. In South Dakota there were rancher Linda Hasselstrom and Dan O'Brien, a falconer and endangered species biologist. In Missouri there was William Least Heat-Moon (a.k.a. William Trogdon), a best-selling travel writer who spent nearly ten years exploring one rural county in Kansas. In Iowa living among the Amish there was Mary Swander, whose environmental illness forced her to grow organic vegetables and harvest edible prairie plants.

Each of these writers was born and raised in grass country, urban or rural, and remains by choice. Each expresses in his or her work a unique sense of environmental and communal responsibility, a daily, conscientious effort to, as Wes Jackson phrases it, "become native to place."[23] In their writing there is no easy back-to-the-land connection, no simple regional association. Because they live inside their literary subject, what they write about these places is complicated and challenged by relationships to family, friends, and neighbors and by the land itself. Their lives, as presented in their nonfiction, ask tough questions of readers as well, inviting them into the risk of commitment, displaying in full view its rewards and costs. Their inclinations are wide. They all express at times the flush of discovery, sharing what they see and learn from the land around them. Yet they also exhibit the grief and sometimes rage of those who have witnessed, and continue to witness, the destruction of prairie communities, both natural and human. And as personalities on the page, they can be, as Worster predicated, contradictory and unpredictable. It is perhaps because of these things that they are not, with the exception of Heat-Moon, immensely popular literary figures.

Yet it is this very complexity that draws these writers closest to the grassland places in which they reside. They seem to acknowledge this connection, often seeking to articulate the ways the land gives shape to inner nature, defining who they are against the backdrop of the world. During and after the 1993 Iowa floods, as I read their stories alongside stories of the land, I found in both the familiar tension between migration and entrenchment, wildness and domesticity, presence and absence, body and earth. Rather than simple personae, I found that what the author Robert Kroetsch had written was true, that "the consequence of the northern prairies to human definition [is] the diffusion of personality into a complex of possibilities rather than a concluded self."[24] And possibility was what I was most interested in. In a region where the land is often seen as flat and uninteresting, its future already written in the furrows and pastures it has become, I held before me, like Margie at the visitor center, the possibility that the pieces might be made whole, a prairie place once again. Also, the possibility that however broken, this land still had the power to inspire, to surprise, to create and demand a rebirth of the self. That, after all, is the original meaning of the word "nature" — *to be born.*

Reading these authors' books moved me closer to that inner transformation. It soon became clear, however, that words on a page would not be enough; I needed, if possible, to visit the writers in person. Like Berry I was exploring a notion of regionalism in which living was as important as writing, so I felt it was essential to locate the literature in relation to actual lives, communities, and landscapes. I wanted to observe the overlap and tensions, if any, between these authors' published convictions and their daily existence, to see how they made those convictions "come to be." As a writer and lifelong resident of the grasslands, I also had questions about what it means to be at home — or not at home — in this bioregion, questions no book could answer.

So I wrote letters to these four authors, sharing with them some of my concerns and experiences. They were all generous in their responses, and soon we had set up times to meet during the summer of 1994. In South Dakota, immediately following my stay at Buffalo Gap, I would meet with Dan O'Brien and Linda Hasselstrom. In August I would interview William Least Heat-Moon in Missouri, then travel to Chase County, Kansas, to see the Flint Hills prairies and talk with local citizens about Heat-Moon's best-selling book, PrairyErth. In September I would visit Mary Swander at her one-room schoolhouse near the Amish community of Kalona. My journey, both personal and literary, became guided by this constellation of grounded selves. I hoped to learn much from them.

Wallace Stegner may have been right, though, when he said it is our own trails, however faint, that matter most. I thought about this as I turned south toward the Badlands, the wet, blurry expanses folding away from me in the evening's last light. I was looking forward to the long trails I would walk there and in the prairies, the discoveries I would make, the connections I might begin to nurture. I was awake with anticipation, aware that I was at the beginning of something. Yet I had already traveled a great distance, learned much through the lives of others, carried by language. I had become apprenticed to the stories I'd read, they had become my memory, guaranteeing that whatever new self was being born, it would be, at once, a self alone and in conversation with others; one alive in the present yet called back to the past by the land and the longing we share: *We'll find them yet. They are not gone forever.*

A buffalo burger or an Indian taco? I sat at a booth in the Lodge Restaurant, just inside Badlands National Park, trying to decide which to order — it would be my last restaurant meal for a few days. The young, red-haired waitress stood above me, her pen tip resting on her pad, her eyes set in judgment. Pressured, I opted for the taco. She scribbled it down and left me alone.

Through the restaurant window I stared at a jagged butte just across the road, admiring how the thick mist and slate of dusk softened its edges. I wondered if it was the same butte I'd chased my sisters around during our family vacation in 1975 when I was nine. That chunk of South Dakota was both new and old country to me. Old in the sense that I have some family history there, some personal history. My great-great-uncle Tom James had been the railroad station master at nearby Custer, and in 1961 my parents had honeymooned there. During that honeymoon trip my parents visited scenic spots, and Mom learned to "talk antelope" by puckering her lips and making kissing noises—at least that's what she told us. During our own childhood trip to South Dakota, my sisters and I begged Mom to talk to the pronghorn antelope we occasionally spotted through our windows, giggling at her as the green Buick Electra knifed through the summer's heat. At Wall Drug my father bought me a little plastic viewer shaped like a TV, which when held against the light revealed some of the exciting things we'd seen: the "wild" donkeys of Custer State Park, Mount Rushmore, a buffalo herd, the Corn Palace, the Lead gold mine, the giant dinosaur statues in Rapid City. Those were the stories I was most interested in then, the ones I carried back home to Iowa to share with my friends. Now, after almost twenty years, I'd come back to find what I'd missed.

It would be dark soon, and I wondered how I was going to find my campsite. I unfolded the map on the table and located the little green square of free grass that Margie said was mine to claim. To get there I would have to follow the snaking Badlands Loop Road until I came to Bigfoot Pass, where I would supposedly find a gravel road leading north into Buffalo Gap National Grasslands. My place was on that road, two green squares up from the park border. It looked like it had a couple of creeks nearby, which meant, I hoped, animal activity: coyote, bobcat, badger—anything at all. The following night, still searching for that wildlife, I would return here to Cedar Pass amphitheater to participate in the "Night Prowl." "A naturalist will help you unravel the mysteries of the prairie at night," the announcement read. It seemed promising. The naturalist turned out to be a grumpy ranger who led a line of us into a small canyon. The moon that night would be a delicate crescent with Venus shining nearby—a beautiful and rare alignment that has served as a sacred symbol for many cultures. Our ranger pointed instead to the more distant constellation of Cassiopeia, a giant "W."

"Look," he said, "another Wall Drug advertisement."

Just as I was getting ready to walk away in frustration, another ranger, wrapped in a bison robe and carrying a dim lantern, approached our circle. He shook a large bone at us and began to tell "an old Sioux story" about four ghosts who tried to scare a night traveler. One by one the ghosts confronted the man, their eyes glowing, and each time they failed to scare him. In the end the fearless man steals their spectral horse and rides it triumphantly into the village.

"The moral of the story," the ranger said in a dramatic whisper, "is not to be afraid of the night. The night is beautiful." Then he walked back into the darkness, and we were instructed to return to the parking lot.

Driving back to my campsite from the Night Prowl, moving beneath the bright sweep of the galaxy, I would spot a burrowing owl standing in the road, its long legs white as moonlit grass. The night's one wild astonishment.

But all of that would occur tomorrow. At the moment, as I pulled out of the restaurant parking lot, the night did not seem very beautiful. It was totally black and my stomach was cramping, which I blamed on the Indian taco, the Indianness of which I could not determine. Gradually, though, my mind and body settled into the rhythm of the road as I moved, slowly, around this curve and that, softening my expectations. It was, for a while, like any other night ride, when the physical journey becomes the sway of gravity, the green glow of the dash, the low timbre of the wheels. Then the road becomes measured not by visible miles but by amplitudes of thought. Personality becomes a mere suspension, occupied by a chorus of voices, selves and potential selves, conversing, interrupted only by a burning sip of coffee-to-go. During those first miles into the Badlands, I could have been anyone, even someone who belonged there.

I put both hands on the top of the steering wheel, leaned forward, and focused on the sliver of headlight. Along its borders were luminous slips of grass fading into the darkness. Walls of earth, its stratified layers — red, yellow, brown — rose higher and higher, pressing against the road. It felt like I was sliding beneath the planet's crust — which, as it turned out, was an accurate sensation. Tomorrow, while traveling the same road in daylight, I would read informational signs explaining how the Badlands were created, how it is that through wind and water the place takes you beneath the surface of the prairie, as deep as thirty million years. Surrounding me in the colorful layers of rock and soil was a warm ocean (brown) beneath a jungle (yellow and red), beneath a grassland still gracing the tops of buttes. Tomorrow I would begin to learn names: Grass Butte, Pinnacles, Sage Creek.

But tonight it was all nether region, the dwelling place of incredible creatures, real and imagined. A place where the embedded bones of bison, rattlesnake, and bear—prehistoric saber-toothed tiger and giant alligator—might leap again into life. A place where the ordinary prowled alongside the fantastic.

For a moment I thought I had missed my cutoff, but as I came around another butte I spotted the sign and turned onto gravel. The road rose gently, the walls of earth fell away, and suddenly, caught in the headlights, were taller grasses and barbed-wire fencing and open sky. One crossroads, then another—this was the place. I pulled the car onto the narrow shoulder and got out. A light rain was falling—not what I had expected in that reputedly arid country. I retrieved my lamp, which cast a shocking brightness onto the road, and pulled my tent from the trunk. After sliding beneath a barbed-wire fence, I headed out across the prairie. The earth offered a surprising resistance, occasionally turning my ankle. Hard ground. I decided to camp on a small rise about a hundred yards from the road, close enough to make an easy escape. The lamp made me feel painfully conspicuous, so I assembled the tent hastily, sure that I was visible for miles, a beacon for every kind of evil. I fell twice into prickly pears, their thorns driving into the soft center of my palm.

It took a good thirty minutes to get everything set up. Finally, blessedly, I was able to turn off the lantern, but the darkness offered little comfort. I lay on my back for only a few minutes before I was up again, peering through the mesh at the invisible prairie. The painful throbbing in my hand was getting worse. I felt, as I said, vulnerable and exposed and alone. I yearned for the morning, my first glimpse of the open grasslands. What would they look like, feel like? Here is what I hoped: that a great vastness would open before me, full of the color and complexity of my dream prairies, alive with songbirds and hawks and coyotes and pronghorn. I wanted to see something so magnificent it might, as Albert Pike had said, throw me back upon myself, change me instantly and forever.

Here is what would actually happen: I'd wake to see a Hereford cow grazing on yellow sweet clover, a European invasive, about fifty yards away. Yet there, too, like a promise kept, would be a prairie coneflower—several of them within reach. I would walk around, discovering that the open spaces were not so open, a ranch house and barn were within sight. But closer, near my ankles, I would find the wild things hanging on: the reptilian prickly pears, the yellow and purple prairie coneflowers, the sideoats grama, its seed head shaped like an arrow's feather. The day would eventually carry me back into the Badlands, into the Sage Creek Wilderness area where I would unknowingly pitch my tent in a buffalo wallow and be warned of the danger by a park official. The next morning I would take a long hike across milky Sage Creek and into a prairie dog town. Near its borders I would lay down, munch a breakfast bar, and watch in amazement as a bison bull wallowed in the dusty earth. Not much later I would discover that standing just beneath me in the deep arroyo had been another bison bull. If he had decided to walk up the embankment, he might have stepped on my head.

Thus I would become sensitive to the layers of the prairie, where surprises can live and grow. Moving on I would observe how the taller grasses—Indian grass, even bluestem and compass plant—flourished in the low places, while the buffalograss, short and crisp, clung to the upland. Inside a deep, brushy draw I would hear a rattlesnake's warning and slowly step back out. Following a bison trail up to a high, hot place, I would view the impressive, serrated edge of the distant Pinnacles, their strata bleached white in the sun. Up there I would run out of water, feel thirst, become lost, but eventually find my way back down through juniper thickets, acrid in the heat. In the open valley near my campsite, I would watch another bison bull roll in the dirt of the prairie dog town, the small residents barking furiously. The centuries-old conversation, continuing.

But again, all that would occur later. Tonight inside my small tent was the beginning, and there must always be a beginning to any new story of our lives on the land. For those few hours the prairie held me, suspended and totally bewildered, in its grasp, the familiar land once again full of fear and mystery. I continued staring into the dark until, gradually, the rainy mist began to lift. Far in the distance I spotted tiny points of light moving just above the earth. I gazed at them, feeling the old longing—the eyes of bison in the moonlight? But there was no moon, and it didn't take me long to determine they were the headlights of cars traveling on Interstate 90, the same interstate I'd followed from Iowa. At first I was disappointed—after all that effort and worry, I had not traveled very far from the highway. I was not lost in the prairie and probably never could be. Then I imagined the people in those cars, driving along the edge of the grasslands. To them I was part of the dark unknown, something wild that might run out of the night and into the thin wedge of their headlights. And for me as well, this was the first, most startling miracle of the prairie: my presence in it.

I lay back down to sleep, the great land all before me.

CHAPTER 2

Reaching Yarak *The Peregrinations of Dan O'Brien*

"Look at this," Dan O'Brien said to me, pointing to the young Cooper's hawk on his arm. "She's reached yarak."

The hawk's name was Alice—as in "Alice Cooper's Hawk"—and at the moment she did indeed seem as electrified as her heavy metal namesake. The speckled brown feathers on the back of her neck were elevated, her wings drawn tight, her eyes dark and hyper-attentive. Dan explained that "yarak" is what falconers refer to as the "killing trance," a state of excitement that indicates a raptor's eagerness to hunt. To illustrate, he instructed me to walk along the outside of the windbreak. When I scared a small bird from one of the shrubs, a simultaneous, lightning fast shadow passed before me. When my eyes caught up, I spotted Alice lodged in a nearby Russian olive —wings outstretched, thorns protruding between her feathers. It looked painful.

"Is she okay?" I asked.

"Okay?" Dan replied. "She's *dead*."

"Oh no," I responded, horrified.

"No, dummy, not Alice, the sparrow." Dan pointed to the small, bloody ball of feathers clutched in Alice's talons.

My unfamiliarity with this moment—a native grasslands preda-tor killing its prey—was a big reason why I was in South Dakota visit-ing Dan's ranch for the second time. I was there to learn about a bio-region I had lived in all my life but about which I knew very little. For Dan, however, this moment and many others like it had been at the center of his life and writing for nearly twenty-five years.

Few writers have done more to restore a degree of wildness to the grasslands than Dan O'Brien. His love of the wild began early, during his childhood in Ohio. "From the beginning," he writes, "the migra-tion of wild things fascinated me. . . . Crows and geese would come from nowhere to gather, in the spring and fall, near Lake Erie, and they spoke to me as surely as the stars and the magnetism of the earth spoke to them. They drew me near and I watched them, never know-ing exactly why I was watching, but knowing that their wildness was a vital element of life." For O'Brien this vital element was most evident in birds of prey, the raptors. As a boy he became fascinated with hawks, even raising a fledgling red-tail when he was twelve. However, his most profound experience with a raptor occurred in 1965, when he was eighteen. While visiting a beach on the Gulf of Mexico, he watched, for the first time, a peregrine falcon hunt its prey:

The peregrine was a dark unfamiliar blur and I could think only that perhaps it was a stray artillery shell or a meteorite that would crash into the waves after it passed through the flock of birds. . . . It came out at the bottom of the flock and flared with grace and purpose at the top of the waves. The air passing though the falcon's wings made a whooshing sound. After its first stoop, the falcon turned on its tail and climbed effortlessly several hundred feet above the rattled sanderlings. From this position, it controlled them, covering distance in a way that mocked physics. It loomed in the salty air high above, lingered for an instant, then rolled and dove. The second stoop was lethal and the falcon, with a sanderling in its talons, mounted again without so much as a wing flap. In a minute it was gone, leaving just the memory of something alive, moving as fast as imagination allowed, commanding the upper air and, incidentally, the earth below.[1]

That moment marked the beginning of a lifelong fascination with falcons: a dedication to hunting with them, to preserving them, to living like them.

O'Brien's efforts to preserve the species began in the early 1970s. He was in his twenties and had just moved to South Dakota, escaping his native Ohio where the shootings at Kent State had left him feeling vulnerable to the human violence and chaos of the time. As friends continued to be drafted, O'Brien thought it would be impossible to escape the war. Due to a childhood hearing loss, however, he failed his military physical and wasn't drafted. Then the Peregrine Fund came knocking.

The Peregrine Fund was a nonprofit organization based at Cornell University, dedicated to saving the species from extinction. This was a different kind of war, and in the 1970s it received little public attention. But it was a war nonetheless. DDT and local bounties had ravaged peregrine populations, leaving only three known pairs in the entire Rocky Mountain West. There were only twenty known pairs in all of America. Dan's job was to relocate — or "hack" — young falcons from breeding facilities into the wilds of the Rocky Mountain area. The work was exhausting and dangerous, requiring long weeks of hiking, climbing cliffs, and monitoring and protecting the birds. Gradually, thanks to the efforts of O'Brien and many others, as well as a national ban on DDT in 1972, peregrine numbers rebounded. The process of officially removing them from the endangered species list began in the summer of 1995, and now nesting pairs are found all over the West and Midwest, including metropolitan skyscrapers.

O'Brien moved to the Dakota grasslands for literary reasons as well, the most important of which was to study writing with John Milton at the University of South Dakota. Milton was, according to O'Brien, "the first person to talk seriously to me about the importance of place in literature."[2] And like Milton the most important place for O'Brien was the northern Plains. It was the native range of his beloved falcons and their prey, but even as a child vacationing with his family in the Black Hills, O'Brien felt at home on the open prairies. Those prairies have been essential to his life and work ever since. In his collection of short stories, Eminent Domain (1987), as well as his three novels, Spirit of the Hills (1988), In the Center of the Nation (1991), and Brendan Prairie (1996),

O'Brien explores the complex and often adversarial relationship between human interests and the grasslands environment. However, *The Rites of Autumn: A Falconer's Journey across the American West* (1988) was, at the time, the only one of his books to directly explore his own relationship to that environment.[3] For me this work of autobiographical nonfiction raises important questions about what it means not only to appreciate and protect the all but invisible cycles of grasslands wildlife but also to participate in those cycles—to live them.

The Rites of Autumn begins on a mountain cliff in Montana, where a golden eagle kills two out of the four young falcons O'Brien has just hacked. In the few minutes it takes to descend the cliff to recapture the remaining fledglings, an eagle picks off one more. Ironically it is O'Brien's hearing loss that prevents him from saving the bird—he cannot hear the shouts of his distant colleagues. The experience also exposes the tension at the heart of his relationship to nature. On the one hand O'Brien believes the eagle cannot be blamed for killing the birds; it had to feed its own young. On the other hand he blames himself and has difficulty accepting the loss, emotionally:

The term "survival of the fittest" makes perfect sense when read from a college textbook or discussed over coffee, but the reality of it can be demoralizing. Nothing makes you feel more insignificant than to witness a golden eagle swoop down to pluck a clumsy young peregrine falcon from the air. It is a grisly thing to see and only underscores the fact that nature is extraordinarily unforgiving. . . . And even when you think you understand it, when intellectually you see this is the way it has to be, it is still difficult to shrug your shoulders and accept it.

O'Brien, however, does not accept the fate of all the young falcons. After the failed release, the standard procedure would have been to capture the remaining bird and, because it would be imprinted and dependent on human care, transport her to the breeding facility in Boise. Instead, after lengthy reflection O'Brien decides that he will try to give the falcon "the chance to become what its genes had prepared it to be." "And it occurred to me," he continues, "that it would be a necessary privilege for me to go along."[4] O'Brien decides to teach this young raptor, which he names Dolly, how to be wild by hunting her along her natural migratory route, the great corridor of grass from South Dakota to the Gulf of Mexico, where he hopes to release her into the southern draw of her species.

The Rites of Autumn is the narrative of this journey with Dolly. It starts in the sage-land flats of Montana, then moves south through the Rocky Mountains of Wyoming, the grasslands of Dakota and Nebraska, and the arid plains of the Llano Estacado. As O'Brien and Dolly travel and hunt, O'Brien educates readers about birds of prey, Plains environmental history, and the grand migrations that are the Plains' natural identity. He also introduces us to other falconers dedicated to preserving and restoring the grasslands. One falconer gave his entire retirement savings to the Peregrine Fund, while another, a rancher, helped implement grazing restrictions on native grasses in his county, one of only two counties in the nation to do so. What distinguishes this book, however, is not just O'Brien's critical look at the endangered grasslands but also the way he turns that critical eye inward, questioning the motives behind his own connection to Dolly and to the environment they share. "So what did I think I was doing?" he asks, referring to his unusual role as surrogate parent to Dolly. "Was I just another silly human with an anthropocentric view of the world?"[5]

For me, O'Brien's connection to Dolly was far from arrogant—it required careful training, scientific knowledge, and what O'Brien calls "affection." This affection is personal, but it is also based on history and biology. "Peregrines and men have a special history," he writes, "a tradition of association rivaled by only two other animals, the horse and the dog. But the peregrine stands apart because it has never been domesticated. Though the degree to which a horse or dog has forgotten its ancestral ways determines its attractiveness to mankind, the opposite could be said of the peregrine." Humans are also drawn to the falcon, O'Brien claims, because it shares with us "the same aesthetic taste" in landscape. "[Peregrines] nest in the most beautiful places on earth," he states. "In the days of their rapid decline, when peregrine nests were few and very hard to find, it was commonly known that the best way to find a peregrine eyrie was to go to the nearest tourist trap and look at the postcards of local places of beauty."[6]

This shared "aesthetic taste," especially for the prairies, is part of

O'Brien's affection for the peregrine and because of its biological origins seems more akin to "biophilia" than anthropocentrism. Biophilia is defined in part as the human "affinity and reverence for living things, attachments that are not simply inculcated by culture but deeply ingrained in basic genetic makeup." As a species we evolved inside an intimate relationship to our savannah-like environments, where the sound of water and the smell of grass and trees and the presence of rich animal life had deep, even mortal significance. According to some it still does. In one recent experiment, participants from all over the globe were asked to rate the attractiveness of various kinds of landscape, and most of them preferred "open, grassy environments with water and scattered trees — just like the savanna habitat that was home for millenniums to ancient human ancestors." In losing those habitats and species we face, according to the sociobiologist E. O. Wilson, "an enormous psychological and spiritual loss." David Orr agrees that by systematically destroying natural diversity we are waging "a war against the very sources of mind."[7]

The Rites of Autumn, in contrast, presents a man who, through a close relationship with a wild bird, becomes reunited with those sources. And what he finds there is a fundamental, inner tension between wildness and domesticity, between migration and stasis. "It has occurred to me that this state might be addictive," O'Brien reflects while driving Dolly to the Boise breeding facility. "I know people, and indeed am one myself who, when things aren't going exactly right, feel the need to jump into a pickup and drive several hundred miles in one direction or the other." At the same time, "There was something in me that did not want to leave the ranch, that wanted to walk around my 760 acres of dry pasture every morning for the rest of my life, to get to know the neighbors again and buy a quarter horse colt to work with on a daily basis. But by then Dolly was ready to go, and the federal permit had come through. I was committed."[8]

Throughout the rest of the narrative, O'Brien finds himself torn between his commitment to Dolly and his commitment to the ranch and his partner, Kris — two different commitments to home.

O'Brien's inner conflict finds its analogue in the history of the surrounding grasslands. The tension between nomadic and settled civilizations, according to Richard Manning, "erupts wherever grasslands exist." Manning argues, however, that it is the freedom of motion that best defines grasslands ecology, especially the migrations of native wildlife and hunter-gatherer societies. O'Brien's treatment of Plains history highlights similar tensions, especially within the lives of historic men who themselves were wanderers in the wild. Crazy Horse, for instance, the "last of the free Sioux," and John Colter, a famous free-trapper from the early nineteenth century. "John Colter was defined by his movement, his freedom," writes O'Brien. "It seemed no fluke to me that within three years of the day Colter surrendered his life-style, he was dead." Likewise, "What made Crazy Horse triumphal was his wildness, his unconquerable freedom." The possibility of this freedom is part of what attracts O'Brien to a migratory life in nature, away from other kinds of commitment. "[Kris] had asked me once what I was looking for," he recalls. "I had mumbled a reply that probably didn't satisfy her. But she never called me on it; she knew I didn't have a good answer. Then I looked around my little camp; the dogs sleeping peacefully, quail cooking over a fire, and the sea beyond. This was part of the answer, I was sure. But only part."⁹

The quail cooking over the fire underscores that for O'Brien, the essence of the native grasslands, its freedom and wildness, is defined by the cycles of not only migration but also predation. "We had begun to hunt," he proclaims after first eating grouse that Dolly has killed. "As José Ortega y Gasset says in *Meditations on Hunting,* we were now more than spectators of nature. We were part of it; physically and spiritually we were finding our way back." O'Brien goes on to distinguish between his own predatory relationship to nature, one that "is not a matter of outwitting or overpowering animals," and the envious, controlling relationship inflicted by others. It is the envy of wildness, of its freedom and defiance, that has led much of human civilization to want to subdue and destroy nature and those most closely associated with it. As an example O'Brien cites the murder of Crazy Horse at Fort Robinson, Nebraska, an act "very much like that of a farmer who, after witnessing a peregrine falcon stoop from the heavens to catch a duck, creeps up on it while it feeds and kills it with a rusty pitch fork."¹⁰

The stories of Crazy Horse and Colter, while attracting O'Brien, further reveal his ambivalence over connecting himself to wild things in a modern culture that seeks, consciously or unconsciously, to contain and destroy them. Too often such a commitment leads to despair, as the end of *Rites of Autumn* illustrates. On Padre Island off the coast of Texas, O'Brien is about to release Dolly for good — "she was as close to a wild peregrine as I could make her." If all went well she would join the migration of her species to South America, then return with them to the northern Great Plains in the spring or summer. In this spirit of hope, he releases Dolly into the tropical sky. Minutes later he sees her strike a power line and tumble to the earth. She is alive but crippled — "her migration, and mine, was ended."[11]

Though the physical journey is over, O'Brien's inner journey continues: "A thin strand of steel had decided Dolly's fate. That was one thing I did not have to worry about. But the next day or two, I would have to make some decisions about myself." In the end it appears he has decided to live close to the ranch, with Kris. Dolly is also settled there, spending the rest of her days in "a large airy chamber, with padded perches and a view of the Black Hills." She will never be wild. Likewise, O'Brien's understanding of his own relationship to nature remains elusive. "Sometimes I see injustice in what happened to [Dolly]," he writes. "Sometimes I want to say that the eagle in Montana was a natural hazard, but the power line in Texas was unnatural, man-made, and so unfair. But I am not so sure. From time to time I believe I have become wiser. Usually I feel I have learned nothing." As he observes the autumn migrations, however, there is clearly a touch of sadness, a continued longing to join the resplendent flow of life across the grasslands:

And, when I see the north wind pushing the prairie grass in front of it, I know that it is pushing peregrines too. I know that peregrines are riding it southward. But not Dolly. And not me. We may catch a duck and cook it over an open fire. We may sleep outdoors and watch meteors streak through the belt of Orion. But we will be staying here. We will live out our lives in the center of the continent, surrounded by the movement of birds. We will remain lodged between the greens and browns of the earth and the endless blue of the prairie sky.[12]

O'Brien's desire to merge with wildness is nothing new in American nature writing. It is, however, newly applied to the contemporary American grasslands. If David Orr is right, if by extinguishing native plant and animal life we are waging "a war against the very sources of mind," then no American population is in more psychological and spiritual jeopardy than those of us living in the Midwest and Great Plains. Because the native grasslands of this bioregion remain, as Dan Flores has said, "pathetically underprotected ecologically, . . . [c]itizens of places like Texas and Kansas are today among the most divorced of all Americans from any kind of connection with regional nature."[13] Within such a place, O'Brien's traditional narrative becomes unique and essential. For residents like myself who have never seen a peregrine falcon or any other large grasslands predator on the hunt, it has the potential to create powerful, albeit vicarious, feelings of biophilia — feelings that might lead to action.

At the time, however, what most affected me while reading The Rites of Autumn was not the inclination toward environmental activism. Rather it was the endnote of longing and ambivalence, the acknowledgment of hazard and risk and doubt in his relationship to nature. Standing as I had near the banks of Otter Creek Marsh back in Iowa, just after the floods, watching the fall flight of pintails and wood ducks, of Canada geese and red-tailed hawks, I too had felt ambivalent. My time in graduate school would soon be ending, and I would have to decide what to do. I felt on the one hand a familiar urge to cut free from earthly bonds, to live a writer's life of motion and freedom. On the other hand I felt an emerging desire to stay in one place, to commit to a more grounded notion of home. Reading O'Brien's book helped complicate this polarity, distinguishing between a human migration based on the love of wildness and one that simply moves us from one house, one city, one state to the next — an exhaustless process of reentrenchment involving little regard for ecological relationships.

Yet the question of how to "make it come to be" remained, intensifying during my camping experience in the Badlands and Buffalo Gap. While there I again found myself suspended between relationships to home. I missed my wife, my family, my friends, even the house where I spent my childhood — all those things that define who I am. Yet the openness of the terrain, the severe shift in temperatures, and even the slow movement of the bison helped me see that the native identity of the place was movement, not stasis, not farms and housing developments. On the prairies, as Richard Manning has stated, the cause of environmental jeopardy may, in fact, be our root-edness. But what would it mean to re-create a self—even a society —in the image of those prairies, to embrace a wilder, more migra-tory and predacious lifestyle? *The Rites of Autumn*, for me, explored some of the complexities and contradictions such a life forces on the daily, more commonplace commitments to loved ones, to commu-nity, even to writing. How is it possible to live successfully within those contradictions, to live "lodged" between earth and sky, be-tween stillness and motion? These were some of the questions I car-ried with me from the Badlands to Dan O'Brien's ranch, just north of Sturgis, South Dakota.

* * *

I drove up the mile-long gravel driveway, Bear Butte towering a thou-sand feet over the acres of emerald grass, and parked in front of a small ranch house. That day in June 1994 Dan was between movie work in Colorado and a fishing trip to Montana and would be leaving the ranch before dawn the next morning. Clearly he had not totally relinquished a migratory lifestyle, and I felt lucky to have caught him. Erney, Dan's friend and assistant, pulled up on a noisy four-wheeler.

"Are you the guy from Iowa?" he asked. He was wearing blue cover-alls, his gray hair and beard blown thick by the wind. Bright, inquisi-tive eyes appeared crevassed above his high, sunburned cheeks.

"Yeah, that's right."

"Glad you made it," he said, extending a rough, thumb-less hand. "Dan should be along shortly. We've got to move them cattle today." He took off, rumbling toward the eastern pastures.

A few minutes later Dan rode up to the house on a tall, chestnut horse. He was slim and muscular, his skin dark from the sun. I intro-duced myself, and we shook hands.

"Nice to meet you," he said. "Can you ride a horse?"

The question caught me off guard.

"Uh . . . sure," I said, trying to sound matter-of-fact. Actually, I hadn't ridden a horse for over a year, and that was on a slow, guided trail in Montana at a family reunion.

"Good," he said. "We could use some help with the cattle." He tied his own horse to a post and walked around to the back of the house. I followed. He retrieved a saddle and blanket and placed them on one of the other horses standing outside. Erney returned just as I was mounting the dark and slender yearling.

"You should get along fine with this horse," Dan said. "She's from Iowa." He winked at Erney.

As we rode slowly toward the pastures, Dan explained a little of the history of the ranch, which was just over seven hundred acres. He had purchased it back in the 1970s when it was a piece of overgrazed, degraded rangeland — a "calf-killing son-of-a-bitch," as the previous owner called it. At first, to survive financially he ran a small cow-calf operation, but it has since become a less labor-intensive yearling operation.[14] The cattle remain a secondary concern. The point all along has been to transform this piece of land into a falconer's paradise. That has meant restoring some of its original ecological integrity, restocking the area with native grouse and other quarry, and bringing back indigenous grasses. The cattle serve an ecological purpose as well, grazing the warm-season grasses from May until August, when they are sold in time for falconing season. Dan explained that to avoid overgrazing, he and a neighbor had created a system of fences that allows their small herds to rotate across both properties — a strategy informed by the historic movement of buffalo and other wild grazers across the open prairie. The result, as I could see, was lush grass and wildflowers and plenty of cover for wildlife. I sat tall and confident in the saddle, surveying the gentle land around me.

"Do you mind if we pick up the pace a little?" Dan asked.

"Not at all."

He started his horse into a gallop and mine followed. Though I had ridden fast-moving horses before, I was completely unprepared for the challenge of tearing across the open prairie. The ground was dry, uneven, and bumpy, and the horse kept lurching to one side then the other. I was literally bouncing out of the saddle. Soon my left foot slipped out of the stirrup and I felt myself sliding off. *I am going to die*, I thought. Desperate, I dropped the reins and grabbed the saddle horn. Dan finally turned around and, seeing my predicament, reined his horse. My horse slowed down as well.

"You okay?" he inquired.

"Yeah," I replied, panting, pulling myself back to an upright position. "Yeah, just fine. I just got a little out of sync back there."

Dan smiled—my fear must have been obvious. He turned his horse and we continued, slowly, toward the herd. Moving the cattle was easy; the horse knew what to do, methodically guiding the cow through the gates and into the next pasture. But it was too late to play the good horseman. All pretense had been erased during our tear across the prairies—the rough, unfamiliar surface of the land indelibly printed on my mind and body. I would be sore for days.

When we returned to the house, a middle-aged couple was waiting to talk with Dan. The man was big, over six feet tall, with long blond neck hair. He was wearing a sleeveless shirt and had some kind of medieval shield tattooed on his shoulder. He was interested in hawking and Dan agreed to show him his setup. Dan led us all to the large steel building where he kept the birds and equipment. Inside was a small room full of electric collars, check cords, falcon hoods, telemetry equipment, bath pans, and wood falcon blocks. There were also postal scales to weigh the birds. Dan explained that it was important to keep them at a proper hunting weight; they wouldn't hunt if they were overfed. Erney added that the birds required the meat equivalent of about a robin a day. It soon became clear to me why falconing had long been considered the sport of kings: it takes a lot of money and time.

Back outside we observed the falcons perched high in their large breezy chambers. Dan declined to bring them out from behind the fencing, saying he wouldn't be hunting with them until the fall, after they were finished molting. Though the birds remained in the shadows, I could feel their eyes glaring at us.

"Is one of them Dolly?" I asked.

"No, she's at the breeding facility in Boise," Dan replied. "But that bigger one there is her offspring."

Erney explained that they usually get their birds from Boise in June, "as babies," then release them on the property. They fly free for about a month, and then he and Dan recapture them. Sometimes they hunt with the same bird for years, but more often it just flies off during a chase, never to return. It was that balance between wildness and tameness in a bird that, for Dan, marked successful falconing. The visitors seemed to have a different view of things.

"I just love the feel of a hawk on my arm," he said.

"Yeah," his wife replied, adjusting the strings on her halter. "It just looks so cool."

"Have you worked with birds before?" Dan asked.

"Well, I used to raise magpies," the man replied. "In fact, this year I found a nest of them and brought one home with me. When I came back the next day to get the other one, it was gone and the nest all scattered. What I figure is the mother smelled me and moved her baby."

Dan looked at Erney.

"Actually, it's more likely a raccoon followed your scent to the nest and killed the bird."

"Oh."

Later that evening after the couple had left, Dan and Kris prepared a dinner of herring salad and grilled pork, and we all sat down at the picnic table on their deck. Erney was there along with Kris's sister, Charlotte, visiting from Boise. Dan asked Erney what he thought about the tattooed man.

"He'll never make it in hawking," he replied. Dan nodded.

"How do you know that?" I asked.

"Just an intuition," Erney said. "You've got to have a lot of money and time and know how to work with these birds, and he doesn't seem to have any of that. And it takes a different kind of mentality, too, a hunter's mentality, not a pet-keeper's mentality. If you want a parakeet, get a parakeet. But a hawk's a different thing. A hawk's a wild animal."

Dan agreed: "Hawking is not a hobby — it can't be if it's done right. It's a way of life."

I wanted him to elaborate, but the conversation drifted elsewhere. After we cleared the table, Kris said that she and Charlotte were returning to Rapid City. Kris works as an anesthesiologist at a local hospital there and spends most of her time at the house she and Dan own in town. Dan, in contrast, drives the hour to the ranch every morning to write and work with the birds and his hunting dogs, Spud and Mel. Kris has striking, dark features and a powerfully athletic build. She and Dan are marathon runners.

"Do me a favor," she said to him, "give me a phone call over the weekend, okay? You're a hard guy to get a hold of sometimes."

"I think I can do that," he replied, smiling, and they walked to her truck together.

When Dan returned he retrieved some beers from the fridge, and we sat down at the picnic table for the interview. I started by telling him how much I admired the beauty of his land and what appeared to be the ecological integrity of his life on it. It was the kind of life I fantasized for myself, but one that also mystified me: how did a boy from an Ohio dairy farm end up with such a fierce attachment to grasslands wildlife?

"Well, the answer is both personal and literary," he replied. "On my father's dairy farm, I had been exposed to more wildlife than many of my peers, especially birds of prey. So that's where it began. As far as this country, I remember coming out here as a kid with my family and thinking, 'I'm home.' I returned here when I was fifteen with my brother, and we went clear to the mountains, just to hang out. My brother loved the mountains, but I always liked the grasslands. I always liked where you could see. I tried living in the Black Hills for a while and it was good, but I didn't like it as well as living here. Anyway, I moved to South Dakota in 1970. I was about to get drafted, and at the same time I had just finished reading *Lord Grizzly* by Frederick Manfred, which is all about the awesome power of the Great Plains landscape. I came here to learn more about that landscape and to learn, from John Milton and Manfred, how to write about it. I was also interested in falconing, and this is a great place to do that."

"So South Dakota offered a chance to return to a landscape you love," I said. "But in *Rites of Autumn* you also mention the draft and suggest that coming out here was an escape as well. Is that accurate?"

"Oh yeah, definitely. I think for me, and for many from my generation, there occurred a jarring realization early on that the world wasn't the way we had been told it would be. If you were born in the forties and grew up in the fifties like I did, Christ, everything in the world was perfect and we were going to inherit the greatest country on earth and technology was going to provide us with everything we ever wanted. Then the sixties came along and for those of us caught in the crack of being young and male, it became clear that not only was our notion of the world a bunch of bullshit, but we were probably going to die fighting a war no one understood. I mean we had really thought we were free, that that was what it meant to be an American. Turns out we weren't even close to being free. So I think that's part of why I ended up out here, and why others ended up in the West as well, like Rick Bass. We were trying to break loose again. I wanted to be away from Kent State, away from all the goddamned factories where my high school friends ended up working. I wanted open country, so I moved to South Dakota. I've been hiding out here ever since."

"You mentioned Rick Bass," I continued, "another writer who lives in the West and writes about environmental issues. Clearly you both aren't hiding out as writers; you've been pretty prolific. What's the nature of your life here as a writer, the benefits and challenges? Have you made any sacrifices to live in such a rural area?"

"Well, yeah, kind of," he replied. "But I don't buy this stuff about the suffering American writer—I really don't think most Americans know what suffering is. I mean this Saint Dostoyevsky stuff, that's a crock. Sure it can be difficult work, and I threaten to quit each time I finish a book, but then it's kind of like remodeling your house or getting a divorce—after a while you forget all the bullshit you went through and you do it again. Another thing I don't buy is this stuff about how midwestern and western writers have it tougher than other writers, that they don't get any respect. If anything, writers out here get a break. I mean, you know, I have a fax machine and a telephone, so what's the difference? Sure, I'm not writing about Holocaust victims who fall in love in Manhattan but, you know, big deal—I'm not sure everyone wants to read about that. At the same time, I'm not preoccupied with how many people want to read about grass. If I did, I'd go crazy. Still, when I travel around on book tours, I'm amazed at how many readers *are* interested in grass."

I asked him if he receives much support from readers in South Dakota.

"I'm from here, so I get a lot of support from the arts council and so forth. But if no one in South Dakota ever bought another book of mine, it wouldn't make any difference on my financial statement. I sell maybe a couple hundred books here or a thousand, so these aren't the people reading my books; my audience is somewhere else. For some unknown reason I'm popular in France—I've had French guys actually come out here and interview me. I think part of it is that people romanticize what they don't have, and France doesn't have this western landscape. But people living here all their lives aren't interested in reading about it."

"Does that bother you?"

"Not really. Most of the people in this state don't read the kind of things I write anyway. And I'm glad they don't. If my neighbors read my stuff, it would change my relationship to them and I'm not sure I want it changed. When I talk with them, I talk about cows and grass; I don't want to talk with them about writing."

"So you don't see your writing as having a regional mission?"

"First of all, I don't really consider myself a regional writer. Too often writers use that term 'regional' as a crutch and then whine about how New York doesn't pay any attention to them. I bet my sweet ass that if they wrote a good book, New York would pay attention to them. To be honest, I don't think that many good books have come out of this area. But when it's a good book, it doesn't matter where it comes from. I mean look at *Moby-Dick*—who the fuck wants to read a religious book about whales? Yet he pulled it off. He pulled it off. And when you write a good book like that, no one is going to call you 'regional.'"

"I'm not sure I'm following here," I said. "Are you saying that the term 'regional' is derogatory, because what I was trying to say was..."

"No, I don't think of it as a derogatory term," he continued, "I just don't think it means anything. I mean what's a region? New York's a region. And what's a regional book? A lot of people call *Dakota* a regional book, but that's about someone from New York who moves to the prairies? Kathleen Norris is a friend of mine—I call her 'the weird sister'—but she's as New York as they come. And what about *The Solace of Open Spaces* by Gretel Ehrlich—that's not about this country, kiss my ass, that's not about this country at all. The term 'regional' is so arbitrary. The classic example is Richard Ford. When I first knew him he was called a New England writer, *The Sports Writer* and all that stuff, and then he wrote *Rock Springs* and suddenly he was a western writer. Now he lives in New Orleans, and I bet he'll be called a southern writer after his next book. So talking about 'regional literature' is fun—God knows I've taken a lot of courses on the subject and loved them—but I've become really skeptical of it. Anyone can write about horses and cows and grass, but the trick is writing about it well. *That's the trick.*"

"But are there any writers you would call distinctly western," I asked, "those whose work is recognizably connected to a particular landscape? What about Frederick Manfred; didn't you say it was his work that, in part, led you to live in this country?"

"Okay, now you're talking about something different. If what you're talking about is not this general, abstract term 'regional' but rather something more specific like 'western short- and mixed-grass prairie writers,' then yeah, there are some distinctions to be made—those writers are a different breed of cats. But there aren't that many of them. Manfred was one and Stegner, writers who lived in the West most of their lives and really understand the subject matter. But just knowing the subject matter and living in a place doesn't make you a good writer. I mean, I go to these writing conferences every once in a while and these people will come up to me and tell me how they've written a story about their grandfather who works with pigs and how they can't get it published. I'll say, well, maybe there's something in the writing that isn't working, and they'll say, 'Naw, that's just the way those sonsabitches are on the East Coast; they never give us regional guys a chance.' You never heard Stegner and Manfred whining about that; they just wrote great books."

"It's interesting that you mentioned Stegner," I said, "because he certainly defined for himself a sense of regional responsibility. He felt that the way people wrote about the West influenced the way it was settled, the way it continues to be settled, often in detrimental ways. I don't think it was just about writing a good book to him; it was about writing a responsible book. Do you agree with that at all?"

"Well, yeah, I don't like the fact that so many people are moving out here, and I think the popularity of western literature has encouraged that movement—it certainly did in my case. Of course, people in Ohio feel that way, people in New York feel that way—there are just too many people *everywhere*. No one likes change; you want it all to stay the same—the place where you kissed your first girl, the old swimming hole, everything. But I just get so tired of all the bellyach-ing. I was talking to Jim Harrison [author of *Legends of the Fall*] just a few nights ago, and he agreed. Every time I get together with people who've lived in the West as long as I have or longer, we just talk about how bad things have gotten, and it gets you down because no one is listening. No one is listening. The wilderness here is history, and people should start figuring out a way to deal with it."

I was a little confused at this point. *Rites of Autumn*, for me, had been about lamenting change, especially the destruction of grass-lands ecosystems and wildlife. Also, Dan's work with the Peregrine Fund certainly wasn't about just accepting the extinction of wildlife, just "dealing with it." It was about fighting that loss and then writ-ing about it, educating others. It was about responsibility. Didn't he think, I asked, that writers owed something to the places and com-munities where they lived?

"No," he replied, "I think writers should do whatever they want to do. That's the way it works. I don't think there should be any rules. Everyone has different reasons for writing: some want to entertain, some want to make money, some want to become famous. There are a million other motivations. In my case—and I'm not particularly proud of this—but in my case, I'd like to change the world, make it a better place. I do care a lot about the grasslands, and I learned a long time ago that the only thing that really works for me is the stuff I really feel deeply about. I feel deeply about cows and grass and fal-cons, so I gotta stick with that. That's how place gets into my writing; it's what I care about most. It's not a matter of choice. Other writers gotta go with what works best for them."

"I guess I don't really buy that," I said. "In *Rites of Autumn* you're critical of what you call 'Walt Disney Biology,' a romantic notion of nature in which no one takes responsibility for displacing and de-stroying wildlife with irrigation systems, hobby farms, and suburban sprawl. It seems to me that in your books you don't just accept the ignorant actions of others, you get angry and point out that igno-rance. Are you saying that it's okay to bash suburbanites for being ignorant of their surroundings, but not okay to bash writers?"

"No, I'm not saying that," he replied. "I bash writers all the time. Like the other day I read this goddamned book about a coyote—I

won't even tell you the name of it. It got good reviews, so I picked it
up. I read fifty pages of it and put it down—the coyote hadn't eaten
anything but vegetables for the first couple weeks. That's a stereotype
just as damaging as the stereotype of Indians as bloodthirsty savages.
But when writers and academics go around talking about 'responsibility' and 'stereotypes,' what they usually mean is this politically
correct bullshit. I mean look at the treatment of Indians. I live here
where Indians and Indian cultures are a really big deal, not just a literary big deal, and the politically correct notion of Indians as these
mystic nature people is wrong. I've lived here long enough to know
what it would be like to live here in a tent, killing shit with sharp
sticks all winter long. Those people were not a bunch of tree hug-
gers. And also, just because you're an Indian today doesn't mean you
know how to live on the Great Plains in an environmentally sound
way. Sure, Sioux culture may have a mystical connection to the Black
Hills, but does that mean they'd be able to take care of it any better
than the park service? Not necessarily. And yet writers and academics
keep perpetuating that stereotype. I could spend my whole career
criticizing those writers or that vegetarian coyote person, but then
I'd never write myself. I just write the best, most accurate books I can
and hope people will choose to notice. I can't worry about what other
writers are doing."

"What about writers who share this bioregion with you," I asked,
"like Linda Hasselstrom and others who share your environmental
sensibilities? Do you feel at all connected to them, part of some larger
mission to, as you said earlier, make this a better place?"

"Well, Linda and I have been fond friends for twenty-five years, but
we don't come from the same place on a lot of things. We have differences of opinion, like about grazing cattle on public lands and her
deep belief in the family ranch. I think the family ranch is a great
concept, but the reality is something different. Basically, the worship
of family ranching has left some of our most valuable resources in
the hands of some of our most ignorant people. Just because your
family has lived on the land for generations doesn't mean you know
shit about it. I mean my neighbor, a family rancher, is convinced that
hummingbirds migrate on the backs of geese. Sure that's funny, we
can laugh at that, but that same neighbor believes that it's his Chris-

tian duty to graze all his grass right down to the ground. He says that God gave him that grass and that if he didn't graze it all it would be a sin. And that's a pretty prevalent attitude among a lot of these ranchers. They don't want to hear about science, even if it means they ruin that piece of ground and run themselves out of business. They don't care; they just want to go to heaven. And even if you don't subscribe to that arrogant version of Christian speciesism, it still takes a hell of a lot of scientific knowledge to keep from hurting this fragile land. I've got a lot of friends who say it just takes common sense, but that's a crock. My goal is to live my life on this place and not leave any trace, not even a track. That would be the ideal. But to do that I'd need to know a lot more about the ecology here than I do now, and a lot more about myself."

"What do you mean 'know a lot more about yourself'?"

"Now here's something Linda Hasselstrom and I agree on. Most of us in America go around denying who we really are, denying our roots in the animal world. I mean it's a deep, deep denial. I think that one of our jobs, not really our job, but one of the things our writing *can* do is address that denial. We are essentially predatory, meat-eating animals—we smell, we have canine teeth, we can be mean, we can be cruel. To pretend that we don't possess these qualities, to hide behind, say, vegetarianism as a political statement or Christian morality, is an arrogant speciesism that puts racism and sexism to shame. It's dangerous. It's destroying the world. I want to plug back into the opposite thing, something closer to animal existence."

I asked what he meant by "plugging in."

"I have this idea—and it's nothing new—that a person really needs to be connected, plugged into the physical, natural world. Most of the people in this country are plugged into television or their jobs, but that leaves them insulated from what is real. What I mean by 'real' is dirt, air, water, fire—the physical, natural world. Some people start out being plugged in as kids but then lose that connection, like my brother. My brother probably has more to do with my outlook on life than any other person. I mean, he climbed Mount McKinley back in the sixties and was in one of the first Outward Bound courses. When we were in high school, we'd go mountain climbing in Colorado. But then he went to college, got married, had a cute little boy and girl, and went to law school. He's basically happy, but he longs for something more. When he comes out here to go hunting his desperation is just so clear to me, but he's trapped by the culture. Most of us are trapped by the culture because we're afraid to embrace this other thing, this freedom. Of course, it'd be better if we just didn't have the choice."

I asked him to explain, and he replied that he was working on another nonfiction book about falconing.[15] In this new book, he said, he wants to further explore what it means to "reconnect" to wildness as an individual and as a culture, a process of identifying with predation as well as migration.

"I'm interested in the possibility of changing culture by talking about this process. I don't mean phony reconnecting; I don't mean like when kids have an ecological project, an environmental day at school where they go out and paint faces on trees—which is what they do. That's antithetical to what I'm talking about. Instead they should go out there, chop a tree down, and eat the baby birds that are living in the top. Only something like that could truly change them. It's not enough to look at something in a zoo; you've got to get your hands on it. That's the same kind of thing as Earth Day. I was the chairman of the first Earth Day here in the 1970s—I mean, it was wild. It wasn't like go out and plant a fucking tree, give me a break. It was more like you should go out and wipe out an entire town, knock down all the buildings. It wasn't benign. It's not looking down on animals or vegetation but getting right down there in the blood of it. But how do you express that?"

At this point we had had a lot of beers and Dan was, quite frankly, beginning to scare me. He must have sensed this, because he suddenly shifted the topic to the beauty of the evening, calling attention to the distinctive "whoomph" of nighthawks, the first of the season.

"I love those birds," he said, looking east into the lush grasslands, golden with sweet clover. "They go way up, and have this big long stoop, and it makes that haunting noise. That's why the Indians called them the thunderbirds. I have a friendly argument going with Linda Hasselstrom about how they make that noise when they stoop. No one knows for sure. I guess it's just one of the mysteries of this place."

It was getting chilly, so Dan left to find us some jackets. When he returned, we stood against the deck railing and watched the moon rise.

"So how old are you, John?" he asked.

"Twenty-seven."

"Jesus, that's young," he said. "And you're getting a Ph.D.? Why?"

"I can't really remember right now."

"I don't blame you. I was in your shoes once. After I got my M.F.A. I was completely broke and Kris was working down in Denver, so I entered the English Ph.D. program there. I did that for a year and, my God, it was hard—reading Joyce and learning foreign languages and all that. I enjoyed it, don't get me wrong, but I was glad to be saved from it. I was at the point you are now, wondering what to do with my writing, when I won the Iowa Short Fiction Award. So I got a book published and then a novel, and, well, I'm still going. I dance along the fringe of academic life; I still teach a lot, but I've seen how it kills people. I've had good friends who were and are good writers, but then they get a university job, make fifty thousand dollars, and never write another thing. Talk about being insulated."

"About this insulating thing," I replied, "you're not exactly living like a wild animal here. I mean, how does that hot tub over there fit in with your goal of 'getting down in the blood of things'? And even if you aren't in academia, doesn't the act of writing itself separate you from the native essence of this place—writing is sedentary, it's a product of civilized society, not nomadic existence. How do you reconcile that literary life and the life of chopping down trees and eating baby birds and all that?"

Dan smiled, continuing to look out into the grasslands.

"I don't reconcile them. My life's a bunch of pretty obvious contradictions—haven't you figured that out yet? Sure, I may be a little closer to the natural cycles out here, but for all the talking I've done tonight, I'm essentially stuck like everyone else. And I worry about that. That's part of why I took another job with the Peregrine Fund this summer—for six weeks I can sleep on cliffs, get rained on, work with falcons, and be free for a while. But it's only temporary, and that's how I want it. I have a wonderful home here, and Kris, well, she means a lot to me. Like I said in the book, I'm suspended between these two worlds. I have friends who do live that migratory life, who are forty-five, fifty years old and have never lived in a house, never been married. I admire those guys. I admire Erney; he doesn't own anything. When he showed up here he didn't even have a driver's license. I admire him and those others, but I couldn't live like them. I just couldn't. Could you?"

"Probably not," I said, and went on to tell him that one of my reasons for traveling to South Dakota was to connect, however briefly, with what remained of the prairie wilderness.

"There's no wilderness left here," he replied, "so don't fool yourself. I mean, people talk about how this ranch is so isolated, but I hear cars and cows and airplanes. This place isn't isolated; it isn't wild. But at the same time, this ain't tofu country and it ain't ever going to be tofu country. Sure it's nice right now, but try coming back in February when you can't get out of your driveway for three weeks. There's still something wild and powerful in the land here, more than some other places, and that's what sustains me. Speaking of, did I tell you about my basset hound?"

"No, you didn't."

"When I first moved out here, I had this basset hound. He was a great hunting dog, but he got into the habit of roaming the land around here, sometimes for days at a time. Every once in a while he'd show up, like the time when my other dogs had cornered a cat. They were just barking at it, scaring it, when all of a sudden here came the hound, bumping and scraping his way toward all the excitement. When he got there, he just walked right past the other dogs, chomped down on the cat, and broke its neck. Just like that. We called him the 'prairie gator.' Anyway, the older and more crippled he got, the longer he stayed out on the prairie. The only way we knew he was alive was we'd hear him howlin' at the moon. Then he just disappeared. Something in this pissy little stretch of land changed that dog, made him a little wilder. It still has that power, even if most of us aren't able or willing to plug into it."

Behind us a warm breeze caressed the acres of yellow sweet clover and prairie grasses. Bear Butte, where Crazy Horse received his name and sought spiritual renewal, rose a thousand feet out of the southeastern horizon. Beside it the moon hung in the lavender sky. The air was full of birdsong. Dan seemed lost in the pleasure of the moment as well, despite having weathered almost twenty-five winters there.

"Look," he said, pointing to a small rise directly east. Two large-winged birds rose above the horizon then descended, circling and swooping at each other.

"Marsh hawks," he explained.

"Why are you so drawn to birds of prey, to falcons?" I asked.

"I want to be a falcon," he replied. "I want to see the world the way a falcon sees the world; I want to be as noble as a falcon; I want to be faithful to my mate; I want to raise young on a cliff; I want to hunt for my food. Falcons really do symbolize ideals that are beyond most of us, certainly beyond me. Whether releasing them in the wild or hunting with them or writing about them, those birds take me to a place I can't go on my own. And until you've been to that place, however briefly, I'm not sure you've really lived."

Before I left Dan's ranch, he and Erney invited me to return sometime in the fall when they were flying falcons, which I did the next year. In the interim I thought a lot about our conversation. Dan had proven to be a warm and generous host, but also, in ways I hadn't expected, an elusive personality. On the one hand he seemed uncomfortable talking about literary responsibility for the environment, and yet on the other his entire life had been informed by a deep sense of that responsibility. And all that talk about killing baby birds and wiping out towns and hunting shit with spears—I wasn't sure whether it was simply hyperbole or emerged, instead, from his ongoing desire to "plug in" to the latent wildness in himself and in the land around him. I sensed it was the latter, but I didn't yet know enough—about him or myself—to be sure.

I was, however, brought a little closer to understanding during a stay at South Dakota's Wind Cave National Park in late September 1995, just before my second visit to Dan's ranch. Most people visit the park to descend into its famous whistling, limestone caves—that's what my family and I had done back in 1975. Few people realize, however, that it is one of the most beautiful restored mixed-grass prairies in the country. I certainly didn't. Not until I ventured out into the miles of big bluestem, little bluestem, sideoats, and prickly pear. You can walk anywhere you want there, in any direction, no fences. And I walked for hours, through the grass, past woody draws full of juniper and snowberry, past shiny red mineral deposits where I watched free-roaming pronghorn and bison lick the earth to replenish their bodies. An hour or two later, still walking across the open prairie, I heard a kind of dull squeak. Then another. I followed the sounds for about a mile, my breath misting in the cold air, until I came to a crest overlooking a small valley. There, in a grassy clearing between wooded hillsides, was a bull elk resting in the sun. He tipped his head, his huge wrack falling backward, and let out a high-pitched, screeching rush of air that ended in a deep, nasal snort—his bugle call. More bugling came from the trees and soon two additional bulls emerged and crossed the valley. When I shifted my position to the north, I could see the cause of the commotion—a group of elk cows standing on the hillside. Their dominant bull was being challenged. The bull was clearly agitated, bugling furiously, rubbing his antlers against small trees, mating in quick succession with two of the cows. He was ready for a fight.

I knew what I was witnessing, yet I couldn't believe it. The only wild elk I'd ever encountered was at a great distance, through binoculars, against the jagged backdrop of Idaho's Sawtooth Mountains. At Wind Cave I was reminded that elk were native grasslanders, the great stags of the prairies, now pushed into the highlands by hunting and agriculture. But what I experienced in that moment was not about factual knowledge, not about appreciation or empathy. In this way it was different from watching birds at Otter Creek Marsh in Iowa or pronghorn at Buffalo Gap. It was, instead, a moment of crystalline clarity, of cohesion, and yet also a dispersion of self, a negation of consciousness. I was consumed. The experience carved out a space in my life that can never be filled—except by the sight of those bugling elk. There is no leaving that emptiness; I carry it around with me wherever I go. It gnaws at the surface. And when I try to describe it to others, I not only want to verbalize I want to embody: the shivering fury of the bulls, their urgency, their heat. My voice rises in the telling, I exaggerate, I gesture wildly. I make a fool of myself. And when the conversation moves on to other subjects I want to interrupt and say: "Wait! I've seen the elk—*remember?*"

What must it feel like, I wondered, to carry around a space carved out of you by encounters with the native predators of this place, encounters far rarer in the grasslands than stumbling upon elk? The gray and Mexican wolf, the mountain lion, the grizzly bear, the peregrine falcon—creatures extinguished, or nearly extinguished, from their native prairie habitats by human ignorance and government-sanctioned slaughter. In 1915 the U.S. government began its infamous "predator control" campaign, mostly to rid the western rangeland of wolves. Richard Manning notes that "[b]etween 1916 and 1928, federal, state and grazing association agents killed 63,145 animals." This included the eradication of the entire wolf population in the Plains, along with "169 bears, 1,524 bobcats, 36,242 coyotes, . . . 18 mountain lions, [and] uncounted badgers, beavers, civet cats, blackfooted ferrets, foxes, martens, minks, muskrats, opossums, raccoons, skunks, weasels, porcupines, rattlesnakes, prairie dogs, ground squirrels, jack rabbits, eagles, and magpies."[16] The federal Animal Damage Control (ADC) program continues the killing. In fiscal year 1990 in seventeen western states, ADC employees intentionally killed more than 809,000 animals, including 91,158 coyotes, 7,065 foxes (four species), 250 mountain lions, and 236 black bears.[17]

To connect in any meaningful way to such predators, I thought, is to carry around a sense of loss, a sense of emptiness, as big as the land itself. Little wonder Dan O'Brien feels the need to talk about killing baby birds, about hunting with falcons, about getting down in the blood of prey—what else is left on the prairie to fill that emptiness but our own bodies and imaginations?

I arrived for my second visit to Dan's ranch at night, in the middle of a September snowstorm in 1995. The next morning, however, was sunny and by noon all the snow had vanished. Dan was regularly hunting with the falcons, and I was looking forward to joining him for the next few days to see this legendary raptor in action. Our first day out was silver and still, nearly perfect. Dan had two falcons—a female peregrine named Little Bird and a male Barbary named Dundee. Both had been given to Dan as chicks by a local breeder. Dan and Erney had released them on the property in June and recaptured them about a month later. During my last visit I had only seen his peregrines from outside their large, fenced-in mews. Now that they were out in the light I could fully appreciate their striking beauty, their deep blue wing feathers and tan, speckled undersides. Their eyes were dark and wild and stared right through me. They were mesmerizing.

While driving slowly through the grasslands around his ranch, looking for a good duck pond, Dan asked me if I had ever seen falcons hunt.

"No," I replied. "I don't think I've seen any raptor hunt."

"You're in for a treat, then," Dan said. "This female I have, Little Bird, is an awesome hunter. Fierce. The first time I picked her up, she dug her talons into the flesh of my palm and took out another chunk with her beak. It's real easy sometimes to see why they're related to dinosaurs, you know?"

Not really, I thought. That wasn't the kind of relationship I had with birds. Sure, I'd been dive-bombed by red-winged blackbirds while riding my bike in the Iowa countryside, and once, while driving down a highway, I'd almost been killed by a pheasant that flew in my open window. But I didn't share the stories of these "dangerous" encounters with many of my adventure-loving friends — people who regularly climbed mountains or ocean kayaked — and I didn't share them with Dan.

It wasn't long, though, before I once again revealed my inexperience. Dan parked by a pond where a few ducks had congregated. When I got out of his truck, I slammed the door. The sound reverberated out across the pond, but luckily it didn't scare the ducks. When I walked around the side of the truck, Dan was standing there, smiling.

"Sorry about the door," I whispered.

"You know what Iowa stands for don't you?" he replied.

"No."

"Idiots Out Wandering Around."

I laughed quietly — at the moment I couldn't argue with him. Dan retrieved Little Bird from the back of the truck, removed her hood, and released her. She circled tightly around the pond, slowly rising. Then she caught a thermal and seemed almost to vanish into the sky. In *Rites of Autumn* Dan remarks that falcons can become hypnotized when soaring, so entranced that they forget about food and just float, sometimes for hundreds of miles. This is when the falcon is most wild, when it is least likely to return to the falconer. He had lost many birds that way.

Dan told me to sit on a little rise while he went ahead to flush the ducks. The best way to watch a falcon stoop, he said, is to watch either the falcon or the ducks, not both. I chose the falcon. I could barely see her, hundreds of feet up, in the crystal light of the autumnal equinox. While watching her I considered the near extinction of her species — it seemed incomprehensible that such a bird was regularly shot and poisoned, especially given its ancient relationship to humans. "Man emerged from antiquity with a falcon on his wrist," writes Roger Tory Peterson. For centuries falcons have inspired poets and writers, including Rilke and Yeats, and more recently Terry Tempest Williams. The language of falconry itself was poetic. At the moment, far above me, Little Bird was "reaching her pitch" or "waiting on" or, my favorite, "finding the pride of place." Dan was right — as a metaphor, it was hard to beat a falcon.

I heard the commotion of the ducks, then watched Little Bird roll and stoop, diving so fast she was almost invisible. Her aim was straight and stunning, and she knocked one of the mallards into the dirt. Dan ran toward Little Bird, waving me to follow. When we found her, she was mantling the freshly killed duck, plucking feathers from its broken neck. Dan let Little Bird consume some of her hard-earned prey then, with some fresh meat, lured her back onto his gloved fist, replaced her hood, and retied the leather brace with his teeth.

"What did you think of that?" he asked.

"Beautiful," I replied. "Beautiful."

It's all I could say.

Later that night Erney cleaned and cooked the duck. As I ate the dark, rich meat that Little Bird had provided, I experienced what I thought was "plugging in." The circle of predator and prey, of creation and consumption, had been completed.

After dinner Dan suggested we hunt with Alice the Cooper's hawk before it got dark. Erney refused to go with us, calling Alice a "little savage" because she killed prairie songbirds "sometimes just for pleasure, it seems." Erney wasn't alone in disliking this raptor. William

Vogt, in his descriptive caption to Audubon's painting, wrote: "The depredations of this bird often draw ire upon the head of other hawks, most of which are allies of man and deserving of complete protection."[18] In the accompanying illustration Audubon portrays the Cooper's hawk chasing down a bluebird of love. Dan, however, liked this new bird, partly because it was such an aggressive hunter. He got Alice out of the mew. She was not as stunning as Little Bird—her liver-spotted feathers made her look like something closer to the dog world than the world of raptors. But she made up for her looks with eagerness.

As we walked along the shrubby windbreak, Alice was quick to reach yarak—neck feathers elevated, black eyes hyper-attentive. She killed a sparrow almost immediately, and (as mentioned earlier) I wrongly assumed that she'd injured herself on the thorns of a Russian olive. Dan quickly lured her back onto his glove, pinched the head off the sparrow, and, because it was worthless for the hawk's nutrition, threw it aside. We kept walking and flushed another sparrow, which Alice also killed. Then another. We moved to the backyard where Dan retrieved a large white bucket. As Alice watched from the woodpile, he tossed the bucket into the air and out flew a baby rabbit. The rabbit took off—Alice gave chase but, to my relief, missed her prey. At that moment it was unclear to me who, exactly, was in yarak: Dan or Alice. Finally, after killing a pigeon that Erney reluctantly tossed from the bird house, Alice had had enough. Dan left her alone with her dinner.

The following day Dan was scheduled to fly his falcons for a Ted Turner film on Crazy Horse. He was hesitant at first, but when the director promised to list him in the credits as "Falcon Wrangler," he couldn't refuse. The site was to be the 777 buffalo ranch south of Rapid City, where parts of *Dances with Wolves* were filmed. While driving there Dan talked about western literature, but my mind was stuck on the killing spree I'd witnessed the previous evening. What was the point? Was it connected in any way to what Dan termed his "affection" for raptors? If so, I wasn't sharing it. Unlike hunting with the falcon, watching Alice kill didn't seem to have any poetry, any larger ecological lesson. Still, I had to acknowledge that there was part of me that had felt enthralled by Alice, by her power and purpose. In all my days of living in the Midwest, I had never encountered such a predator up close. As Dan's truck moved past billboards and farmhouses and electric wire, I worried that I might not ever again.

Just before reaching the 777, Dan pointed to Linda Hasselstrom's house, nestled in a grassy hillside. This was almost a year after I had visited with Linda on her ranch, and I mentioned to Dan how much I admired her sense of belonging, her commitment to that one piece of land.

"Well, maybe you can explain it to me," Dan replied, "because I can't really understand why she doesn't just sell the place. Now that she's living in Cheyenne, the ranch has become a huge financial burden to her. It's killing her. And she's not around to look after it like she used to. I'm not sure that's such a great arrangement for the health of that land. I mean why not sell it to the 777, let it go back to buffalo? If they offered me the amount they offered her, I'd sell in a second, give it to the buffalo, and buy another place."

For a moment I was stunned — sell his ranch, his home, his place of solace? Then I recalled the spirit of the day: Crazy Horse, the buffalo hunter, the nomad.

"Crazy Horse didn't own anything," Dan said me as we turned past the gates to the 777. "And still his people loved him, fought and died for him. I'm interested in that. We took a wrong turn as a people when we embraced capitalism. It just doesn't work. We're dragged down by our need to own things, to stay settled."

In *Rites of Autumn* O'Brien laments that Crazy Horse was not celebrated as one of the truly great Americans. Now, at least on Ted Turner's television network, he would be. As we approached the busy movie site, Monte, the stunt coordinator ("trainer for the Esso Tigers," he boasted), approached the side of the truck and explained that they wanted to film one of the falcons in flight for "a vision sequence."

"This is what Crazy Horse sees when he dies," Monte explained, his silver hair pulled back into a tight ponytail. Earlier in the day at Reptile Gardens, a local tourist site, the crew had filmed a bald eagle hopping across a coffin. Another "vision sequence."

"Crazy Horse wasn't buried in a goddamn coffin," Dan spat as he retrieved Dundee from the truck.

The director called for a few practice runs to check timing. Dan, who was now a couple hundred yards out on the prairie, released Dundee, who flew in a wide, speedy circle, crossing almost directly in front of the camera.

"Shit," the director said, spitting out some tobacco. "That bird's too fucking fast." He shouted to Dan and Monte: "Can you slow it down a little?"

"No," came the distant reply.

"An ugly bird, an ugly day," the director said to his assistant.

Clouds interrupted the shot, so they waited for the setting sun to reemerge. When gold exploded from above the Black Hills, Dan once again released Dundee, and the director finally got his "vision sequence."

To reward Dundee for his patience and to lure him back, Dan released a white pigeon he had brought with him from the ranch. However, instead of flying out over the prairie, it turned and flew in the direction of the film crew. Dundee rolled, stooped, and killed the pigeon right in front of the camera.

"Jesus Christ!" the director exclaimed. "Did you see that?"

The film crew gathered around the feasting, bloody Dundee, experiencing perhaps the most authentic vision of the day.

"Is that a real pigeon?" a young assistant asked.

"No," I replied, glad to have fun at someone else's expense for a change. "But he plays one on TV."

The next morning Dan retrieved Alice from the mew, this time to see if she was quick enough to kill meadowlarks.

"Erney claims she isn't," he said. "But I bet she is."

Unlike the previous evening, when she'd pursued the baby rabbit, I was prepared to be fully on Alice's side, to root for her not because I would be eating her game or because she was the subject of poetry but rather for the simple privilege of seeing her hunt and kill in a place nearly robbed of all its wildness. To paraphrase Dan, she took me to a place I couldn't go on my own. I scared up bird after bird, but Alice seemed uninterested in hunting for our pleasure. She was not in yarak. Finally, though, she took to a meadowlark and snagged it. As we approached Alice mantled her prey, hiding it with her wings. Dan gently coaxed her back onto his glove, and then, suddenly, the "dead" meadowlark exploded into flight. Alice hadn't killed it after all.

We continued walking, but Alice showed little interest in pursuing any more songbirds. Instead, she kept looking over her shoulder into the sky. I began to anthropomorphize, associating her look with thoughts of freedom and flight. But when Dan and I looked deeper into the blue we noticed the barely discernible shape of a red-tailed hawk, soaring. It was not freedom that had turned Alice's eyes from the hunt but fear. Our hunt was over.

As we walked back to the ranch, I tried to imagine a time when the prairies might once again be filled with the native migrations of predator and prey. And I continued to wonder what it would be like, as prairie people, to take part in those migrations, to wander out beyond the safety of our individual enclaves. There is an old German word, *vogelfrei*, which loosely translates into "free as a bird." Far from the often positive connotations of this phrase, *vogelfrei* refers to the state of being cast out from the tribe—so free you will die in the open, unburied, to be picked apart by birds. It is a state of fear and vulnerability and movement that might, I suspect, make us more observant of the natural world around us, more humbled by its fierce embrace.

But true connection may require something more than fear. It may also require a kind of self-sacrificial knowing, a giving over of the self, the flesh, to the place. What would it mean to risk being hunted and consumed like all the other animals, here in this land without fang, without claw? What would it be like to be those animals, "[f]ulfilling themselves," as James Dickey writes, "without pain":

> At the cycle's center,
> They tremble, they walk
> Under the tree,
> They fall, they are torn,
> They rise, they walk again.[19]

Is it in animal death only that all our contradictions are brought together, migrating into the earth, then back again? Is it in animal death only that we are made whole?

On that autumn day in South Dakota, walking among the tall, soft grasses within sight of the ranch house, it was difficult to feel anything but peace. Dan was silent, caught up, I supposed, in the still beauty of the morning. Alice, perched on his bobbing fist, continued to look over her shoulder at the soaring hawk. I looked as well, imagining — with fear and longing — some future day on the prairie when I, like her, might know the wild instrument of my own humility.

CHAPTER 3

Not Just Any Land *Linda Hasselstrom at Home*

"I don't think I would have been a writer without this place," she said
as we stood on a rocky hill just south of her family's ranch. "Now
that I've moved away, I don't know what's going to happen to my life
or my writing. I feel like I'm floating." "Floating" was not a condition I associated with Linda Hasselstrom, a writer whose work was
so rooted in that short stretch of South Dakota prairie that even I,
a first-time visitor, felt vaguely at home there. Even the horizons
seemed familiar: the dark wave of the Black Hills to the west, the
small gray town of Hermosa to the north, the great expanse of the
777 corporate buffalo ranch to the east. In between it all, surrounding us as we stood on that hill, was the one-mile radius of buffalograss prairie that Hasselstrom has called "the circle of [her] world."[1]

Hasselstrom had lived on those grassy acres since childhood, working cattle with her father, John, and later with her husband, George,
who died from cancer in 1988. Her daily life on that small ranch — its
personal, cultural, and environmental lessons — had been at the cen-

ter of all her autobiographical writing. But since her father's death in 1992, financial circumstances had forced her to move to Cheyenne, sell the cattle to a neighbor, and rent out her parents' house and the house she and George built together. She still owned the land, but at the time of our visit in June 1994 she had not walked through her pastures in nearly two years. "I couldn't bear it," she said. And yet, at least for that morning, there she was: hands on hips, left leg forward, eyes gazing out over the bright and airy acres as they had so often in her books, in her life. Floating? I stepped back a few yards, raised my camera, focused, and took the picture I wanted to see: a writer, grounded.

Perhaps more than any other Great Plains author, Linda Hasselstrom's writing emerges from a life settled within the traditional work and culture of the rural grasslands. This was evident to me from the very first time I saw her books, lined up side by side in an Iowa City bookstore. The titles — *Windbreak: A Woman Rancher on the Northern Plains* (1987), *Going Over East: Reflections of a Woman Rancher* (1987), and *Land Circle: Writings Collected from the Land* (1991) — all called attention to an interweaving of self and land, writing and ranching. I immediately thought of Wendell Berry, the Kentucky farmer and writer, who since the mid-1960s had been calling on families to return to rural places, work the soil, and in the process "improve both the land and themselves." But the setting of the Great Plains — the vast rural interior of the nation — made Hasselstrom's titles even more interesting to me than Berry's. At the time I could think of only one other woman writer living in the Plains who was also a working rancher: Gretel Ehrlich, author of *The Solace of Open Spaces*. Ehrlich, who moved to Wyoming in the late 1970s to work on a film project, ended up staying after the death of her partner. Slowly, through her work as a sheep rancher, she began to heal her personal loss and shed her outsider status by becoming a part of a place where "[a] person's life is . . . a slow accumulation of days, seasons, years, fleshed out by the generational weight of one's family and anchored by a land-bound sense of place."[2]

As I read Hasselstrom's books, however, I became immersed in a perspective quite different from Ehrlich's — and from Dan O'Brien's.

Unlike them Hasselstrom had lived within the "generational weight" of a family ranch since childhood and had continued living and ranching there as an adult. In grasslands literary history, such a settled life for a native, Euro-American author is unconventional—many spent their childhood here but eventually left to write about other, more distant subjects. In 1930 Ruth Suckow, who lived most of her life in her home state of Iowa, referred to such artists as "a whole tribe of aesthetic nomads, a flock of cuckoo birds, always trying to make their homes in the nest that other birds have built." She continued: "Many have gone clear abroad; but even more are now abroad in their own country. New York, of course, is the stronghold; but there are a handful of other American cities where they may find an exotic, and therefore artistic, atmosphere—San Francisco, New Orleans, Santa Fe. . . . The chief trouble of our 'civilized minority' has always lain in the fact that, in general, it's been desperately timid and unoriginal, not escaping from a pattern but seeking to unite itself to one ever older and more impregnably established."

This sense of cultural inadequacy is verified by other Plains writers. Hamlin Garland, for instance, claims to have been taught as a boy to worship New England artists and intellectuals. "Writers," he states, "were singular, exalted beings found only in the East—in splendid cities. They were not folks, they were demigods, men and women living aloof and looking down benignantly on toiling common creatures like us." Wallace Stegner recalls comparing his own background growing up in the prairies of Saskatchewan with that of an English novelist friend:

I had grown up in this dung-heeled sagebrush town on the disappearing edge of nowhere, utterly without painting, without sculpture, without architecture, almost without music or theater, without conversation or languages or travel or stimulating instruction, without libraries or museums or bookstores, almost without books. I was charged with getting in a single lifetime, from scratch, what some people inherit as naturally as they breathe air. . . .

How, I asked this Englishman, could anyone from so deprived a background ever catch up? How was one expected to compete, as a cultivated man, with people like himself? He looked at me and said dryly, "Perhaps you got something else in place of all that?"[3]

But what is that "something else" gained by writers who have grown up in the rural grasslands and chosen to stay? What is its value and its cost? Linda Hasselstrom's writing offers an important response to this question. As a family rancher Hasselstrom recognizes that her working relationship to the land has the power to complicate many of the misguided myths associated with the region. "Broad generalities and shallow theories confuse and anger me," she writes. "Reality hinges on practicality, on knowledge that has daily use." This goes for writing as well as ranching: "Merely traveling through a region does not create intimacy, as Midwesterners have seen eastern writers prove often in our history; you must put down roots, become involved, be battered and tested by the terrain, the weather and the people, before you can speak with authority of a place."[4] In this way ranching has always been, for Hasselstrom, intimately related to her authority as a regional writer.

Hasselstrom, though, doesn't just theorize about regional literature in her books; she portrays what it has meant for her to enact those theories — "make them come to be" — at a daily level on a piece of earth shared by family and neighbors who have known her since childhood and on which she is economically dependent. For Hasselstrom, that enactment began at nine years of age when her mother married John Hasselstrom, a rancher whose family had lived in South Dakota since the late 1800s. John adopted Linda and brought her and her mother to his ranch just south of Hermosa. Linda's first glimpse of a prairie blizzard was intimidating: "I could hear nothing but the moaning wind, see nothing but a few brown and white cows, who looked at me, snorted, then turned and ran ahead. Suddenly I felt very small, alone and terrified — until, dimly, I saw the tall, slightly bent figure of my father, almost lost in the blowing snow. He was striding along, looking sure of where he was and where he was going." Her father became the dominant influence in her childhood, teaching her the work of the ranch and inspiring her, through his example, to make her own commitment to the land: "I had pledged my soul . . . to acres of tawny grass and dry creeks that would absorb my blood and sweat, as they had my father's, and still look parched."[5]

Unlike her father, however, the land also inspired Linda to write. During her initial year on the ranch, when the physical landscape began to spill into her young imagination, she wrote poems and stories about her experiences. For the rest of her childhood and adolescence, she threw herself simultaneously into ranch work and writing. Both endeavors defied the gender roles her mother and grandmother had prescribed for her, and neighbors saw her merely as a "rancher's daughter" with no voice of her own. Nevertheless, she continued to write and to do as much ranch work, if not more, than the hired men and was proud when her father bragged to neighbors that she could "mow as much hay as a man."[6] Ranching, she believed, was her destiny, and though she planned to attend college, she contemplated a lifetime spent working at home.

After graduating from high school in Rapid City, Hasselstrom attended the University of South Dakota where her interest in writing was openly encouraged, but after one year of graduate studies she chose instead to follow her mother's advice: marry a non-rancher and move away. Hasselstrom and her husband, a divorced philosophy student with three children, moved to Columbia, Missouri, where both enrolled in graduate school. Her professors, while recognizing her literary talents, discouraged her desire to return home to write about ranch life: "[P]rofessors, who were mostly male, urged me to abandon my provincial attitudes and think about larger issues — things like Truth, Beauty and sonnets. . . . My professors smiled indulgently at my rural ideas, and joked that I actually believed South Dakota was the center of the universe."[7] Their skepticism was shared by many of Hasselstrom's artist friends who thought the heavy physical labor of the ranch would prove disastrous for her writing, exhausting her and limiting intellectual growth.

When Hasselstrom's marriage began to falter due to her husband's numerous affairs, they decided to return to the ranch to try to salvage the relationship. They built a fifteen-by-twenty-foot addition onto her parents' house and she once again immersed herself in the cycles of ranching. While her husband worked on his own writing career, Hasselstrom worked on the ranch and taught at a college eighty miles away to pay his child-support bills. However, her husband quickly became dissatisfied with life on the ranch, and a year later they moved to Spearfish where he took a traveling job with the South

Dakota Arts Council. When Hasselstrom once again caught wind of affairs, she filed for divorce.

Thirty years old and alone, Hasselstrom returned to live with her parents. Several townspeople and even her writing friends scoffed at her for "wasting" her education. She soon discovered, though, that her personal losses had rejuvenated not only her interest in writing but also her deep connection to home. Once again, as it had been when she was a child, the physical landscape merged with the imaginary, inspiring her to write:

When I was divorced, I retreated to the ranch, the only thing I had left. My parents were there in summer, and in winter I lived alone. I was thirty years old, and everything for which I had prepared myself by going to college and marrying the "right" man and getting an education so I'd have "something to fall back on," had failed me, and disappeared from my life. I didn't trust anyone or anything — but the land. . . . [S]uddenly I realized that the things I really valued about South Dakota were its air, its water, its space — and its land. During the next few years I talked more to cows than I did to people, and listened more than I talked. I read a lot about the relationship of people we call "primitive" to the land, and the land healed me, and I began to write seriously and well for the first time.

Several years later she married George Snell — the first man to accept both her "need to write and [her] compulsion to stay on the ranch" — and they built a house together just a quarter-mile from her parents' house.[8] Home at last, Hasselstrom settled in for what she thought would be a lifetime of writing, ranching, and caring for the land.

During the nine years that followed, balancing her work as a writer and a rancher proved to be challenging. It required strict scheduling and a simultaneous ability to deal with surprises. One minute she'd be working on an essay or a poem and the next she'd be reaching into a cow's birth canal. George's help was essential. By doing extra work, he cleared time for her to write. Hasselstrom, though, was finding it difficult to publish her nonfictional accounts of life on the ranch. Editors and agents from places like Florida and New York suggested her work was uninteresting and "unbelievable."[9] She contemplated giving up writing for good.

Then she saw the film *Heartland*, which portrays the efforts of Elinore Pruitt Stewart to survive on the Wyoming grasslands at the turn of the century. To Hasselstrom the film presented a powerful and authentic portrait of women who have, in their own ways, faced the inevitable grief of living in that country and found the resilience to stay. Stewart's determination reminded Linda of the ranching women around her and helped her re-locate her own story in "the stories of women . . . who chose ranch life among numerous other options." Linda walked out of the theater "determined to keep writing, whether a single word was ever printed or not." In the mid-1980s she organized one year of diary entries into a manuscript. Finally in early 1987, after twenty-six rejections and nearly three years of revision, her book — *Windbreak: A Woman Rancher on the Northern Plains* — was published by Barn Owl Books and received favorable reviews, including one in the *New York Times Book Review*. More satisfying for Hasselstrom, though, were the letters from ranch men and women who thanked her for "chronicling their lives" and reminding them of "why they chose to stay."[10]

Hasselstrom also received letters from rural artists who admired how she successfully "juggled" her traditionally contrasting roles as rancher and writer.[11] In *Windbreak* she accomplishes this by locating both roles in the daily facts of the ranch — the freezing winter mornings, the beautiful and often bloody process of spring calving, the silent moments of reflection that lead to essays. Yet she also admits to feeling isolated from literary company and conversation.[12] In contrast to absentee writers like Hamlin Garland, Hasselstrom works through these tensions from her position *within* the landscape and the community. She sees herself as a bridge-maker, bringing writers and rural citizens together and modeling a lifestyle that finds value in the work of both the body and the mind. She describes, for instance, a gathering at her house where her ranching neighbors conversed with Leslie Marmon Silko and other artists over dinner. "I love to create an atmosphere where those meetings can happen," she wrote in her diary for that day.[13] Likewise, the form of the book brings outside readers into the daily rhythms of ranch life: sections are organized into seasons and each entry begins with a weather report. In this way the daily story of the land always qualifies and shapes the daily story of her life. Nature always comes before narrative.

In *Going Over East*, published the same year as *Windbreak*, Hasselstrom continues to explore issues of belonging and responsibility but expresses a stronger sense of doubt about her long-term relationship to the ranch. The book is organized around a trip to summer pastures with George and his teenage son, Michael. Each chapter is marked by a particular gate through which they must pass on their way to check the cattle. So, like *Windbreak*, the form of the book brings together the craft of writing with the rituals of ranch life. But whereas *Windbreak* begins with a detailed map of the ranch and weather reports, both of which orient readers within a specific geographical place, *Going Over East* begins by orienting readers within the landscape of family history: "When we head over east I become, more than at any other time, a composite of a hundred years of history here; the spirits of earlier dwellers in the land seem to follow my pickup like dust. Things I remember from my own past mingle with things my father has told me about his youth, and his father's. A history of this piece of land would require some mingling of the dry official records with the varied and fallible memories of those who have lived and ranched or farmed here. No single truth is possible."[14] Each crumbling homestead or rusted machine not only evokes personal memories but also teaches practical lessons about living responsibly, and irresponsibly, in that arid country — lessons she shares with George, Michael, and her readers.

It is Hasselstrom's individual connection to the land, however, that proves to be the most difficult lesson to share with her family. In the introduction to *Going Over East*, Hasselstrom states that she is traveling to summer pastures in large part to "try to explain to [George and Michael] something of what this dry, hot land has come to mean to me." By the end of the book, Hasselstrom acknowledges that her efforts have probably fallen short: "I love the country, but I feel guilty when, as now, George and Mike seem to see nothing in it but hard work for small rewards. For me, the sight of an eagle floating over a pasture is reward enough for a week." Hasselstrom's thoughts about home and family soon give way to questions about insanity, transience, and disinheritance:

When the wind has been howling in the window frames for three days, I can understand the pioneer women who went insane in their dusty sod shanties, without a tree or stalk of green in sight. I wonder if I am one of them, or will be when I am *old — if I am still on this land. I wonder if I will have to choose between this land and a husband who is talking of getting a job in town, getting away from the endless isolation of winter, the silence, the wind, the cattle. I wonder if our son's cowboy dreams will evaporate as he learns the cost of TV sets, VCRS, cars, food. . . . What is it that I will inherit?*

"What will I inherit?" she repeats a few pages later. "Perhaps nothing that I don't already have: the knowledge and love of the land I have gained from my father and from my own absorption in this unique world."[15] But these abstractions — knowledge, love — give little solace within a narrative intended to explain, however incompletely, why she needs and expects to stay on the land. She goes on to talk about holistic ranching, bioregionalism, and how South Dakota remains, for her, "the center of the universe," but the easy sense of belonging expressed at the beginning of the book has dissipated.

Hasselstrom's connection to home becomes even more complicated when George dies from cancer in 1988, an event explored in her third nonfiction book, *Land Circle: Writings Collected from the Land.* "Suddenly," she writes, "everything I've written about the meaning of my life is being tested." George's death seems to especially aggravate the tension between the personal and the didactic in her writing. She is, for instance, noticeably absent from the title and subtitle. And in the first paragraph, Hasselstrom states that she intends to "look beyond the immediate concerns" of her ranch work and family life to "explore other aspects of being a woman and a rancher concerned for the future of the land and culture around me." The rest of the book shifts, sometimes suddenly, from the personal to the polemical and ends by asking readers to write their elected officials. Contradictions emerge, including her attitude toward aging. In an essay titled "Hairs on My Chin," Hasselstrom reflects: "I must learn, now, how to get old alone, but I won't be altering the natural signs of age: I have sunsets to watch." Later in an essay titled "Rolling Up the Hoses," George's death inspires a much different attitude toward aging: "And what does Time do? Grays your hair, jostles chunks out of your memory, plays nasty tricks like taking away the memory of whole nights you spent crouched by the bedside watching his face, watching his chest move, his lips whisper love."[16] This ambivalent, sometimes embattled relationship to time may explain why *Land Circle,* unlike her other books, is not organized according to the progression of days or seasons.

Even so, the ongoing connection among her life, her writing, and her land continues to sustain Hasselstrom in *Land Circle*. At times in the book she claims that her sanity was saved by her knowledge of the land, by her writing, and by sympathetic letters from her readers.[17] The land also provides her with a healing metaphor for the self, one that embraces contradiction as well as commitment: "The land has invested me with its personality, its spare beauty and harshness, and I have invested it with my love and care." The land is likewise at the center of her identity as a woman: "The female is the Earth Mother made flesh. . . . We are closer to the earth, more intimately involved with it than a male can ever be." She also states that she is as close to the land "as to a sister." By the end of *Land Circle*, the land appears to have become *everything* to her:

I wasn't born on the land; I was reborn here when I moved from a small city to a ranch at the age of nine. I was adopted by the land, and began developing a personal land ethic the first time I looked out on the empty, rolling prairie around my home. Although I have left the ranch where I grew up several times — to go to college, to marry a philosophy student — I have always returned. My second husband, George, joined me in working the ranch with my parents, and now that I am a widow, the land is still most of my family, as well as my spiritual guide.[18]

Here, at the end of *Land Circle*, is where I initially left the events of Linda Hasselstrom's life. A few months later in October 1993, I had a chance to hear her read at a conference in Wichita. She was part of a panel titled "South Dakota Writers" with Dan O'Brien and Kathleen Norris. After being introduced she confessed to the audience that she had moved away from South Dakota and was now living in Cheyenne but didn't give any explanation. Then she read a poem about the ranch.

During the months that followed, it was difficult for me to imagine that Hasselstrom no longer lived on the acres of "tawny grass and dry creeks" to which she had "pledged her soul." I kept thinking about absentee writers like Garland and Cather and wondered how different Hasselstrom's fate was from theirs. How different, really, was Cheyenne from New York for a writer who had dedicated her life and literature to one spot of Dakota earth? Was true harmony between a writer and the rural grasslands possible only in the ghostland of literature and not in real life? Was the new story always destined to become the old? The following June, driving south from Dan O'Brien's ranch near Bear Butte toward Rapid City for our interview, past the Harley Davidson shops and Wall Drug signs and the irrigated bluegrass pastures full of recreational horses, I wondered if indeed all expression of the place was, in some unavoidable way, doomed to be the voice of transience and exile.

* * *

When Linda Hasselstrom arrived at the Rapid City café for our interview, she was wearing a long denim skirt, cowboy boots, and a white t-shirt. A few strands of shoulder-length blond and gray hair were hanging over the outside of her wire glasses. When I introduced myself she offered a firm handshake — "Call me Linda" — and invited me to get something to drink at the counter. She said she had visited this café several times before and noted that they had recently changed the art on the walls. It was more western this time, even a few grassy landscape scenes, and she approved.

The occasion for our interview indicated how much her situation had changed since the end of *Land Circle*. She had driven that day from Cheyenne to Rapid City not to check on her cattle or to fight prairie fires but instead to be filmed by a group of video artists from New York who were putting together a PBS series called "The U.S.A. of Poetry." Even so, one of the first things Linda expressed when we sat down was anger over the drivers she had seen throwing cigarettes out their windows. "I've stopped and fought fires started by less," she said. She also expressed a rancher's concern over the weather that day, which struck her as a "hail breeder." It was as if she had never left.

But she had left South Dakota, and our conversation soon turned to the reasons why. Linda explained that even before George died they had planned to move off the family ranch. George wanted to pursue another college degree, but more than that, Linda's father — the man whose tall figure had first anchored her to the land — had become so verbally abusive that neither of them could stand it.

"I'm convinced now," she said, "that my father had Alzheimer's for probably ten years because he would make statements that were completely out of character. I mean, he'd get vicious sometimes, and the next day he'd be a pretty reasonable individual. But it got worse and worse."

At one point her father referred to George as the laziest man he'd ever met and called Linda a "worthless bitch." For the sake of her own sanity, she decided to leave with George. But before they could move George became mortally ill from cancer. After his death, Linda continued to live on the ranch, though her relationship with her parents disintegrated even further:

"My father, both my parents acted as though I was nine years old again, and they had to take care of me. If I didn't call them every night, they'd come up to my house at nine o'clock to see if I was there. I tried to be real patient with this because I knew they were completely thrown by the idea of my husband being dead, but then they started telling me what to do. Finally I said, 'Hey, I'm forty-five years old, you can't do this.'"

Soon after, Linda's life as a family rancher and her life as a writer irreversibly clashed:

"I said to my father, 'We need to work this out so that I have time to write and some time to do workshops and make some money. Then I can also help you with the ranch.' I said, 'I think I can stay here but we need to work out a schedule.' He wouldn't hear of any schedule. I had to drop everything at a moment's notice and help him. I wouldn't do that. Finally, he said: 'Now you can quit this writing stuff, it's just nonsense, and you can stay here and help me.' And I said: 'Fifty percent partnership, otherwise no deal.' He said, 'No,' and then he said, 'So long.'"

In the spring of 1992, after nearly forty years on the ranch, she moved to Cheyenne to live with a friend, a place she saw as a temporary refuge until she discovered a way to return. But the personal losses continued to mount, further distancing her from home. A few months after she left the ranch, her father died. Then she lost her best friend and neighbor, Margaret, who'd contracted AIDS from a blood transfusion. Then she had to move her mother to a nursing home in Rapid City. Though her father had left her nothing, Linda suddenly found herself managing the ranch. Her financial situation, however, as well as a new personal relationship in Cheyenne, made moving back complicated, if not impossible. She decided to rent her parents' house to a young ranch hand and his wife and rent her own house to another writer. A neighbor bought her cattle and leased much of her pasture. She has become, she said, her "own worst nightmare — an absentee landlord."

"It's very strange," she continued. "I mean in the last five years: my husband, my father, my best friend, and those houses. I'm just trying not to make any fast moves, because I think you have to give yourself time to adjust."

Adjusting to her new home in Cheyenne has been difficult. Although Cheyenne is a city of only fifty thousand — a far cry from the metropolitan nightmares she's criticized in her books — she claimed that the noise of the city had disrupted the normal cycles of her life and writing. Even worse, the city had disrupted her boundaries of personal responsibility — she could no longer rush out of her house at midnight with a shotgun to check out strange noises. Her responsibilities as a writer were also changing. In her books she often used her dual perspective as a rancher and environmentalist to promote compromise between those political extremes. Now that she was off the ranch, she wondered if her opinions might lose their persuasiveness.

Linda confirmed, however, that her sense of regional responsibility as an artist, though often appreciated by local citizens during her time in South Dakota, had not been without consequences. Her environmental opinions, which she expressed openly in her writing and lectures, elicited public criticism and sometimes threats of violence. Yet despite her statewide and regional notoriety, Linda found that very few people within her own community of Hermosa had actually read her books. She claimed her decision to write nonfiction rather than novels was partly to blame. A few years ago, for instance, a romance novelist committed copyright infringement by stealing direct quotes out of *Windbreak*. After the dispute became public, a neighbor dropped by to give Linda a copy of the romance novel, which the woman had read and enjoyed. That neighbor had never read *Windbreak*, nor had she recognized the romantic landscape described in the novel as her own.

But local disinterest in her books, Linda claimed, had proven to be a kind of blessing — "It enabled me to be here longer than I might have." Recognition of her writing, however small, had already alienated her enough:

"For instance, there was my essay in *Life* magazine where I mentioned the little local café. The next time I went in there, one of the guys was getting ready to tell a story, a good story, and there was little ol' me getting ready to take notes as I'd done thousands of times in there. All of a sudden there's this silence. So I kind of looked over there, and he turned around and looked at me and said, 'Now, I don't want to see this in any goddamned magazine neither!'"

His attitude was, according to Linda, shared by many in the community, including her parents:

"I was in Cheyenne when Teresa Jordan was there to introduce her memoir [*Riding the White Horse Home* (1993)]. She enjoyed a tremendous response, hundreds of her neighbors and friends came in. They hadn't read the book yet, so some of them got twitchy during parts. But they supported her. I'm curious about what the difference is, because I wouldn't expect that to happen in my community. Partly I think it's because they know my father was dead set against me writing about the family. He kept saying, why don't you write about something else — don't write about me, don't write about ranching, and don't write about the community."

Her father's response is a familiar one in Great Plains literary history. After Mari Sandoz won a writing award, her father, Jules, a Nebraska Sandhills pioneer, flashed off an emphatic note to her saying: "You know I consider all writers and artists the maggots of society." ("Why wouldn't he?" asks William Kittredge. "Hadn't [writers] told nothing but lies about the strenuous facts of life where he had lived?")[19] Linda recognized that her father's response — like Jules's — was the result of years of hard physical labor, economic hardship, and a real sense of powerlessness shared by many of his neighbors. She also recognized, however, that her choice to write personal nonfiction aggravated the situation. In fact she was writing about that very issue in her latest book manuscript, tentatively titled "Feels Like Far: A Rancher's Chronicle."[20] She sent me a copy six months after our interview. In this manuscript (the first chapter of which has been removed and published separately as an essay titled "How I Became a Broken-In Writer") Hasselstrom does indeed explore how her autobiographical writing violated "a rancher's standards": "Show no pain. Our business is no one else's. Introspection is a luxury, self-analysis a sign of weakness or dementia." Hasselstrom also acknowledges her own investment in these standards, confessing that while reading her work she is often "horrified by [her] own revelations, tempted to retreat behind the barricade of family secrecy traditional on the plains."[21]

Linda's distance from the ranch and her family, despite its many disadvantages, appears to have offered her the psychological distance necessary to transgress the "rancher's standards" and to take new risks in her nonfiction. "Feels Like Far" is, in many ways, her most personal work. She is more direct about her experiences as a woman —from a critique of the traditional gender roles her mother pressured her to play to an intimate engagement with the cycles of her own body. She writes openly about the verbal abuse she took from her father and other family members. She also reveals just how deeply she felt alienated from her community. "I always felt," she writes, "as if I were not plugged into the same socket as everyone else."[22]

"Feels Like Far" also provided me with an important personal context for Hasselstrom's earlier work. While she was writing *Going Over East*, she and George were planning to leave the ranch to escape her father's paranoia. While she was writing *Land Circle*, her father was demanding that she give up writing and threatening to kick her off the ranch. Perhaps this is why her parents are absent from the acknowledgments in *Land Circle* and why, near the end of that book, she refers to the land as "most of my family." The very real threat of displacement also clarifies why her books reveal an increasing need to explain the depth of her commitment to the ranch, her need to stay there. The loss of sanity she fears throughout *Land Circle* proves to be the consequence of losing both George *and* the land.

"Feels Like Far," however, is ultimately a book about healing, where each negative is carefully balanced by a positive. It is a balance inspired by the land itself. While focusing with even greater clarity on the indigenous wildlife living on her ranch, Linda also portrays the larger, bioregional forces that move through and beyond its borders, reaching even to her new home in Wyoming. In one chapter Linda recalls the moment when, shortly after moving to Cheyenne, she hears the familiar cry of a nighthawk, a bird she admired during her many years on the ranch. She steps outside and sees dozens of them wheeling above the city, spinning and diving. "Tears pour down my face," she writes. "Remembering what they have meant to me, I decide they are an omen, signifying an end to my questions about the future of the ranch and the direction of my life." Once again, it seems, the land — its ecological cycles, "its life everlasting" — reaches out to steady her.[23]

At the time of our meeting, however, I had not read this new chronicle, and the person talking with me was still clearly struggling with the consequences of her displacement. Whatever reconciliation Linda had accomplished on the page, whatever fragile truce with the past, could not outweigh the fact that she had not walked through her pastures in over a year. For this reason I was surprised when she suggested, near the end of our conversation, that we visit them tomorrow, before her scheduled appointment with the "U.S.A. of Poetry" film crew.

"I think it's about time," she said.

The next morning we met at a restaurant for omelets and coffee. We talked some more about her political activism, but she seemed distracted by smaller annoyances, like the cigarette smoke of the woman sitting behind us. She was anxious to get to the ranch, and when we finally rose to leave I noticed she had only eaten a few bites of her breakfast.

We got into her Ford Bronco, with its "My other car is a BROOM" window sticker, and pulled into the morning rush of Rapid City. Gradually the traffic fell off, and we found ourselves riding south into the grasslands. The gently rolling terrain was spotted with the fuchsia of prairie coneflower, the grass already displaying an edge of summer gold. Linda continued to talk about the alienation she felt from her community. She believed much of it could be blamed on a larger American bias against staying home:

"To not retain the connection to the land, to not go back — there were all kinds of reasons given to me. I mean, it's a life of hard labor. But more than that, it was that you shouldn't have ties to the land, you shouldn't stay wherever your home is. That has been almost a rule of raising children in this country. You don't grow up and stay — that's not being grown up. You particularly don't live in the same place where your parents live. But now we've got hordes of people wanting to come back. I've read countless articles — Kathleen Norris wrote one of them — about people moving into old houses and trying to adopt their grandmothers' way of life. But they're carrying a lot of information from someplace else. I'm not saying it's a bad thing, but they're searching for the kind of rootedness that everybody spent my *entire fucking childhood* telling me was a bad thing, and wasn't grown up. Even some of the very, very good writers that I love and admire, like Barry Lopez, they're always visiting some place besides their home."

Linda acknowledged, however, that by living in her childhood home it was psychologically difficult to separate herself from the role of the child: "I mean I finally said no to my father at the age of forty-five. That's not being too mature from some points of view."

Another, less expected consequence of having lived there so many years was that her home landscape had become, in many ways, a landscape of loss. The Hermosa cemetery is at the center of that landscape, and Linda decided we should visit it before the ranch. George is buried there, as well as her father. It's where Linda will someday be buried, in between those two men. "Just like I was in real life," she remarked as we drove through the gates. The cemetery was on top of a hill, the bluegrass neatly trimmed but starting to brown. George's gravestone is a large, jagged piece of dark granite, standing upright like "a dagger into the earth," she once wrote. She had planted a variety of prairie plants on his grave, each of which was symbolic of some aspect of his personality or their relationship: sego lilies, catnip, Johnny-jump-ups, yellow sedum. But George's grave also revealed how much of that symbolic landscape she had lost since leaving the ranch. Groundskeepers had repeatedly mowed over her prairie flowers, mistaking them for weeds. The sego lilies had never had the chance to bloom. That morning the gravesite did indeed appear dry and patchy, having recently been mowed for Memorial Day.

Linda was visibly upset: "I don't want to be angry, especially since I'm now absentee and can't be here to work on the grave as I have in the past, but on the other hand I just can't take it. I get so sick when I see this . . . I mean, it seems like so little to ask. I've told them they can cut all around it, but inside the stones, leave it alone."

After the cemetery we continued moving through a landscape where it was difficult to distinguish between reality and metaphor, where physical features perpetually gave way to emotions and memory. In Hermosa we drove through a nearly deserted downtown and passed abandoned mobile homes, all of which suggested that the town, like so many in the rural Plains, was suffering from decades of economic and social distress. Hermosa is a place Linda still loves deeply, a place she is protective of, and yet like the cemetery, it displayed the signs of her continuing absence — familiar houses inhabited by unfamiliar people. We drove on, through her hay fields, through acres of lush brome grass, hip-deep and shifting in the wind. Linda said she wanted to preserve those acres for wildlife, but she worried that if she didn't let some locals hunt there, they might set a match to her hay bales. At her parents' house we visited briefly with the renters, a ranch hand and his pregnant wife, who had just put a new washer and dryer in Linda's old living room.

Finally we drove east into the pastures. Just inside the first gate an enormous Angus bull glared at us. The cows were also staring.

"This is a strange vehicle to them now," she explained. "They can get pretty spooked."

Much of Linda's life had centered on her relationship with her cattle, keeping them alive through freezing winters and summer droughts and botched births. It was an intimate relationship, body to body. She had reached into the womb of a cow to safely birth a calf; she had also reached in with a saw to dismember a crooked stillborn. In learning about life and death and responsibility, these animals had been some of Linda's most important teachers. We stopped alongside a large, cream-colored Charolais, and she pointed out the mark of her brand, the H-heart. An Angus grazing nearby displayed her grandfather's 1899 brand on its flank as well as the new owner's bright yellow ear tags, standing out in stark contrast to those fading scars.

Linda seemed relieved when we finally gained the top of the hill. During her life on the ranch, she had often sought out this crest for privacy and perspective. Robert Thacker states, citing Cather, that it has always been the "'great fact'" of the land itself that has inspired and challenged the imaginations of prairie writers.[24] Nowhere was that "great fact" more obvious than from the top of that hill, where one could witness the meeting of three starkly different landscapes: the mountainous upthrust of the Black Hills, its deep cover of pine and spruce; the eroded, saw-toothed edge of the distant Badlands; and the grassy slide of the surrounding buffalograss prairie. In the case of the Badlands and Black Hills, the geographical facts of the land quickly give way to the invisible, palimpsestic layers of history and myth. Those places carry with them some of the most famous names in the American West: Crazy Horse, Custer, Hickok, Calamity Jane, and Black Elk. Together they attract more than a million tourists a year. It is not surprising that Hasselstrom has often defined her small stretch of prairie against those more famous and valued places. "We go to the Black Hills or the Badlands as to foreign countries," Hasselstrom writes, "to show visitors the beauty; the prairie is our world."[25]

But her world had its own rich history, its own stories, as was evidenced by the crumbling foundations of homesteads that could be seen, here and there, from the top of the hill. Linda pointed to one that appeared to be nothing more than a scattered pile of rocks:

"There used to be a family living in that place. Their name was Fuhlbrugge. All my life I heard it pronounced as the 'full buggies.' So I had a mental image of these people with their children spilling over the edges of this buggy being pulled by horses into town. A granddaughter of that family contacted me after she read my book. I hadn't mentioned her family, but she said you must live very close to where my grandparents homesteaded. I wrote back: 'Yeah, come out and take a look sometime at this country where your family started.' They were German immigrants. I could point out to you all kinds of little homestead places, all across here. Those people are gone now but they *were here*, and they had various kinds of dreams."

Her role as the keeper of such dreams and stories, as a bridge between present and past on that spot of earth, had for me always been at the center of her authority as a regional writer. As she led her readers through a landscape that was at once physical and psychological, silent and yet full of human voices, I believed Hasselstrom was fulfilling what Kent Ryden sees as the defining work of the "essayist of place." "Penetrating and describing these visible and invisible layers of history," he writes, "communicating the rich physical and imaginative textures of a landscape, is the work of the essayist of place. This work requires deep imaginative engagement with the landscape and with the lived significances it has accrued over time—it requires a sensitivity to and appreciation of its implicit narratives. Narrative is as inextricably fused to the natural landscape as is history, and to a writer sensitive to the presence of narrative the land's appearance and meaning are irrevocably altered." The essayist has the power, as Ryden puts it, "to write place into being,"[26] into a collective consciousness that will hopefully appreciate and preserve it.

Protecting these "lived significances" was also central to Hasselstrom's work as a family rancher. In her books she often praises the collective wisdom of those living around her, the stories of the land passed down from one generation to the next. The relationship between a family rancher and his or her land is economic, but the generational ties, she argues, make that relationship more intimate, even familial, and thus more likely to inspire commitment and environmental responsibility than absentee or corporate ranching. "The next neighbor's pasture is now called the eight-hundred-acre pasture," she once wrote, "presumably to distinguish it from the five-thousand-acre pasture. Distinguishing pastures by size rather than by family names indicates one of the changes in ranching in my lifetime: the coming of corporate ranching."[27]

It was not that difficult, then, to understand why Linda had refused to sell her ranch to her corporate neighbor, the 777, though they had offered her a substantial sum—enough to live on for years. I could understand, yet I was still ambivalent. Like Dan O'Brien I had my doubts about the family ranch as well as the family farm. Donald Worster argues convincingly that private ownership of rangeland has encouraged as much abuse of that land as stewardship.[28] Others point out that the environmental catastrophe facing the Plains from invasive plant species such as crested wheat grass and leafy spurge will require a selective chemical onslaught few family ranchers can afford. In addition, Hasselstrom's neighbor was not your typical corporate villain. The owner of the 777 rotated his bison herd through thousands of acres so that the grasses and other wildlife remained healthy. I have a lot of hope for bison, not just as a recovering species but as an economic future for the Plains. Bison provide leaner meat, require less maintenance, and are easier on the land than European cattle. There could be no question that bison were made to live in that country. They belong, as do falcons and wolves and grizzly bears and elk — all native prairie species that have been displaced or nearly extinguished by, among others, family ranchers. But for me the 777 also represented a troubling trend toward environmental aristocracy, where access to the experience of nature and thus its physical and spiritual benefits becomes restricted to a few wealthy landowners. Standing there with Linda, it was hard to know what to think.

When I asked her about the possibility of restoring native wildlife to the prairies she seemed receptive. Linda emphasized that she was deeply involved in local environmental issues but added that visiting environmentalists who claim to be speaking for the ecosystem often demonstrate little working knowledge of it, sometimes blaming ranchers for wildlife losses caused by natural forces. In the process they appear to discount the ranchers' environmental sympathies and expertise. It was Linda's father, in fact, who had taught her to respect predators like the coyote, to recognize their essential role in the native ecosystem, and she recalled several angry confrontations with men hunting coyotes on their land. Linda also mentioned, with some pride, that a mountain lion had been spotted on her land and that eagles nested nearby. As for bison, she was torn:

"I mean the 'buffalo commons' is one possibility. Maybe the Poppers are right — we're losing population and maybe what we need to do is just turn the buffalo loose.[29] On the other hand that would mean more and more people jammed into more and more narrow strips. I believe there are responsible ways for people to live out here, ways determined by a renewed appreciation for bioregional forces."

She revealed that she had in fact been talking with organizations that seek to create such a balance between working ranches and environmental interests.

"In any case," she said, "I'm real aware that I can't protect this land forever and that ultimately it's not mine to protect. I figure I've got a chance now to help improve it and set it up in such a way that it will go into hands that will care for it well."

Although Linda could envision a future when her land might return to its natural state, which would include bison and wolves, or become resettled by families living responsibly on the land, she was at the moment more concerned with her own future there. With no children to inherit the ranch—George's son, Mike, hadn't talked to her in over a year—she was perhaps the last Hasselstrom to live there, the end of another family's story on the place. Since her first journal entry as a child, Linda had been weaving her personal story into those acres of buffalograss, using her nonfiction writing to at once express and create her connection to the land. Now she was faced with the unraveling of that essential tapestry.

"I have stories about almost every little place here," she said. "I could tell you something that happened to me on everything you can see here, maybe every hundred square feet to be fairly conservative about it. Some of them are stupid little stuff: I got stuck there, I fell off my horse there, I thought I was going to be struck by lightning over there. Partly it's what happens to you in a place that ties you to it. I'm sure there are people who feel that way about streets in New York City—I'm not saying it can only happen in the country—but it's what makes you narrow-minded about the place. You don't want to see anybody else come in and build a house on the place where you had your first kiss."

The houses below, which looked small and toy-like, no longer seemed to me the romantic icons, the easy metaphors for Linda's deep generational connection to the land. Instead they appeared to represent the awkward realities of her future: in Linda's house lived a writer who didn't ranch, and in her parents' house lived ranchers who didn't write. It was a difficult situation, made all the more so by casual suggestions to sell.

"A number of people have said to me, people who are my friends, they say, 'Oh, you own the land—well, great! You can sell it and buy a ranch in Cheyenne.' I mean it's not just *any* land. Maybe I would come to love some other place, but there's a difference. I wouldn't know it as well. It would be like speaking another language. I know a lot about this place. I can pronounce with some certainty on some things here, and I'm willing to take what I say to the bank. I'll stand behind it. It would take me a long time to get that kind of familiarity with any other terrain, and I may not have that much time. When you're fifty years old, you don't want to assume you'll have another fifty years. You may not."

I stepped back to take a few pictures, then rejoined Linda at the crest. We stood there for a while, silent. As I gazed across the land, my eyes had trouble focusing. For a moment the prairies appeared to have no borders, no limits, and then the dark thread of fence wire would become visible. The scene would be still, and then it would be a flurry of movement—a red-tailed hawk circling, cars on Highway 79, shifting cattle. In my peripheral vision I caught something moving through the grass about a hundred yards away. It was long and low, and its toasted coat blended almost perfectly with the dry grasses. A coyote. I pointed it out to Linda.

"Where? I didn't see anything . . . oh yeah, there he is. Yeah, that's a coyote." She paused. "I should have noticed the cows bawling at him a few minutes ago. I didn't make the connection. See, I haven't been here for a while; my senses are dulled. I would have noticed that before."

Driving back down the hill toward her house, the Bronco lurching over the rocky terrain, there was an awkward silence. When we finally started talking, Linda shifted the topic to my relationship to home. I began to tell her a little about western Iowa, where I grew up, about my own experiences as a writer and student, when she interrupted:

"I think one of the real key things is that for most people a job is a job. For instance, you get a Ph.D., you become a teacher—there are places you would rather teach, you don't want to teach in the Caribbean, but within certain limits you could teach anywhere. You could teach at the University of Iowa, you could teach at the University of Florida, you could teach at the University of Vermont, and there would be certain things that would be the same. What would make the job for you would be your colleagues, your students, your wife, your house, and all the other things you bring to it. But the place is not the job. The job here is the place; it's not something you can leave when you go home at night. I live the job when I'm here — that's how it works when you're doing it right."

"But," I replied, feeling defensive, "that's what I'd like to see the work of writing and the academy become. One of the reasons I'm in South Dakota is to talk with writers who, just like you said, can't separate their writing from their place."

And here, characteristically, I wanted to reach for some outside literary authority, perhaps Wendell Berry. "To assume that the context of literature is 'the literary world' is, I believe, simply wrong," Berry asserts in his essay "Writer and Region." "That its real habitat is the household and the community — that it can and does affect, even in practical ways, the life of a place — may not be recognized by most theorists and critics for a while yet. But they will finally come to it, because finally they will have to. And when they do, they will renew the study of literature and restore it to importance."[30] What came out instead was more personal:

"That's how it is with me. If I hadn't stayed in Iowa long enough to care about my connection to home, the way it has shaped my identity, I'm not sure I would have learned to care about the prairies or any other landscape. I'm not sure I would have found the reasons to write."

I'm just like you, I wanted to say. I understand your loss.

But when we reached her house, the one that she and George built, it became clear how truly unlike her I was. Her deep personal connection to that land, her grief in the face of its loss, were ultimately unfathomable to me. We got out and walked around the house, which they had built at a slant to deflect the bitter northwest wind that swept through in winter. We examined the irrigation hose that her neighbors had accidentally ripped up. It took her ten years to lay the hose, to adjust each hole so that it dripped perfectly on all the native shrubs and small trees that made up her windbreak — one of the central metaphors for her life on the ranch. Now a few of those trees were dying.

Linda met these newfound changes with humor, telling me stories about the railroad ties that she had stacked into a zippered snow guard along the north of the house. When she was first widowed, local bachelors used to drop by to "chat." When she became bored with their conversation or wanted to put an end to their courtship, she'd ask them to help her stack ties. Almost always, it chased them off.

"One of my best friends referred to these as 'the ties that unbind,'" she said, laughing.

When we reached George's cairn, her despair became more obvious. The cairn was a small stone structure with bone-white antlers placed on top. George had built it, and after his death friends had often left tokens there in his memory. It was one of the many small monuments she had maintained there, "between earth and sky": "places where I feel close to my husband's spirit, and to the spirit of the land and air."[31] One side had now fallen over, exposing colorful beads and cigarettes, personal offerings.

"It looks to me like somebody hit this with something fairly sizable," she said, mostly to herself. "It's completely disarranged. The renters haven't had the guts to tell me, and I don't blame them. This is worse than the cemetery."

She coughed, then turned and walked toward the hidden side of the house. Several minutes later I saw her picking up large stones and placing them in the back of the Bronco.

"So why do you think I'm bringing these with me?" she asked, finally. "Am I trying to pick up pieces of the land and move it with me? Is that like taking souvenirs, chipping a piece off Mount Rushmore? Is it the same bad impulse to take something home with you? And if we all take something home with us, it won't be here anymore."

On the way back to Rapid City, the wheels of the Bronco humming on the new blacktop, we joked about the "U.S.A. of Poetry" video crew wanting her to meet them in Milwaukee. "They didn't think it was that far from Cheyenne," she said. Outside, the sun shone silver in the warm, light air, igniting the tips of the western wheat grass. The drive was a welcomed moment of reprieve.

"Back there I drew a conclusion that maybe was inaccurate about you, about your teaching, too," she said. "But I guess that is something I've said before as well. Writing is like ranching; it's tied to particular places. Possibly western Iowa is what got you started, but maybe you'll fall passionately in love with another landscape. I can see it. I was in New Mexico once in my early twenties, and I loved it deeply. Had I moved then, things might have been different. I think maybe there are options that exist up to a point, and then they change. I don't know . . . everything you add, every layer of complication—economics, you have a wife who loves Idaho, you may have children—I mean any number of things can push us in different directions. You can exercise some control, but you can't always make it be the way you want it to be."

That afternoon I watched Linda being filmed for "The U.S.A. of Poetry." Of all the poems she had written about ranching and the grasslands, the director—MTV's "Director of the Year"—had chosen a poem about being in the bathroom, "The Only Place."[32] Bob, the poetry consultant, explained: "Here she is, a woman in South Dakota, writing a poem of universal interest." By universal, I eventually found out, he meant the general "feminist theme" and the "sophisticated religious imagery" of a Tibetan prayer wheel used to describe a toilet paper roll. No grass, no bloody calves, no grouse exploding into flight from snowdrifts. Now it is to be Tibetan prayer wheels, I thought.

"Is a Tibetan prayer wheel round or cylindrical?" Bob asked himself as he moved back toward the camera.

It got stranger from there—the set was inside an actual bathroom. Linda originally requested to be filmed in the bathroom at her home on the ranch, but she reconsidered: "It's not really my bathroom anymore." They finally settled on the men's bathroom at Prairie Edge, a large store in Rapid City that specializes in traditional Native American artwork. The owner of Prairie Edge is the same guy who owns the 777 buffalo ranch. In that crowded hallway, however, the physical and moral context of the prairies and her life on them seemed to dissipate. Even Linda herself—the image of her face reflected by two mirrors and floating on the video screen—appeared bodiless, placeless. Only her voice, repeating the last line of her poem—"Help me, help me, help me"—kept her from fading into the dark margins.

Watching her pale in the fluorescent light of the men's room, I was reminded of a line from Land Circle: "I'm the last one. I'm the zoo specimen, the relic, the survivor who may be captured, dissected, and interviewed."[33] My camera hanging heavy around my neck, I questioned what the next few days would bring to each of us. I would be camping, once again, in the Badlands, deep beneath the surface of the prairie, sinking through millions of years. Then I would drive to my parents' home in Iowa, sunburned and covered with stick-tights, and collapse onto the bed I've known since childhood. As for Linda, I pictured her leaving Rapid City in the morning, slipping her Bronco onto Highway 85 south and cursing at drivers who chuck cigarettes out their windows. I pictured the scene, hours later, when she would pull into her driveway off that noisy street in Cheyenne and come to a full stop. What difference will it make, I wondered, when she discovers familiar rocks in the back of her truck and has to lift them, one by one, into her four-square, city house?[34]

Perhaps all the difference in the world.

CHAPTER 4

Native Dreams *William Least Heat-Moon and Chase County, Kansas*

"You're going to have to get me the polarizer out of the car," Steph said, kneeling, working the focus on her camera. She explained that unlike the mountains near her home in Idaho, the Kansas prairie was causing all kinds of light and depth problems for the camera. If she didn't make the proper adjustments, the spaces would collapse, become two-dimensional, and the sky, almost white in the full strike of the sun, would wash out. She could barely hide her frustration. I told her to forget the photograph, that I thought I could describe the place from memory. In truth, I didn't want to walk back to the car across that hot, rocky expanse with its ground-scratching plants and ragged grasses. If I were going to walk anywhere, it would be forward to find, I hoped, something grand to show her.

This was, after all, the Flint Hills — the largest remaining expanse of tallgrass prairie left in America. They stretch nearly two hundred miles from southern Nebraska, through Kansas, and into northern Oklahoma. East to west, their stony girth varies from twenty to eighty miles, marking the edge between the tallgrass and mixed-grass prairies. They contain some of the richest native plant and animal communities left on the American grasslands, including two of the largest and most important prairie preserves in the country: the Nature Conservancy's Tallgrass Prairie Preserve in Osage County, Oklahoma, and the Konza research prairie in northeastern Kansas. If all went well, Chase County, the county where we were walking, would become the site of a National Prairie Park Preserve.

William Least Heat-Moon had told me about the national preserve when I talked with him in Columbia, Missouri, just a week before traveling to Kansas. In the mid-1980s when he was writing his book about Chase County and the Flint Hills, PrairyErth (a deep map) (1991), the prairie park idea appeared dead. Its recent revival, Heat-Moon suggested, was one example of how the success of PrairyErth might have changed Chase County for the better. He noted that the park proposal had already been far along by the time he published his book, but he felt the national attention it received hastened the process, especially at the federal level. He cited other ways PrairyErth might have influenced Chase, including increased tourism, rejuvenated downtowns, and a revitalized economic base. But the most significant accomplishment, he claimed, was how the book changed the attitudes of some Chase residents toward the communities and land they call home:

"I think what many of them saw in PrairyErth was, well, let me say it this way: when I first went to Chase and they found out I was writing a book, the typical response was, 'Why? What's here? Why would you write about us?' I mean, this is Kansas, a place where they have to put signs on Highway 35 to tell you you're driving through scenic country. But after they read the book, even though they knew a lot of those local stories and certainly knew a lot about the land, I think many of them saw the place in a new way, saw that they really have something special there. And I think with that new perspective came a new confidence and self-esteem that, in part, convinced some of them that they could not only successfully manage such a park but, more important, that they should have a prairie national park in their county. That's what writing the book taught me as well, that there was something unique in those prairies and that I belonged to it."

Here, I thought, might be proof of what I had only theorized when visiting with Dan O'Brien and Linda Hasselstrom: writing about the endangered prairies can help preserve and restore them. And not just their plant and animal communities but also their human communities. Literature, Heat-Moon seemed to be confirming, can make a positive difference in the grasslands.

This had been one of the reasons I had wanted to talk to Heat-Moon, whose inclusion in my literary journey didn't, at first glance, make much sense. Unlike the other grasslands authors I'd intended to interview, Heat-Moon had never lived in the rural Kansas place he wrote about, nor could he claim any immediate family history there. He had grown up in Kansas City and now lived near the university town of Columbia. This contradicted the kind of regionalism I was supposedly interested in exploring, the kind that pertains, as Wendell Berry directs, to "a particular knowledge of the life of the *place* one lives in and intends to *continue* to live in."

I realized early on, however, that any literary journey into the grasslands would have to go through *PrairyErth*. For one, Heat-Moon's book had been a national best-seller, and thus it offered a unique opportunity to see the effect such fame might have on a place. But my primary reasons for including Heat-Moon were less rational. My first reading of *PrairyErth* had struck a nerve at the center of my relationship to home. Initially I thought this was because of the ways it evoked my family's history in the grasslands, especially my Kansas roots. But there was something else in my surprisingly emotional response, a nagging silence that would lead me to travel, alone, to Corder, Missouri. What I encountered there forever complicated any easy notions I had about becoming native to place.

I should start at the beginning. Steph gave me *PrairyErth* in 1992 for my twenty-sixth birthday, a month before we got married. The hardcover edition was so thick that when I saw it wrapped and sitting next to the cake, I thought it was a new answering machine. I opened it and was pleasantly surprised — Steph knew I'd be interested in reading anything about Kansas. My family history in that state was something I had often flaunted when arguing my deep roots in this region. There are six generations of Kansans on my father's mother's side; it is where my grandparents fell in love and where my father was born. Within my family this Kansas branch has always been the most legendary, the most privileged during our genealogical conversations. Unlike my mother's Iowa heritage or my Grandpa Price's Missouri roots, my Grandma Price's ancestry is elevated to the level of regional history and myth. There is a town in north-central Kansas, I was frequently reminded as a boy, named Harlan, after my great-great-great-grandfather Judge John Harlan. His son, my great-great-grandfather Cal Harlan, helped write the musical refrain for "Home on the Range," now the state song of Kansas, and was the first to play it in public. Every time I heard that song, whether during a school choir concert or on national television, I swelled with pride.

So, in 1994, when I decided to visit Chase County after my interview with Heat-Moon to talk with residents about *PrairyErth*, I saw it as an opportunity to reunite with that proud Kansas heritage as well. I also saw it as an opportunity to solidify my future in the region. Stephanie would be joining my travels for the first time that summer, and there was a lot at stake in her presence. From the beginning many of the most serious negotiations of our relationship had been negotiations of place. Four years earlier she had, for the sake of that relationship, moved from her home state of Idaho to Iowa, working for a year at a local fast food joint to earn state residency and lower tuition. At that time we had often talked about moving to the Rocky Mountain West—her home region but one that I also loved. Somehow, that talk had become a promise.

Lately, though, my sense of belonging to the grasslands had started getting sharper, making demands of its own. I was beginning to think that maybe I didn't want to leave. I had not told Stephanie the extent of these new feelings—I wasn't sure I understood them myself—but I was hoping the land might be of some help. The trip to the Flint Hills seemed to offer an ideal chance to show her, up close, the magnificent prairie landscape, the biological richness and overwhelming beauty that I had been exclaiming about since traveling to South Dakota in June. I knew it would still be a difficult sell. While visiting Idaho Steph and I had walked many miles together through the sage-brushed canyons and lacy waterfalls of the Owyhee Range near her family's home and in the Sawtooth Mountains beneath a thick, fragrant canopy of white pine and spruce. Her connection to those wild landscapes needed no explanation—to me or to anyone. Those landscapes spoke for themselves. I, on the other hand, felt I had something to prove, and I hoped the Flint Hills tallgrass would do the proving.

Though we glimpsed some magnificent prairie from the car window on our way to Chase County, our first walk in the Flint Hills was, as I already mentioned, a disappointment. The plant life seemed sparse, trampled on. And for a tallgrass prairie in August, everything seemed, well, *short*—there was no bluestem that I could see, no switchgrass or Indian grass. On the way out to this spot, which had been recommended to us by a local resident, Steph had read aloud passages from *PrairyErth* where Heat-Moon describes the Chase prairies as being huge, lush, and pristine. Now the place seemed like a bad joke. Steph half-heartedly took a few photos, then we continued walking, identifying plants with our field guide. Instead of finding stalks of gayfeather, aromatic asters, and false indigo as Heat-Moon had, we found ourselves looking up plants like broomweed and curlycup gumweed and other indicators of overgrazing. We became especially intrigued by a poinsettia-like plant sporting broad green leaves with striking white fringes. It was everywhere. "Snow-on-the-mountain," the guide called it.

"What a beautiful name," Steph mused as she picked a stem and placed some of its milky sap on her tongue—something she'd often done with sweet mountain wildflowers.

"Hold on," I said, reading further. "'An invasive, it grows in degraded and disturbed places. Its sap is poisonous and has been known to kill cattle if ingested in large amounts. Also known as 'Wolf's Milk.'"

Steph spit violently, then kicked a dry cow pie at me.

"So remind me," she said, red-faced, "why are we here?"

Steph's question struck a fundamental chord not only in our relationship but also in my relationship to the work of William Least Heat-Moon. In reflecting on my stubborn attraction to *PrairyErth*, I had always seemed to come back to that basic question: *Why here?* This is owing, in part, to the fact that Heat-Moon begins his book by asking that very same question: "For years, outsiders have considered this prairie place barren, desolate, monotonous, a land of more nothing than almost any other place you might name, but I know I'm not here to explore vacuousness at the heart of America. I'm only in search of what is here, here in the middle of the Flint Hills of Kansas. I'm in quest of the land and what informs it, and I'm here because of shadows in me, loomings about threats to America that are alive here too, but things I hope will show more clearly in the spareness of this county." Here he is standing at the top of Roniger Hill, just a few miles north of where Steph kicked that cow pie. It is a place that represents for him not just the deep and diverse history of this "vacuous" place but also a more personal "blood" connection: "The Roniger brothers were bachelors, farmers, and collectors of stone artifacts from their fields lying below, and they believed this hill sacred to the people living around it in the time when Europeans were building cathedrals and sending children off to take holy cities from desert tribes. To me, this ridge is singular and, at night, almost unearthly, and I come here, in a friend's words, as *a two-bit mystic,* but I believe I've found my way onto the top by some old compass in the blood."[1] The focus of this passage is both historical and autobiographical, archaeological and imaginative, and the way it sweeps around from the distant past to the present, from the public to the private, is representative of the grand sweep of PrairyErth as a whole. Seen one way, PrairyErth is a history. It is a giant-sized excavation (622 pages, 14 chapters, 76 subchapters) of the conflicting historical forces —natural and human, local and national, Native and Euro-American (among other cultures)—that have shaped the past and present of Chase County. The result is a book that offers readers a deep historical and geographical map of this out-of-the-way place, a map intended, as Heat-Moon said in our conversation, to reveal new reasons for Chase residents and others to save this place from contemporary forces of decline.

That historical dimension, what it had to tell me about Kansas, was what first drew me to PrairyErth, but I gradually came to see that the book was also an experiment in refashioning the self, in trying— even as an outsider— to become native to place. The necessity of such an experiment was being confirmed by much of what I was reading in environmental theory. Irene Diamond, for example, writes that the "hope that the earth might be reclaimed for all grows from the basic wisdom that to reclaim the earth we need to recreate ourselves. We must reimagine who we are as persons and create an appropriate politics." This seemed particularly important and difficult when reclaiming the prairies, a landscape often seen as harsh and uninspiring and one that has been almost totally destroyed. However, while perusing autobiographical nonfiction I had discovered writers who were doing just that: reimagining their identities in relation to the grasslands, then acting on that new, personal connection. Linda Hasselstrom, for one, writes that "[t]his land has invested [her] with its personality, its spare beauty and harshness." Bill Holm, a Minnesota essayist, writes about his "prairie eye," which has influenced his preferences in landscape, architecture, and literature.[2] This reimagined connection, at the level of identity, was one of the main reasons why these authors returned to the prairie places where they grew up and now write from inside that commitment.

But unlike Hasselstrom and Holm, Heat-Moon did not grow up in the place he writes about in PrairyErth, does not own property there, and does not have family living there. Before the 1980s Heat-Moon knew the Flint Hills only incidentally; he first encountered the grasslands when he was twelve, traveling through with his father on the way to somewhere else. Like many who have known Kansas only through a windshield, he "found the grasslands little more than miles to be got over." When he returned from the Navy in 1965 he encountered the prairies again, but this time he saw them differently: "I believe that two years of watching the Atlantic Ocean changed the way I viewed landscape, especially levelish, rolling things. I also began to see the prairies as native ground, the land my hometown sat just out of sight of, and I began to like them not because they demand your attention like mountains and coasts but because they almost defy absorbed attention." Within PrairyErth this new way of seeing topography leads, in only a few pages, to a new way of seeing himself: "At last I realized I was not a man of the sea or coasts or mountains but a fellow of the grasslands. Once I understood that, I began to find all sorts of reasons why."[3]

As someone also hoping to see himself as a "fellow of the grass-

lands," I became drawn to this aspect of Heat-Moon's work, the process of connecting one's identity to the land. I also empathized with
his role as outsider to the prairies. Inside a region where almost all
of the prairies are gone, aren't we all in a sense ecological outsiders,
even those who have lived their entire lives in one locale? Aren't we
all faced with the practical and imaginative challenge of overcoming
the distance between self and place?

In another sense, though, Heat-Moon claimed not to be an outsider to the Kansas tallgrass. The ancestry of William Least Heat-
Moon, also known as William Trogdon, is mostly Anglo-Irish but
includes a small part Osage Indian. In *PrairyErth* when Heat-Moon
states at the top of Roniger Hill that he has come to Chase County
out of some "compass in the blood," he partly means this Osage
Indian heritage; his ancestors once hunted on those grasslands.
Though Heat-Moon does not live in Chase, he appears to be lay-
ing claim to a mystic connection between his tribal ancestry and
the land that defines it, perhaps acting on what the Chickasaw poet
Linda Hogan has described as "a magnetic pull of place, of people,
land, home, for indigenous people." Heat-Moon asserts that these
two racial ancestries — European and Native American — correspond
with two different "men," two different ways of imagining and
living: "I've carried one name for all my life [Trogdon] and another
one for twelve years less than that [Least Heat-Moon], and I've come
to see that while the two names attach to the same man from the
epidermis out, on the inward side . . . the names point to men of different inclinations. . . . One is a kind of dreamer who often darkly
transmutes and even undoes the work of the more orderly man, the
one who always squeezes the tube from the bottom, always wipes his
shoes before entering."[4] Throughout the book, while exploring the
historical and geographical complexity of Chase County, he is also
exploring the complexity of his own identity, the tensions among his
different ways of seeing the land, of traveling through it, of articulating it, of belonging to it.

Any understanding of these defining tensions should begin, I
believe, with an understanding of the author's two names. William
Trogdon was born the youngest son of Ralph G. Trogdon, a Kansas
City lawyer with a small amount of Osage heritage. Ralph was active

in Boy Scouts for many years and was named Chieftain Heat-Moon in the Scout-created tribe of Mic-O-Say in 1959. "Heat Moon" was a name invented by Ralph who, though he knew of his distant Osage heritage, did not know any of his Indian family names. When his eldest stepson, David, entered the tribe, he took the name Little Heat Moon. When William entered the tribe at the age of thirteen —shortly after he and his father drove through Chase County for the first time—he became, in turn, Least Heat Moon.[5] Despite the small amount of Osage blood in their family, Ralph insisted on educating his sons about their Native American heritage through story and ritual. When William entered college, however, he almost forgot about the name.

William didn't publicly reclaim the Heat-Moon name until the early 1980s when he was in the process of writing his first book, *Blue Highways* (1982), a narrative of his thirteen-thousand-mile journey along the back roads of small-town America. His journey began with the loss of his wife and his academic job. "With a nearly desperate sense of isolation and a growing suspicion that I lived in an alien land," he writes, "I took to the open road in search of places where change did not mean ruin and where time and men and deeds connected."[6] During his journey Heat-Moon talked with hundreds of people, explored the histories of many small communities, and discovered, along the way, a renewed connection to both his Osage and Anglo-Irish roots.

When Heat-Moon finally returned home to Missouri, he faced change with a new sense of direction—due not only to a reconnection with his two ancestries but also to a "re-emergence" of an Osage relationship to time. In an interview with Hank Nuwer shortly after the publication of *Blue Highways*, Heat-Moon said: "You can see throughout *Blue Highways* the emergence, the re-emergence, I should say, of the Osage notions of time. The notion is that time is circular and cyclical, rather than linear. The Anglo notions of cause and effect —the rational approach to life—get subsumed to Indian notions that are a little more mystical and cyclical."[7] These ancestral notions served to anchor Heat-Moon's identity against the mid-life forces of change that had at the beginning of his journey threatened to overwhelm him.

But the "re-emergence" in Blue Highways of an Osage notion of time wasn't as spontaneous as perhaps that term implies. In another interview, this time with People's William Plummer, Heat-Moon explained how Blue Highways went through eight drafts over nearly four years and was rejected by several publishers. Then, "suddenly," one winter evening

it popped into my head that what was wrong with the book was that I was trying to write it purely from an Anglo point of view. The book already had all the Indian information, the history, the anger in places. But the narrator was looking from just one side and sounded hollow to me. I was not drawing on the Indian heritage my father, Heat Moon, had taught me. The next morning I couldn't wait to get started rewriting. The title page no longer said "by William Trogdon." It said "by William Least Heat Moon." I excised about 100 pages about Bill Trogdon's failed marriage and his dissatisfaction with life as an academic. And I added a new chapter explaining that the author was part Osage, a man who stood in two worlds.[8]

Heat-Moon's choice of name, his choice of identity, was thus due not only to an unconscious resurrection of a distant past but also to a conscious decision to rerepresent that past in himself.

This choice is not without precedent in Native American literature. Like Heat-Moon, the Kiowa writer N. Scott Momaday has explored how his divided heritage influences the way he imagines and writes about the relationship among the Plains landscape, his Native ancestry, and his identity. In his memoir The Names (1976), Momaday claims any "idea of one's ancestry and posterity is really an idea of the self" and that identity is a matter of both choice, or "formulating," and being "entered upon" by time. As an example, he tells the story of his mother, part Cherokee and part Euro-American, who decided as a young woman "to see herself as an Indian": "That dim native heritage became a fascination and a cause for her, inasmuch, perhaps, as it enabled her to assume an attitude of defiance, an attitude which she assumed with particular style and satisfaction; it became her. She imagined who she was. This act of imagination was, I believe, among the most important events of my mother's early life, as later the same essential act was to be among the most important of my own."[9] Clearly there are some distinctions between Momaday's experiences growing up in or near Indian communities and Heat-Moon's middle-class white experience in Kansas City, but both writers, like Momaday's mother, see their assumption of a Native American identity as a choice (one of several) as well as a mystical connection. It might also be argued that it is a choice forced on them by the largely successful efforts of Euro-Americans to destroy and assimilate Native American cultures. Because Heat-Moon is one remaining heir to those threatened cultures, his chosen identity can be seen as an important act of resistance.

But "going Native," as a friend once quipped, also helped Heat-Moon sell a lot of books. There is no evidence of such a correlation, but nonetheless, while talking with academic colleagues who had read *Blue Highways,* I repeatedly encountered suspicion of Trogdon's transformation into Heat-Moon. Some just found it superficial while others argued passionately that in appropriating for his own ends a Native American name he was trivializing the struggle of "real" Native Americans who had earned the right to their names by, among other things, facing the daily hardships of racism, poverty, and/or displacement. These readers felt that what Heat-Moon demonstrated was not just a doubleness but a duplicity, a kind of literary confidence game.

The issue came to a head for me when Heat-Moon spoke in Iowa City, a year or so after the publication of *PrairyErth.* That evening the auditorium was packed with several hundred people, and his talk was being aired on the radio statewide. Heat-Moon, whom I could barely see from my seat near the back, began by telling us that he hadn't expected to be reading to such a large group and that he was so nervous he might have to use the podium as a urinal. We laughed and Heat-Moon carried on the good cheer with humorous stories about Chase County. Then, nearly an hour into his talk, somebody asked him about the two names listed on the cover of *PrairyErth* (though "William Least Heat-Moon" graced the front of the cover, "William Trogdon" was the name printed in bold beneath his photo on the back). "Good question," he said, then explained that while writing *PrairyErth* he had, in essence, been inhabited by another self or selves whom he called "Heat-Moon." He claimed that after he finished writing the book, at the moment he put the final draft in the mailbox, the Heat-Moon self seemed to leave and he became, once again, William Trogdon.

There was a moment of silence. "Is he serious?" someone whispered. Then, along with tentative laughter, I heard a loud *hiss* emanate from a small group of people sitting nearby. Many in my section of the auditorium turned their heads, but by then it was impossible to determine who, exactly, had made the noise. I looked at Heat-Moon, wondering how he would respond, but he appeared not to have heard it.

After the reading the hissing continued to trouble me. I didn't know for sure what motivated it—disbelief? anger? mockery?—but it further aggravated my ambivalence about Heat-Moon's self-created, regional identity. Was it necessary or even possible to re-create the self through language and imagination and then, as Irene Diamond suggests, "create an appropriate politics?" What responsibility do we have for the past, however benign or destructive, that has created us and our places? What, ultimately, do we control in our relationships to home: what is given, what can be created? These questions wouldn't become personally urgent, though, until my visit to Missouri and Kansas over a year later. In the meantime I reread *Prairy-Erth* with another, less subjective question in mind: Do Heat-Moon's efforts at reimagining his identity have any positive consequences for the place he is writing about?

I noticed immediately that *PrairyErth* is a kind of sequel to *Blue Highways*, a travel narrative, but one in which the narrator steps off those highways and into a more extensive physical and imaginative exploration of one place. Also, like *Blue Highways*, *PrairyErth* is about a dual identity but less about the discovery or creation of that identity than about a test of its applications. At times Heat-Moon foregrounds what he suggests is a Native way of imagining, as well as a desire to keep "Anglo civilization and its disruptions of the prairie contours far enough away so they soften and simplify into mere silhouettes." In general, though, Heat-Moon is not interested in more divisions but rather, as he says himself, in "connections." The form of *PrairyErth* itself reveals such a blending. While seeking an organizing image for his book, Heat-Moon settles on the decidedly European "grid" found on his U.S. Geological Survey map of the county. Each quadrangle on that map becomes, in *PrairyErth*, an individual chapter, defining its geographic and often thematic boundaries. And yet, just after announcing the selection of the grid as his structural motif, Heat-Moon asks us to "attach" to that image an "old Indian story" that denies the Anglo system of grid-like boundaries and affirms a more interdependent relationship between self and nature.[10]

Throughout the book Heat-Moon is seen setting up what appear to be clear distinctions between these two, often racially informed ways of seeing the land, only to collapse them into one another. This occurs in his treatment of form but also in his treatment of character. Slim Pinkston, for instance, is one of the last "real" cowboys in Chase County, but he nevertheless appreciates the ecological value of burning the prairie. Heat-Moon remarks that "[g]ood cowboys like the Pinkstons know the cycle must be served before the dollar, and nothing benefits the old turning so well as what might seem its great enemy."[11] Though Slim himself doesn't identify his ecological sensibilities with Native American influences, they do represent an appreciation for the interdependent, cyclical forces of nature that Heat-Moon associates elsewhere with Native perspectives. Seen this way, Heat-Moon's portrait of Slim, like much of *PrairyErth*, reads not as a triumph of Native American ideology over Anglo (or vice versa) but as an imaginative merging of the two—appropriate for a writer whose identity is tied to both ethnicities.

But again, does Heat-Moon's individual, imaginative effort have any consequences for the endangered natural and human communities of Chase County?

PrairyErth can be read to a large extent as a rumination on how individuals have imagined the landscape and people of the Plains and how those ways of imagining have shaped Chase County. Thomas Jefferson is the preeminent example. "[I]t was from [Jefferson's] mind," writes Heat-Moon, "that came the township-and-range system—the great American grid, an expression of eighteenth-century rationalism if ever there was one." The influence of "Tom's grand grid" can still be seen in the landscape in the fencing-off of the prairie as well as in the destinies of those who have lived there—the "vassalage" of farmers who have lost their land to absentee landlords who exploit ownership laws based on this grid system. Native American cultures have also been threatened by attempts to transform them into Jefferson's "Christian farmers."[12] Jefferson appears to have suffered from what Heat-Moon refers to elsewhere as "shortsightedness": an ignorance of the land itself and, by extension, an inability to understand the harsh complexities that would arise from Euro-American settlement.

Heat-Moon's treatment of Jefferson is just one example of how his own ways of imagining Chase County seek to avoid what the anthropologist Harland Padfield has recognized as "a fundamental illusion of American culture: the persistent celebration of rural life in the midst of its destruction." This is particularly challenging in the grasslands, where the "empty" spaces have so often been seen as an invitation to fill them, unquestioningly, with what we want to see, with the myths that shape our own lives and culture. The geographer James R. Shortridge confirms that though popular perceptions of the Midwest's physical boundaries have fluctuated since the late 1800s, its use as a symbol of the pastoral values of "morality, independence, and egalitarianism" — the simple life — has remained consistent. This collective way of imagining the Midwest, Shortridge argues, has served to protect the illusion of a cohesive national myth, one that also associates the East with "America's technological might" and the West with America's "youthful vigor and freedom."[13] Too often, though, it has allowed the human and ecological complexity of the region to be conveniently forgotten.

As a teenager in Iowa during the 1980s farm crisis, I watched as high school friends were uprooted, as parents were lost to despair or even suicide, as neighborhoods were torn by racial and economic strife. Since then simplistic celebrations of midwestern life have often angered me. Heat-Moon, however, portrays a place that like my own home county has long been in the cross fire of powerful, mostly destructive economic interests. He explores, for instance, the history of railroad ownership in the area and reveals that currently, three-quarters of Chase County is owned by nonresidents, a percentage that is increasing. These absentee landlords take their profits out of the county, contributing little to the quality of life there, but their most devastating effect is on the inner lives of local citizens: "The nature of this landownership ulcerates the lives of many hard-working people with an insidious jealousy often turning into a meanness of spirit, an infection that gnaws at hospitality, friendship, and their sense of community; and, unquestionably, nineteenth-century federal land policies still drive out their children, especially the ones with energy and imagination."[14] Heat-Moon talks to these children, granting them a national audience my adolescent peers and I never enjoyed. In the chapter titled "Up Dead-End Dirt Roads," he interviews several Cottonwood Falls high schoolers about their future in the county. Though I grew up in a larger community of twenty-five thousand, what these kids said to Heat-Moon resonated with what I had thought and heard in the hallways of my own high school. Some of the Cottonwood teens talk about their pride in the community's "togetherness," their desire to stay despite pressures from family and friends to leave, and their sensitivity to outsiders who see their home as a "hellhole" full of "Podunk[s]." In contrast Shannon Lopez, a Hispanic student, recounts how she and her family endured racist comments from local townspeople, including teachers. She wants to move to a city because she's been told, "If you're not full-blooded white, you shouldn't even be over here."[15] Jeremy, a black student, claims he, too, has heard racist comments but that he is accepted for his musical talents, as long as he doesn't date a white girl. Regardless of their individual experiences in the county, nearly all express fear over its economic future and an acceptance—sometimes reluctant—that they will have to leave.

Their fatalism is shared by many of the adults Heat-Moon interviewed, including Lloyd Soyez who speaks about the increasing difficulty of surviving as a family farmer without extensive government subsidies and an outside job. Others, like Frances Staedtler, express despair over the decline of the community and a longing for the past —"I'm afraid I can't go on. It's too much remembering how we all were in those days, when we were strong enough to fight it. We were together." Fidel Ybarra, however, finds no solace in memories of that same past, a time when Mexican railroad workers were housed in freezing shanties and denied service in restaurants.[16]

Heat-Moon also talked with members of the native Kansa or Kaw tribe, a people who inhabited the Flint Hills for ten thousand years but were evicted by whites using "odious methods governments and churches condoned, by an ethic that taints every Pioneer Mother statue put up by the Daughters of the American Revolution." Tribal members on the Kaw Reservation in Oklahoma reveal a grasslands place that, like Chase County, is now struggling with internal conflicts and a diminished sense of community. Only six full-blooded Kaws remain — four-fifths of the tribe is less than a quarter-blood — and the majority live away from the reservation. The most vicious, sometimes violent conflicts over tribal leadership have been between those with more and less Kaw heritage. In addition only a few of the tribal members know the traditional language and rituals. Corrosive economic interests are, once again, partially to blame. "Except for the spiritual aspects," Heat-Moon says, "what the bison once was to the Kansa, bingo is today." Similar to Chase residents, Kaw tribal members like Jesse Mehojah, a ninety-year-old full-blood, speak with sadness about the past and trepidation for the future: "We were a proud tribe. To be the last — I don't even want to talk about it. If I'm the one, I'll be a lonely Indian. When your people are gone, what have you got? A void."[17]

For me, Jesse's words — and the "ruinous tension" over "blood quantums" within the surrounding community — also resonated with Heat-Moon's personal, imaginative efforts to reconcile his Native and Euro-American identities. Heat-Moon seems to suggest that his experiment in identity, his rejuvenation of a Native way of imagining the land, might be a model for others living in the grasslands — including those without Native heritage — who seek to resist and even reverse some of the more destructive forces of change. It's a task made all the more difficult by the historic eviction of the native tribes. "When the Kansas Indians were pushed out of the state," Heat-Moon writes, "they carried with them the last perception of wind as anything other than a faceless force." In this diminished cultural light, many elements of the prairie ecosystem have become similarly denigrated, including the buffalo gourd or, as the Osage called it, *mon-kon-ni-ki-sin-ga*, "human being medicine," which they used to cure headaches. When Heat-Moon asks a farmer about this low-lying, foul-smelling plant, the farmer responds, "Some goddamn old vine." His response is, for Heat-Moon, indicative of the loss of "the mystic properties" of prairie plants and their healing uses.

The answer to this loss is botanical knowledge but also a new appreciation for the land's sacredness, its spiritual integrity — even that of rocks: "To [aboriginal people], rocks were concentrations of power and life. . . . But here, when a bottom farmer limes his fields with 'inert' granulated rock, in his chemistry there is no informing poetry, no myth. Yet, to think of rock can be to dream origins and be reminded of the old search for the philosopher's stone, that elixir basic to all substance."[18] The sense of both loss and hope in this passage, the tracing of saving myth through not just Native American traditions but also European, demonstrates the kind of leap of imagination Heat-Moon believes is required to appreciate and care about the native land. In the process we create an opportunity to connect our own confused heritage to the bedrock of familiar earth.

Heat-Moon states that "[p]eople connect themselves to the land as their imaginations allow," and within *PrairyErth* the most striking breakdown of that collective imagination is the failure to create a prairie national park in Chase County. The idea began in the twenties, but came to a head in 1973 with the formation of a group called Save the Tallgrass Prairie (STP). Though the park had the support of "[e]very major conservation group in America" and was being seriously considered by the National Park Service, it was successfully resisted by a group of ranchers called Kansas Grassroots Association (KGA). According to Heat-Moon, the arguments of the KGA, both formal and informal, were that the park would drive people off their land, drop acreage from the tax rolls, lower beef production, invite unwanted tourists — minorities, in particular — and damage the land through incompetent federal mismanagement. "After the words *communists* and *coloreds*," Heat-Moon writes, "the most potent is *feds*."[19]

While Heat-Moon presents many of the complex issues surrounding the prairie park, its failure, for him, comes down to another failure of imagination — shortsighted notions of the relationship among time, place, and identity. Chase residents, Heat-Moon argues, connect to nature primarily through cattle, "but the linkings go no further back, and the residents don't picture themselves as children of the Permian seas. They understand their living in the hills but not the hills living in them, and so the deeper links are broken and don't inform their conscious life."[20] In place of these deeper links,

many residents get caught up in superficial divisions between in-
sider and outsider, oversimplifying and degrading the discussion
over the land. Part of what gets lost in the fray is a chance for the land
itself, the native prairies, to help heal those psychological and social
divisions.

Ultimately that is what is so sad for the park activists, for Heat-
Moon, and for many residents themselves — that these "*good people*"
lost not only "a rare and nonpolluting opportunity to broaden the
county's economy and share more of American prosperity" but also a
chance to counteract how their home place has been wrongly imagined by others, "to put the lie to the nightmare Kansas of *In Cold Blood*,
The Wizard of Oz, Pike's 'desert,' drought, and grasshopper infestations.
Here was an opportunity to show the beauty of the native land and to
ease that Kansan defensiveness deriving from outsiders' ignorance of
the place." Heat-Moon, however, observes Kansans who are still trying to save the park idea, to preserve the heritage of both ranching
and the prairie ecosystem and as a result "show people how all lives
here sooner or later depend upon natural diversity. They are trying
to point out how the worst tyranny will come not from a federal park
but from an impoverished people and a depleted land."[21]

This effort to change how others imagine the relationship between
self and place is, once again, a reflection of Heat-Moon's personal
quest. It also seemed to clarify the connection between Heat-Moon's
inner experiment and the outside world, between what he refers to
near the beginning of the book as "shadows in me" and "threats to
America." This connection centered, for me, on memory. The French
historian Pierre Nora claims that western civilization is suffering
from a collective loss of memory, a disconnection from "experience
still lived in the warmth of tradition, in the silence of custom, in the
repetition of the ancestral." Heat-Moon acknowledges something
similar to Nora's sense of loss: "The American disease . . . is forget-
fulness. A person or people who cannot recollect their past have little
point beyond mere animal existence: it is memory that makes things
matter." One response to this loss according to Nora is to seek out
"sites of memory": objects and places that are "created by a play of
memory and history," between the conscious reconstruction of and
the unconscious connection to the past. Chase County appears to

be such a site for Heat-Moon, a place where the interrelationship among history, memory, imagination, and survival is especially clear:

I carried my cottonwood stick and my usual haversack, but my real equipage was a mind full of stories I'd heard about Osage Hill, pieces of the real hill, . . . isolated pictographs that can remind a person and involve him in more than they actually were themselves; they were small configurations that had to be continually reinfused and reinvoked to keep them from becoming indecipherable. I believe Indians fear loss of meaning — that is, memory — beyond all other losses, because without it one can love nothing. After all, love proceeds from memory, and survival depends absolutely upon memory.[22]

Within PrairyErth the necessity of individual, imaginative efforts to re-create the self, to rejuvenate lost memories, is even more directly addressed by Wes Jackson, an internationally recognized and respected Kansas writer and plant geneticist. During his interview with Heat-Moon, Jackson claims that American culture has failed to "assess technology against a moral standard," resulting in "the end of the fossil-fuel epoch; disastrous soil erosion; chemical contamination of our food, air, and water; the development of an ozone hole as big as the United States; global warming. Keep naming them." Jackson argues that in order to ensure our lasting survival as a species, we need to imagine and implement new, farsighted methods for producing necessities. He imagines, for instance, a "new Chase" where consumption of fossil fuels is supplemented by more diverse human and animal labor, especially on farms. Success, however, will also require "a new sense of who we are," including a different relationship with each other and our shared places, one based on ancient counter-memories that transcend us/them divisions. Jackson explains: "We've probably always had a little something in us causing us to wish for a neighbor's land rather than a neighbor, and a society built around a fossil-fuel-powered industrial paradigm made that possible, and thereby validated greed in ways seldom available before. Now the time has come to call that avarice for what it is, sin, and then maybe we can find ways to reward another Paleolithic instinct, the urge to help a neighbor. That too is in us."[23]

Jackson's scientific efforts to create "perennial polycultures" — efforts that may someday result in an economically viable, perennial seed crop that mimics native prairie ecosystems — provides a model for this new sense of individual and communal identity. In this new community what are often represented as opposites — the past and the present, humans and nature, traditional and technological cultures — will be made to cooperate, to connect, in the name of diversity and sustainability. Informed compromise will be the rule, not the exception. *PrairyErth* contributes in part by helping cure what Jackson calls "ecological illiteracy."[24] However, *PrairyErth*'s main contribution, as I saw it then, was to model the psychological and literary process of creating "a new sense of who we are," to demonstrate how apparently contradictory ways of imagining can be made to merge, to work together within a divided culture, a divided individual.

Full circle, the grand sweep of *PrairyErth* brought me back in the end to this divided individual, to Heat-Moon's ongoing quest to recreate his identity. This is how the book began, up on Roniger Hill, where he questions what brought him to the Flint Hills. The answer not only involved following a mystic "compass in the blood," the lingering memory of his Native American heritage, but also reimagining himself into a "fellow of the grasslands." Now, in the final chapter, "Circlings," Heat-Moon is no longer standing on a hill for the grand view but walking along the old Kaw trail with a friend, testing, as he has throughout the book, that new way of seeing himself and the land. This friend, Scott Chisholm — a man with some Ojibway heritage — has also been renamed by Heat-Moon as "the Venerable Tashmoo," a name that "seems to combine a vaguely Christian honorific with a historic northeastern Native American name." Together, these middle-aged, reinvented men seek to attain "participatory history" — "an effort at joining in, at trying to recapture a sense of what's gone before us, to act on history."[25]

Mostly, however, they do a lot of talking and tossing around philosophical one-liners ("Maybe this isn't Kansas. Maybe this place is only in Kansas."), with Heat-Moon playing guide to Tashmoo, teaching him how to connect to the prairies as an outsider. ("How do you know when the prairie is in you?" asks Tashmoo. "When you see a tree as an eyesore.") At one point Tashmoo makes a desperate dash to a café to get a burger and a milkshake, forcing Heat-Moon to follow. But then, suddenly, "memory" happens. Around the campfire, sharing whiskey, they feel the presence of "Old Ones":

A circled presence, like miasma, pressed in, and how long it remained I don't know, but a meteor, the slowest falling one I ever saw, dropped right across the Great Bear like a thrown spear, and then the circle seemed to loosen, and things regained their accustomed positions, dispositions. . . . Tashmoo emptied his toddy: In all my life I never encountered anything like that. What brought them in?

—*Memory.*

Ours or theirs?

Yes, I said.[26]

So the book ends. Though Heat-Moon's final quest for memory is at times awkward and self-conscious, it is for him essential. If America, if the human species, is to survive, then it must work actively to rejuvenate and reconstruct geographically specific, ancestral paradigms — deep maps — that move it toward a grand harmony of people and places.

This rejuvenation begins with the individual journey, with the singular act of self-creation represented, perhaps, by William Trogdon's decision to rejuvenate the William Least Heat-Moon name. Whatever the consequences for the larger world, it was clear to me that the "Heat-Moon self" had led Trogdon to write one of the most important books on the prairie in American literature, a book that had had a profound impact on my own commitment to place. That fact alone suggested that what Heat-Moon had written about names was true, that they have the power to shape who we become in relation to the land around us. He writes: "Many tribal Americans believe that a person turns into his name, partakes of its nature in such a way that it is a mold the possessor comes to fill. When names lose their first meaning, as they have to most Americans of European descent, that mold becomes only a handle for others to move us around with."[27]

Names determine, and as Heat-Moon's name became the vehicle for his own connection to the prairies, as he worked to articulate the land and its people — to reinvoke positive, ancestral memories — he appeared to be encouraging his readers to participate in a similar process: "(A suggestion: when you finish reading, go outside and find a living thing you do not know the name of and look at it closely and give it one of your own making; then it will become yours to carry into dreamtime because memory depends finally upon what we create for ourselves, and, until we become nomenclators of a place, we can never really enter it.)"[28] PrairyErth, seen in this light, is an invitation to us all to rename ourselves into place.

* * *

After a brief correspondence, William Least Heat-Moon generously agreed to meet with me for an interview in August 1994 at a brew pub near his home in Columbia. To prepare I reread PrairyErth, and once again Heat-Moon's experiment in regional identity led me to reflect upon my own. This time, though, instead of drawing me toward my Kansas roots, it drew my thoughts toward Missouri. Not that far from Kansas City, where Heat-Moon had grown up, was the small town of Corder where my paternal grandfather, Roy Price, had been born and raised. Roy's father, Tom Price, and grandfather Robert James had worked in the infamous coal mines of northern England and Wales and then, in the late 1800s, immigrated to Missouri to work in the Corder mines.

I knew very little about coal mining in the region. That kind of work—the blackened faces, the dust explosions, the violent labor disputes—didn't fit into the sentimental, agrarian myths that, despite my experiences during the 1980s farm crisis, still held a firm grip on my ways of imagining the Midwest. The dark and troubled history of coal mining belonged primarily to Appalachia, not here. It didn't take me long, however, to discover the significant role the industry had played in developing the Midwest and Plains. Coal mining in Iowa and Missouri had provided the economic foundation for countless communities, fueled the western expansion of the railroad, and driven the rapid industrialization of such prairie towns as Kansas City and Omaha. In Corder, I thought, might be found an overlooked chapter in the environmental history of the grasslands, and—inspired by Heat-Moon's "deep map" of Chase County—I decided to go there.

That's what I told myself, at least. The more personal reason PrairyErth moved me to travel to Corder was my name, John Thomas Price.

"John" came from my mother's Iowa grandfather, but my middle and last names (as well as those of my father and grandfather) came from my great-grandfather Tom Price, the Corder coal miner. Tom's name echoed across three generations of men in my family, yet I knew virtually nothing about him. Unlike Harlan, Kansas, which I had visited for family reunions, I had never visited Corder. The only family members I'd known who'd actually lived there were my deceased Grandpa Roy, who had rarely talked to me about his Missouri boyhood, and his mother, Elizabeth — Tom's wife — whom I had known briefly when I was a child. My sisters and I had called her "Granny," and her rare stories about Missouri tended to rotate among the adventures of Jesse James, a graphic description of a human scalp she'd seen in a general store, and an eyewitness account of the public hanging of a bank robber. She was especially fond of telling me the hanging story after I'd misbehaved. I'm not sure whether she was encouraging me to become a better person or encouraging me to, like Jesse, become better at not getting caught.

In any case, Granny's stories did little to inspire a sense of connection to my Missouri roots — if anything, they frightened me away from them — and no one else in my family seemed eager to bridge the rift. Consciously or not, my parents and grandparents appeared to have made a choice to privilege our Kansas heritage. It had never bothered me — "Home on the Range" made a glorious family legacy — but now I wondered what had been lost. Perhaps this absence, this silence at the heart of my own ancestral memory, was why I felt so drawn to PrairyErth. Whatever the answer was, I knew that if Heat-Moon was right, if names determine our relationship to place, if they are the mold we come to fill, any effort on my part to understand and connect to the grasslands had to go through the coal country of northwestern Missouri.

Though it was morning, the air over Interstate 70 was already hot and thick. I was alone in the car, rehearsing a few of the questions I planned to ask Heat-Moon the next day during our interview in Columbia, but the smell of asphalt and exhaust, the rumble of semis, kept disrupting me. It was with relief that I turned north toward Corder, the highway noise quickly being replaced by the buzz of cicadas and birdsong. Ragged fields of grass and corn ran against prominent groves of oak and hickory. Occasionally, in the ditches, I spotted isolated strands of big bluestem, goldenrod, and switchgrass. The view reminded me that the history of Missouri, its identity, was defined by shifting, often violent political and ecological borders. During the Civil War Missouri was one of four slave states that remained loyal to the Union. Still, many of its citizens fought for the Confederacy, including a few, I was sure, from right there in Lafayette County.[29] Slavery, like coal mining, was not something that fit easily into my ways of imagining the Midwest, but if I needed further confirmation all I had to do was visit the nearby Lexington Historic Battlefield or the Confederate Memorial at Higginsville.

The landscape reminded me that Missouri was also the site of an ecological battleground. Unlike Iowa—which had in the early years of white settlement been predominantly tallgrass—Missouri had been divided nearly in half between prairie and hardwood forests. It was a sharp, dramatic division created to a large extent by the pre-Illinoian glacial advance, whose scouring reach ended in central Missouri between 500,000 and 2.5 million years ago. But the war goes back even further. John Madson describes the ancient struggle for dominance between these two American biomes as "an incredibly hard-fought war": "This silent struggle between trees and grass is the grimmest conflict ever joined by two major plant groups in North America. It has been going on in some form for perhaps 25 million years across a broad battlefront that has seen countless victories and defeats on both sides—and the intrusions of glacial epochs and corn farmers are only interludes, and of little consequence." Madson states, however, that when Europeans arrived on the scene, this plant war was turning in favor of trees, and if "discovery of the New World had been delayed until 3000 AD, . . . Iowa might have been as timbered as Pioneer Ohio." Settlement decimated forests as well as prairies, but "the net gain," according to Madson, benefited trees.[30] Thanks to cultivation as well as suppression of fire and flood, trees now occupy many places previously controlled by grasses, including the nearby Missouri River floodplain.

When I first read this I thought I had stumbled on another of those morally ambivalent, scientific facts that had the power to keep me awake at night. What *was* the true identity of this bioregion? If environmental forces had intended forest to overcome prairie, then why bemoan its loss? On that Missouri road, however, as I spotted another isolated clump of big bluestem and felt a rush of emotion, the answer was clear: Because I choose to.

The city limits of Corder (population 485) arrived with little warning, the corn suddenly giving way to house and lawn. The main street was quiet, a few cars parked in front of the mostly one-story, modest brick buildings. Several of those buildings appeared old and unoccupied, including Biesemeyer's Food Market. My grandmother Mildred Wagner Price — the Harlan, Kansas girl — had told me to visit Mr. Biesemeyer when I was there, if he was still alive. She'd said he had been a longtime friend of the Price family in Corder and might be able to answer some of my questions. I peeked in the windows of the store and was discouraged to see things in disarray, old refrigerators and metal shelves and cardboard boxes scattered around the dim room. The place was obviously out of business.

As I headed back to my car, I noticed a sharply dressed elderly man walking across the street. I waved and after catching up to him asked if he knew a Mr. Biesemeyer.

"I sure do," he replied, suspiciously. "And who might be asking?"

When I explained that I was Roy Price's grandson, his face lit up. "I'll be tied," he said. "I'm Biesey and am I ever glad to see you."

Mr. Biesemeyer unlocked the door to the old store and invited me to enter. He explained that his family had run the place for over fifty years, beginning in 1933. It was officially closed now, owned by someone else, but he joked that the new landlord couldn't stop him from going there every day to make coffee and talk to folks. It gave him something to do now that his wife had passed on.

We sat in metal folding chairs and spent the next few hours talking about the history of the community and my family. Mr. Biesemeyer had been good friends with my grandfather's older brother, Buddy (whom I had never met), and had spent many days at the Price home, as well as at the home of Granny's parents, the Jameses. He said both families had been kind to him, good people, but he seemed especially drawn to memories of my great-grandfather Tom Price. Tom was, according to Mr. Biesemeyer, a representative Corder man — a tough, hardworking coal miner and dedicated family man. The kind of man that Mr. Biesemeyer had aimed to serve through his general store and meat shop.

"I made sure Mr. Price and the rest of them got only the best, choice meat," he said. "Given the kind of work they did, that's what they deserved."

He explained that during the boom years of the teens and 1920s, there had been three major mines in the area. The largest had been the Imperial where Tom had worked. Like the rest of the miners, Tom had entered the shafts before sunrise and emerged after sunset, a life of darkness I could hardly comprehend. And because the shafts were unusually deep and narrow, the miners spent most of their time crawling on their hands and knees to retrieve the rock. With no health care, no retirement, most of these men worked until they went lame or died of cancer or black lung. My great-grandfather might have died there as well if the mines hadn't closed in the 1940s when many homes and industries stopped using bituminous, or "soft," coal—in part because of the thick, poisonous clouds of smoke it had created in some cities. The local mines were covered over and the men left to fend for themselves. Now in his sixties, Tom found work as a night watchman for the railyards in St. Louis, another brutal and dangerous job, returning to Corder on the weekends. Eventually he and Elizabeth moved to Tekamah, Nebraska, where shortly after he died of cancer.

For Mr. Biesemeyer, though, the memory of my great-grandfather will always be entwined with the Corder mines.

"I can still hear him coming," he said, shaking his head. "Can hear them all coming."

"Hear them?" I asked.

"Yes, in the winters, after dark. When the miners came up from the shafts, the water would freeze on them and make a tinkling noise as they walked. I could hear them coming down the street toward the store at night, tinkling like a bunch of Christmas trees."

That harsh and beautiful image of my ancestor, one I could never have imagined, seemed to linger in the air between us. It was unexpected yet confirmed another stubborn myth I carried with me about the Midwest as a place where work—especially hard, self-sacrificial work—held an almost spiritual, redemptive power. Hearing this story provoked a welcome rush of pride, an admiration for my namesake, as well as renewed guilt over neglecting his memory for so long.

Mr. Biesemeyer stood up and announced that there was someone I must visit — my Grandpa Roy's best boyhood friend, George Dillingham.[31] Though Grandma had never mentioned a Dillingham to me, I enthusiastically agreed, and Mr. Biesemeyer called him on the phone. After he hung up, I shook his hand and thanked him for his time.

"Well, thank you," he said, his blue tie reflecting the bright light of the windows. "This has meant a lot to me. It's as if Roy was right here, talking about the old times. Now that you know where we are, I hope you won't be a stranger."

"I won't," I said, and believed it.

The Dillinghams lived in a nearby town, and when I pulled up to their small white house they were already standing on the front porch, waving. He was bald and slim, though a bit gaunt looking in his black slacks and gray, short-sleeved shirt. In contrast, his wife was red-cheeked and round and wearing a lemon-yellow pants suit. A ray of sunshine beside a cloud. They both embraced me, exclaiming how much I looked like Roy. Inside, after serving me a tall glass of iced tea, the stories began. Mr. Dillingham claimed that he and Roy were inseparable while growing up together in Corder and that he had been "pretty hurt" when Mildred hadn't contacted them about Roy's death, though they had assumed she'd been overwhelmed with grief and forgot. Such an oversight didn't seem like my grandmother, and it made me question once again why she hadn't told me about these friends.

I soon became lost, however, in hilarious stories about the pranks Roy and George used to play on their schoolteachers, and the tall tales told by Tom around the Price dinner table, and my grandfather's famous temperament during high school basketball games. Mr. Dillingham said it had been well-known to Corder opponents that if they got Roy Price mad enough, he would eventually "knee someone in the nuts" and get kicked out of the game, almost guaranteeing a victory for the other team. This was not an image I could easily reconcile with my own memories of Grandpa, a man who had always been patient and affectionate with his grandchildren, no matter how rowdy we were. Still, the story amused me, opening windows of mystery behind an overly familiar face.

"Of course," Mr. Dillingham continued, "you don't see many white boys playing basketball nowadays. It's a colored boy's sport, but it didn't use to be that way. A lot of things have changed around here. Did you know that, today, coloreds could buy a house right next to ours if they wanted? When I was growing up, that didn't happen — we chased a colored family out of Corder once, and they never came back. Time was, those kind knew not to show their face in this county after sunset."

The sudden turn in our conversation completely silenced me. Desperate to change the subject, my gaze fell on several family pictures hanging on the wall. I asked who they were and Mrs. Dillingham recited the names of their children and grandchildren. They were very proud of them, she said. The Dillinghams felt sorry for their grandchildren, though, "growing up in a world like today." They claimed that one had recently been assaulted, right there in town, by gang members from Kansas City.

"People like that ought to be strung up," Mr. Dillingham exclaimed. "That's how it used to be."

"George, didn't Corder have a public hanging when you were a boy?" Mrs. Dillingham asked.

"No," he replied. "What happened was they tied a colored man to a tree there, tar and feathered him and set him afire. He'd raped a white woman."

I stood up, muttered something about an appointment in Columbia, and gradually made my way toward the car. Arm in arm, the Dillinghams waved from their porch and, like Mr. Biesemeyer, told me not to be a stranger.

I was tempted to leave directly for Columbia, to escape the memory of that place and those people, but something compelled me to return to Corder. On the one hand the Dillinghams had confirmed many of the historical facts I had read about in books. Missouri had been a slave state, occupying an ambiguous border between the Midwest and the South. As such I knew racism, including violent racism, had been part of the state's cultural fabric. Likewise, I knew that the

Midwest and Great Plains had never been free of racist brutality—the genocidal tactics used by whites against native peoples had been well documented, as had the history of hate crimes against midwestern African Americans. In the first chapter of Malcolm X's autobiography, he recalls how the Ku Klux Klan attacked his childhood home in Omaha, just a couple of hours from my own hometown. The possibility for that kind of violence still exists in the Midwest, as demonstrated by the rise of hate groups during the 1980s farm crisis.[32]

As I approached Corder, however, these layers of historical awareness proved to be no armor against Mr. Dillingham's story. *They* had burned a man alive. To whom, exactly, was he referring? The Klan? Or was he referring to a more general group from Corder—a group that because of the town's small size might have included my great-grandparents, my great-great-grandparents, or others from my family? I had spent a lot of time with Grandpa Roy while growing up and had never once heard him make a derogatory comment or tell an offensive joke about another race. Nor had I heard my parents say such things. Mr. Dillingham's version of racist violence had always been something I had read about in books or associated with other people—certainly not my own family. Certainly not me.

I drove down the side streets of Corder, searching for . . . *what*? I eventually stopped in front of what Mr. Biesemeyer had said was the old Price home. He had remembered it as a pretty house with a white picket fence and a huge, lush garden in the back. The house I saw, however, was clearly in decline: flaking blue paint, the roof patched and sagging, a rusted car sitting in the front yard. And yet, displayed in the windows were several crayon drawings by children. I knew nothing about that family, but at one time, according to Mr. Biesemeyer, a good and kind family had lived there—my family. Memories of Grandpa Roy seemed to confirm that legacy; I did not want to slander my Corder ancestors by assuming that they knew about, supported, or participated in the torture and murder of a man. I didn't even know if what Mr. Dillingham had told me was true.[33]

A week later, while looking through old Price family photos with Grandma Mildred, I would ask her about the incident. She said that the Dillinghams were "probably just talking, as usual," her tone implying that they may not have been the "close friends" they'd claimed to be. Grandma strongly doubted any such murder had occurred.

"Roy would have told me about it," she said, "and Tom would have bragged about it."

"*Bragged* about it?" I asked, but she wouldn't elaborate.

I would find it hard, that future afternoon, to look through the rest of the photos with her — my great-grandfather, Tom Price, happily posing with his family or with his beloved terriers or with his mining friends. Who, exactly, was I looking at? In those positive images I would see one kind of ancestral memory, the kind I wanted to claim as part of my connection to the grasslands. But what other memories were living there — in him, in his son Roy, in my grandmother's silence? I think I understood, even when parked in front of the house in Corder, that I would never know for sure. The only certainty was that the life of the place, another family's story, was moving forward.

On my way out of town, I parked in front of the unassuming mound of earth that Mr. Biesemeyer had claimed was the old Imperial Coal Mine. I had planned to take a picture from the car but then decided to get out and climb to the top. Surrounded by bean fields, the mound was thick with trees and tangles of shrubs and grasses. I made my way through them slowly, searching for evidence of the mine, but there wasn't much, just a large circular patch of eroded earth that I assumed had once been the main shaft. Railroad tracks ran alongside, reminding me that this hill was an important source of coal for the polluting factories of Kansas City and for the railroads themselves. In the mid- to late 1800s mines from this region had provided one of the last opportunities for trains to purchase fuel for the long trip across the Plains to the Rocky Mountains. If this was one such mine, could those who created it be blamed for helping determine the sad fate of the grasslands, for carving towns and fields out of the prairie, accelerating the decimation of its native communities?

The mound itself reflected that destructive history. Though it was evenly covered with trees and grasses — an echo of the ancient and ongoing battle between those species — the only native plants I could identify were hickories and several tall thistle. The lack of any native grasses confirmed what my books had already told me: no matter what side I chose, tree or grass, the war to conquer the prairies in that place had been over long ago. And yet the prairie's memory, though diminished, endured in the thistles. The scientific name for tall thistle, which I had first come across during the Iowa floods, is derived from the Greek for "swollen vein," a condition it was once used to alleviate, though I doubt there are many who appreciate its medicinal value.

What the thistle most reminded me of, however, were the literal avenues of blood that connected me to my ancestors, to that place —another kind of source. When that hill was a working coal mine, the bodies of my relatives were lowered, again and again, into the earth beneath my feet. Down there, crawling on hands and knees, they had driven their own flesh into the rock, and in return the dust had coated their lungs, choking their organs, threatening to suffocate them or, in an explosive instant, burn them alive as it had countless others. What kind of man emerged from such a place, covered with ice, to limp home through the streets of Corder? To those immersed, daily, in that avalanche of abuse—its devastation reverberating from the cells of their bodies out across the vast interior of the continent—could any act of cruelty be thought unnatural? Could any act of kindness be less than miraculous?

I didn't know. Didn't know what, if anything, to do with these thoughts, these reluctant memories. All I knew was that they were now a conscious part of me, as was this place. There would be no leaving it behind. I sat down and watched the shadows of the grass and trees extend across the hill, then fade into a dusk that had once been, and still seemed, a warning.

* * *

The next morning, just before my interview with Heat-Moon, I went through my notes but was distracted by my experiences in Corder. I thought I might work them into our conversation—hadn't Heat-Moon, at the top of Roniger Hill, also struggled to articulate his conflicted relationship to ancestral memory and place? Hadn't he, while exploring the land, encountered "shadows" in himself and others? Each time I tried to wrangle my thoughts into words, they fell back into confusion and silence. I decided that for the sake of a smooth interview, I would stick to my previously prepared questions.

When I first confirmed our meeting, I had been disappointed that I wouldn't be interviewing Heat-Moon at his home, where I might locate his work inside a more intimate landscape. Once inside Columbia's Flat Branch Brew Pub, however, I felt comforted by the artificial surroundings, the way the local past was simplified into sepia photographs and antique advertisements, framed and hanging on the clean brick walls.

When Heat-Moon arrived, I introduced myself as he sat down in the seat across from me. He was dressed casually, in a blue sports shirt and jeans; his hair and beard were a thick salt and pepper, trimmed short for summer. He put me at ease almost immediately, complimenting my choice of beer and talking about his early days as a magazine writer, during which he'd written an article on brew pubs. As he asked me about my studies, my life — his dark eyebrows raised, alert and interested — I could understand why so many different people had opened up to him during his journeys. In Heat-Moon I sensed none of the condescension of a best-selling author, just someone who enjoyed conversing with others.

It wasn't long before we got around to the issue of regionalism. Heat-Moon claimed that like me, he had not been educated to appreciate regional literature, especially travel literature.

"Things are maybe better now in English departments," he said, "but when I was a student, professors had so little respect for anything that wasn't part of the canon. I went for years thinking American literature was a short list of about fifty texts. Writing *Blue Highways* saved me from that limited way of looking at our literary tradition. It forced me to seek out other voices, and I found out that there were a lot of great books I had never heard of before, especially travel books. I have whole bookshelves of them at home, around seven hundred volumes. Yet there are so many good ones, even I haven't discovered them all."

I asked him why travel literature had been slighted by teachers and scholars.

"Part of it has to do with the fact that travel literature is not fiction, not so-called imaginative literature, and so it's not in anybody's canon. But there is also—and perhaps this has influenced the critical response to my own work—there is also a prejudice against so-called regional literature. That's been going on for a long time. Before the thirties, if you wrote about Pulpit Rock in Massachusetts or about Jewish culture in Jersey City you weren't considered a regionalist, but if you wrote about or painted Iowa cornfields, like Grant Wood, you were one. Then, just before World War II, with writers like Marjorie Kinnan Rawlings, regional art and literature seemed ready to shed this pejorative term 'regional.' Then the war just collapsed everything. Nothing really exciting happened again in the field until the late sixties, the seventies, with writers like Wendell Berry. Looking back, I think *Blue Highways* was part of that resurgence in regionalism. But, I must confess, I'm not sure that term 'regionalism' really means anything."

"How so?"

"Few people agree on what a 'region' means anymore. It depends on your perspective. When I was writing *PrairyErth*, Kelly Kindscher, who worked as a botanist in Kansas, took me out on the prairie to give me some crash courses on flora. He really leaned on me to use some sort of bioregional definition in *PrairyErth*, rather than a political definition represented by county lines. I thought about it, thought about defining it as a watershed, and that would've been fine. But I was already too far along, and in some ways it's easier at this time in our national development to work with something like a county by which information is centrally organized. Besides, most people understand counties—that's how they define themselves, so you can work with them easier. Most people in Chase don't know whether they belong to a watershed or not; that's not what they identify with."

"But isn't that what you were trying to change in writing your book," I asked, "to help them see themselves as citizens of a bioregion, of the prairies, the Permian seas?"

"Oh yes, and I think I've succeeded to some degree. Remember that prairie park controversy? Well, the park has finally come about. I'm not sure about the details, but the new park has an agreement with, I believe, the National Park Service, which will allow local citizens to oversee the project. I think that could be good or bad, depending on who those citizens are — if the right-wing nuts get in there, who knows what will happen. At any rate, the tallgrass prairie there is going to be saved, and PrairyErth had something to do with that."

Heat-Moon went on to explain how his book had helped the prairie park project by getting the attention of Kansas Senator Nancy Kassenbaum and how it had improved county tourism, doubling the visitors to the Cottonwood Falls courthouse. Also, the main street in Cottonwood "looked better now than it ever did when I was working there." But he felt the most important change, as I mentioned earlier, was in the attitude of some of the residents toward the prairies, seeing them as something beautiful, something worthy of a national park.

The apparently positive influence PrairyErth had had on Chase County represented a relationship between literature and place I had not encountered while visiting the home communities of Dan O'Brien and Linda Hasselstrom. Heat-Moon's book had not just exposed the ecological, economic, and psychological wounds left by the past — it had, in observable ways, helped heal some of them. This is what Hamlin Garland had hoped to do with his best-selling books, and recalling the cool welcome his work had received from some in the region, I asked Heat-Moon about the local response to PrairyErth.

"It started," he said, "when the publishers released the book in Chase County, in Cottonwood Falls, at my request. I was prepared to be picketed by the local anti-environmental right-wingers, even though they could not yet have read the book. I was sure my environmental and racial views would elicit some kind of response. Instead, on the day of the release, I was hauled down Broadway in a Model A. At first I thought it would be fun, but when I got up on that thing I felt like a perfect jerk. You can't imagine the chutzpah it takes to parade down a street, waving at people. Anyway, in the crowd, I could see some of the people who opposed the prairie park, people wearing buttons that said 'Keep Grasslands Free' — I always call them the 'Keep Grasslands for Me' contingent. But they waited in the long line to get their books signed with everyone else. They were smiling and happy. I think what pacified them was my donating a thousand dollars to the Chase County Historical Society and a thousand to the local 4-H group. I did it to thank local citizens for their help, and between the historical society and 4-H, that pretty much covered everybody in the county. So those people with the buttons might have believed that I was all messed up on my environmental opinions, but they also knew I believed in their children. I think that earned their tolerance."

"I'm curious," I replied. "Of all the possible monetary donations you might have made — the prairie park, political groups, city hall — why those focused on educating children about their regional heritage? How does that connect with your general hopes for how your work might shape the future of Chase County?"

"I care about the future of Chase County," he said, "and that's what those children represent. I hope PrairyErth continues to make a positive impact on that future, but sometimes I wonder. The chamber of commerce in Emporia has said that PrairyErth has set the tone for economic development in the whole area. I think some business people mean the kind of development found in places like Strong City, which is a large and rather unattractive place already. To fill it with fast-food joints will make things worse. That's not what I had in mind at all. I realize that Chase County needs a new economic base, but I want that base to be built upon conservation and, to use a word some people hate there, preservation. They hate the word, but not the concept; they want to preserve the ranch buildings on the Z Bar [the ranch where the prairie preserve is located]. Those buildings, and the land they sit on, represent who they are. I hope it stays that way."

I asked if his worries over the impact of PrairyErth on Chase County were part of any larger tension he felt between writing a good book and a responsible book, one that would make a positive difference in the lives of others.

"Writers always want to write the best book they can, but sometimes writing the best book you can means writing the most influential book you can. I think Harriet Beecher Stowe wrote the best book she could but also the most influential book she could — we know what Abraham Lincoln said about her. That's one of the key issues I'm dealing with right now as I write this third book about traveling across the continent on rivers.[34] Because of the large readership this book is likely to have, I want it to convince a lot of people that we really need to take better care of our waters. We've got to think of rivers in an entirely different way; we can't continue with this western European notion that we are masters of the planet. That book will offer a chance to express my opinion, but if I choose to speak my heart deeply, if I start pounding my fist and lecturing and preaching, I'll lose my readers, especially the ones who disagree with me. If, on the other hand, I speak to them with reason and—above all—*show* them why they should care, then I have a chance of reaching them. To do that I'll need to speak softly, with some sympathy and understanding for the opposition. That isn't always easy for me. I mean, I believe in environmental issues so strongly, I'm not sure I can maintain moderation or even want to—sometimes you can moderate all the power out of your opinions. So how do you find a balance? That's the challenge facing writers like Terry Tempest Williams, Linda Hasselstrom, Barry Lopez, and myself, writers who are trying to change minds."

In addition to his sense of environmental and social responsibility, I wondered if he felt personally accountable to the individuals he wrote about in *PrairyErth*. How did those people respond to being portrayed by an outsider, about having their private lives exposed to a national audience?

"[Unlike in *Blue Highways*,] I wasn't just traveling through Chase County. I spent many years there, talking with people, and I think an unusual degree of trust developed among many of us, even friendship. Although I didn't always agree with their environmental or racial views, I liked and respected most of the people. I received only one complaint, but it bothered me nonetheless. It was Slim Pinkston, the cowboy. I don't know whether he's read the chapter on himself or not, but he was mad at me after *PrairyErth* appeared. I heard about all this thirdhand from Whitt Laughridge, one of my most important guides to the county. Whitt said to me, 'Slim's mad as hell about what you wrote about him.' 'What was wrong with what I wrote?' I asked. 'Well, he doesn't really know. He's just mad that you wrote about him.' I couldn't believe it. I mean what the hell did he think I was doing sitting there with a tape recorder on his kitchen table for three hours? I told him I was writing a book, and Whitt told him I was writing a book—what did he think I was doing? Whitt said not to worry about it, that Slim can be ornery that way. When I came back a year later, I still wanted to talk to Slim about it, but Whitt told me to just let it lie. I did, but it bothered me that Slim may have thought I'd violated his trust."

"Do you feel any Chase residents violated your trust?"

"There was one man whom I really thought was a helluva sweet guy and who helped me a lot. A good man in almost every way. But during the last eight months I was in the county, I don't know what happened, but he started talking about 'nigger' this and 'nigger' that. He'd never said the word in my presence before. I don't know whether he was trying to let me know where he stood before I published the book or what, but I felt most uncomfortable. I'm glad it took him so long to bring it up, because I had trouble talking with him after that. Racism, for me, is different from environmentalism. With environmental issues, I want and need to listen to the other side in order to understand and interpret. I don't need to hear the other side on racism; I've heard it all my life. I know what it is. Still, I never mentioned his racism in the book, and even if I had I never would have identified him. That's a dilemma for me because in leaving that kind of thing out, people can end up looking a little more generous than they really are. I just have to count on the reader to understand where my heart is."

Here my thoughts slipped toward my own discomfort while visiting the Dillinghams. I almost shared the details of that experience with Heat-Moon, but once again I couldn't find the language. If I had we might have moved toward an even more substantial conversation about the relationship among regional identity, writing, and responsibility. As we seek to reimagine the connection between self and land, what responsibility do we have to also expose the history of human atrocity in the region, especially when it might involve those to whom we feel a sense of obligation, even love? What does that personal history—that ancestral memory—demand of us in the present? Where, ultimately, was *my* heart when it came to these matters?

While I scanned my notes, trying to reorient, Bob Lindholm sat down at our table. Heat-Moon introduced us, explaining that Bob had been one of the copilots for his recent river voyage and that they were going to be examining old maps of the Missouri. Bob said he hoped he wasn't interrupting, and Heat-Moon assured him that we were about to finish. I felt a surge of panic—there was so much more I wanted to discuss—and in the rush, I blurted out a question that came close to expressing the new tension I felt in my own regional identity.

"Why did you choose to write about Kansas and not somewhere else, like Missouri, where you live?"

"The answer is long," he replied, "so I'll do a compressed version. As I mentioned before, the *Blue Highways* trip was a horizontal journey where I wanted to cover a lot of territory, to keep moving, to see a lot of things in a little time. With *PrairyErth* I wanted to write a book at the other end of the spectrum, a book about stopping, exploring one place. In other words, I wanted depth instead of breadth. I also realized that in *Blue Highways* my conception of travel was coming partly from Rand McNally road atlases and that I was thinking in two dimensions, in lines—highway lines. That isn't a very informed way to think about traveling because it ignores the other dimensions. Then, when I was traveling through eastern Montana, crossing those miles and miles and miles of pretty much level ground, and wondering how that state ever got named for its mountains, I began to think in terms of squares. What would it be like, I wondered, to carve out a square-mile cube of eastern Montana, lift it up into the air, set it to the side, look down into that hole, and then, like an earthworm, move over to penetrate that square mile of dirt? How much more would one know about that level surface after having traveled its depths? Well, I let those questions percolate a bit, and eventually they led me to *PrairyErth*. Rather than a square mile of Montana I chose Chase County because it was a fairly neglected place, austere, a blank spot on highway maps. And I liked the name of its county seat: Cottonwood Falls. Loved that name. What's more, the Flint Hills are also the embodiment of the tallgrass prairie, and, well, the tallgrass region is my home."

Before I could ask another question, the waitress interrupted, inquiring whether we wanted another beer. When Heat-Moon said no and looked at Bob, I realized my time was up. I thanked him once again.

"Sure—I wish you the best with your project. Are you heading back to Iowa City?"

"Yes."

"Great place," he replied, then turned toward Bob. "I gave a talk there once, about a year ago. My publisher told me that I was just going to sign some books and that there would probably be around twenty people. I walked in ready for a simple conversation and there were two or three hundred people and a statewide radio audience. It was one of the greatest audiences I've ever had. I mean they really felt involved, and they knew if they didn't help me along, I was going to flop up on that big stage."

I hesitated, wondering whether to mention the hissing I'd heard from that same "great" audience. Finally, I couldn't resist—the event had played such an important role in shaping my relationship to his work.

"It was a great talk," I said, tentatively, "but do you remember when you mentioned being occupied by another self when writing? At that moment, I distinctly heard hissing coming from the back of the room. Did you hear it?"

His face became serious; Bob sat up in his chair.

"No, I didn't hear that."

"I guess my question is, . . ." I started to stumble. "My question is: How do you respond to people who believe you assumed a Native American name for purely literary and financial gain? I mean, how do you respond to those hissers, those people who see you as, well, an opportunistic poseur?"

Heat-Moon took a drink from his pint of bitter. "First of all, John, I utterly reject that charge. Having said that, were I to start again, I'm not sure that I would use the Heat-Moon name."

My face must have registered my surprise.

"Now hang on," he exclaimed, raising his palms. "What I mean is that when I wrote *Blue Highways,* I had no notion whatsoever that more than three or four thousand people would ever read it. I didn't know what I was starting. All I knew was that when the title page of the manuscript simply read 'by William Trogdon,' it felt hollow to me, empty. It didn't hold together. Neither my editor nor I could figure out why. Then I realized—and I've said this before—that the story coming out of me was from both sides of my background, the Anglo-Irish side and the Osage side. It happened at about two or three in the morning while I was working on the loading dock of the *Columbia Daily Tribune*. The answer just came to me—talk about an epiphany—it just flashed in: you're not writing the book from the whole person you are. Once I realized then that the person trying to tell that story was William Lewis Trogdon and Least Heat-Moon, everything changed. From that moment on I was sure I had discovered the right voice, and so I went back and made a few changes—not many really—and changed the title page by adding William Least Heat-Moon. That made all the difference for me, although the published editions of *Blue Highways* continued to also list my Anglo name."

"I don't think some people buy that story about your epiphany," I continued, "or at least don't accept that it's reason enough to assume a racial identity you haven't earned through experience."

"Again, please read the title page and look at the photograph. In *Blue Highways*, the title page lists *both* names; some people forget that William Trogdon appears beneath my photograph.[35] I insisted on that photograph so that nobody would assume that I was Chief Dan George. If you pay attention to all that, you'll see that this guy is, well, let me say it this way: I am not an Indian. I have Indian blood. Those are two different claims, but people often confuse them. So that's why I say if I were to do it again, I'm not sure that I would try to open up that confusion. But if I did that, if I dropped the name, how would I be able to draw upon the person who writes my books, who is definitely not William Lewis Trogdon? That's who you're talking to now. I guess I have enough questions about how the creative mind works, about forces beyond our normal perceptions, to believe that if I didn't honor all sides of my self, I would not be able to use them. Maybe it would still work, maybe it wouldn't, I don't know. All I know is that when I tried to write from the purely Anglo-Irish side it didn't work. It just didn't work because I wasn't capable of reaching inward far enough."

"You suggest that there is a mystical element in this, a kind of passive channeling, but your use of the Native American perspective, the act of reimagining the self in relation to the land, is at times very self-conscious in PrairyErth, especially at the end. . . ."

"Yes," Heat-Moon interjected, "'conscious' is the key word. When I consciously put both feet down in both worlds, then the writing works. And apparently my approach has worked for lots of other people who read my books. I remember talking to John McPhee not long after Blue Highways hit the New York Times best-seller list and telling him that I wasn't sure I wanted to write any more books under that name, Heat-Moon. He said, 'No, now that you've established that name you stay with it.' I have a great deal of respect for him, so I decided that even though it may get sticky, I'll keep using that name. So I have. But it wasn't a decision without consequences."

"So how do you interpret the discomfort some people express about your use of that name?"

"It has to do with crossing interracial lines, I think. You're allowed to cross European ethnic lines, that's alright, but if you start crossing minority racial lines then people get suspicious. This is not as true in the West, but throughout the rest of the country many people assume there is an advantage in claiming an Indian identity. But I have no other racial identity to claim, I'm sorry. In the East—now I haven't heard this opinion in a long time—but in the East, I've heard people say my use of this identity is self-serving and manipulative, while in the West I've heard people say it's stupid, you're opening yourself up to all kinds of prejudice out here. So it depends on what part of the country you're coming from. Besides, of all the writers I know, only one is full-blood Native American: Simon Ortiz. Everybody else is mixed blood, writers like Leslie Marmon Silko and Louise Erdrich and N. Scott Momaday, whose grandmother was white. You don't hear those writers claiming that Native American heritage all for themselves. In fact, it's only been white people who have raised this issue with me, people without that heritage to claim. I find that interesting."

He was probably referring to me, and he was right, it was interesting. What were my real motivations for asking him this question, for caring about the issue in the first place? During the pause there may have emerged a reluctant answer in my mind, the perceived burden of my own racial heritage—how it tied me, unwillingly, to a destruc-

tive history in the region — as well as a simultaneous desire to escape
that heritage. But these feelings quickly found the easier, less com-
promising route to articulation. One that had more to do with the
theories of Pierre Nora — western civilization's collective longing for
memory, the benign "repetition of the ancestral" — than my own life.

"Maybe," I said, "it's because the farther away Euro-Americans get
from their own ethnic heritage, the more they crave and even resent
that kind of connection in others, that kind of power. Is that how
you would define it, as power?"

"Yes, a creative power. And what I fear most is that that power,
those voices, won't be there for me in this new book, the voices who
spoke for me during part of Blue Highways and all of PrairyErth. When I
say voices, I don't mean I actually hear voices, but my mind does put
things on paper that when I read them later don't sound like they
came from me. When I read aloud from PrairyErth, the words don't
sound like me — they sound like someone else. That's the person that
I have got to get hold of to write. When I write as the Anglo-Irish Bill
Trogdon, it's crap. I mean, I have written some things, I can show you
some magazine pieces that are written purely from that Anglo point
of view. I guess 'point of view' is the wrong phrase; rather, they are
written from that Anglo persona. And they're empty. I don't believe
in those pieces; I don't respect them. And if that persona or personas
are not there for this new book, then I'm not going to have a book.
I've been worrying about this for over two years now, but I'm happy
to say that since I got back from this trip checking out the rivers,
for almost eight days straight I've dreamed about rivers. When I start
dreaming about rivers, that's a good sign because it's entered another
level of my consciousness. I'll leave it to some psychoanalyst to tell
me whether that force I'm touching is part of the Osage ancestry or
whether it's from some place in Ireland or the U.S.A. or just from inside my brain. I don't know; it doesn't make any difference to me."

He crossed his hands and leaned into the table: "All I know is that
the ethical, the emotional drive behind that voice has a great deal
to do with the best that Native Americans have presented to us. I
say the best because they've presented a whole lot of shit to us, too.
Drive across a reservation today and look at it — it's some of the most
degraded land in the United States. So there's no point in trying to

make Native Americans into environmental paragons. They're human beings and that's all they are. But when we look at the best that they've done and thought, there's a lot we can learn from them. Same with the best that Thomas Jefferson has done; his best is truly great."

"Does this native persona and the books it has written represent the best you have to offer the world?"

"Yes, I think it does," he said. "I really think it does."

I closed my notebook and started to say goodbye when Heat-Moon interrupted:

"I should tell you one more story before you go. I was once in Rochester, New York, for a book signing, and afterward there was a little reception at someone's house, a barn out in the country. I was standing, as usual, near the buffet table, when George Rudy came up to me. He is full-blooded Sioux and looked like a young version of the man who posed for the buffalo nickel. We were talking, eating some potato chips, and he said, 'I don't know why I'm eating this goddamned white man's food.' So he put down the potato chips and started eating carrots and celery sticks. Anyway, as he said goodbye to me, he closed his parka and a feather went *swish* — shot way up in the air from his parka. *Way* up. And then, as feathers do, it fell slowly and landed on the floor between us. We both watched it, and then he reached down and picked it up. It wasn't a little down feather; it was big and perfectly white. He said, 'Where did that come from?' I said, 'I think it came out of your parka.' He said, 'No, no — I don't understand,' and then walked off. The next day was the second ever *Blue Highways* book signing, and George came right up to me and said, 'I don't want your signature, but this belongs to you.' He reached into his shirt pocket and pulled out that white feather. 'It's yours,' he said. 'The way it flew out last night, I just couldn't figure it out. So I went home, smoked my pipe, and thought about it. I thought and thought about it; visualized it.' Then he said: 'I finally realized that this is your feather, and wanted to let you know what it means: there is something pure in your work.' He gave me the feather and walked off. I've never seen him again. But hearing that gave me confidence about using all my names, all the personas, even though I'd had doubts."

"That's really great," Bob said. "And you've never seen him again?"

"Never," Heat-Moon replied. "But that's what he said. You should call him up. His name is George Rudy and he lives in Victor, New York. Call him up and ask him if he remembers that feather."

"Maybe I will," I said, as I stood up. "Well, thanks again for your time."

Heat-Moon was smiling. "You kind of laid back on this touchy question until I'd had a couple pints down me, didn't you?" He turned to Bob: "That's a good interviewing technique."

Bob was already unfolding the map of the lower Missouri River. Heat-Moon had been reading Lewis and Clark's journals and some other early accounts of that part of the river and was especially interested in the Council Bluffs area of Iowa. I told him I grew up near there. "Oh really," he said, and asked if my family lived in the Midwest. Instinctively, I skipped over the Missouri roots and told him about the Harlan, Kansas/"Home on the Range" connection. I would be visiting Harlan in a few weeks, I said, after I visited Chase County.

"You're going to Chase County? *Great.* While you're there, you should look up Whitt Laughridge, tell him hello for me. It's been a while since I've been back. I wanted to get back this year for the concert out on the prairie. Hey, speaking of 'Home on the Range,' do you remember Jane Koger, the woman rancher I interviewed in *PrairyErth*? Well, just last June she had what she called a 'Symphony on the Prairie.' It was an all-women orchestra brought together for the occasion, and they performed classical pieces right out on the prairie. She guessed five thousand people showed up. The population of Chase County is three thousand. And at the end of the concert, they all stood, all five thousand of them, and sang 'Home on the Range' — not just the first verse but some of the lesser-known verses too. I was told people were choking up left and right. So I guess your family's legacy continues in that song. Does that make you a native of Kansas?"

He was still smiling. I shrugged: "I guess I don't know."

*   *   *

The journey to Chase County was one of the few extended car trips Steph and I had taken together since driving to Idaho to be married two years before. Like then, my mind was full of questions concerning responsibility and commitment. I was interested in finding out how *PrairyErth* had changed Chase County, if at all. I wanted to hear what residents thought about Heat-Moon and his book, about how it portrayed them and their home. I also wanted to walk through the prairies there with Steph, to experience together what I hoped would be close to a tallgrass wilderness. My sense of the need to do so had only increased since the trip to Corder and my conversation with Heat-Moon just a week earlier. I hadn't told Steph about the Dillinghams and how they had complicated my relationship to family and region. I would start to, but then I'd think about what Linda Hasselstrom had said about the possibility that I might have to learn to love another landscape as home, perhaps in Idaho. As Steph gazed out the window at the amber grasses of the Flint Hills, I worried — to what distant place might our marriage lead?

By the time we got to Strong City it was nearly dark, so we checked into a motel. The next morning Steph stepped out to get a paper. "Hey, look at the front page," she said, tossing the *Wichita Eagle* to me. There was an article about the prairie park: "Bipartisan Deal Boosts Flint Hills Park."[36] The article describes how, "after years of partisan squabbles," Republican Senator Nancy Kassenbaum and Democratic Representative Dan Glickman had teamed up to push through a plan to create and finance the 11,000-acre national preserve at the Z Bar near Cottonwood Falls. The National Park Service will buy a 180-acre tract containing the historic ranch buildings, but the compromise agreement "keeps 98 percent of the rangeland out of federal hands, sets up an 11-member board of Kansans to oversee the property, gives farm groups a significant voice in the land's operations, and ensures that taxes will continue to be paid on the property." The plan is meant to "calm the fear of farm and ranch groups" while at the same time protect and educate people about the tallgrass prairie ecosystem, as well as the cultural legacy of both Native Americans and ranchers. As of the publication of that article the plan had not yet been approved, but proponents hoped to pass it during the four weeks remaining in the legislative session. Heat-Moon had been right.

I'd scheduled an interview with Whitt Laughridge for later that morning, but we decided to visit the Z Bar first, maybe walk around the prairies for a while. When we arrived we were greeted by a sign intended to keep visitors away from the historic Spring Hill ranch buildings and the land. Even from a distance those buildings were impressive, all built of Cottonwood sandstone, white in the eastern sun. Especially striking was the three-story, Second Empire mansion, with its towering red mansard roof and wide open porch and triple terrace gardens—an enduring witness to the size of the original owner's wealth, as well as his dreams.

The story of the Spring Hill/Z Bar ranch, as Heat-Moon tells it in PrairyErth, is your typical Great Plains boom and bust. Stephen F. Jones, a wealthy land baron from Tennessee, built the place in the 1880s and eventually ranched seven thousand acres along Fox Creek. Jones, who once employed black servants to feed him and his family on silver trays, ended up selling the place twelve years later and moving to Kansas City. Twenty-five years later he returned to Cottonwood a broken man, reduced to sitting on the town's main street and watching cars drive by. For Heat-Moon Jones's story illustrates the general principle that "[t]he American prairies and plains eat pretension and dreams of aristocracy with the slow patience of inevitability, corrupting, eroding, and quite dissolving them in some places, and in others leaving only a carcass as a kind of memorial."[37]

The recent struggle to establish a prairie national park revealed that this land still carried a heavy burden of dream. In PrairyErth Heat-Moon recounts the practical arguments opposing the original prairie park, such as keeping the land on the tax rolls. Those arguments hold powerful sway in a population so often victimized by national and international economic policies. Heat-Moon states, however, that racist "fright tactics" and "vituperation" also contributed to the success of those arguments: "Farm houses robbed by niggers from Chicago. Watermelon rind all over the streets. Daughters assaulted by New Yorkers. Buildings burned by drug dealers." As one Cottonwood man told him, "If you want to kill off something here, all you do is throw in the word colored." Here may be another illustration of what journalist Osha Gray Davidson establishes as a correlation between "the social and economic unraveling of rural communities" in the Midwest and Plains and the rise in racial and religious intolerance. Unlike Davidson, however, Heat-Moon appears to offer prairie preservation as one possible antidote to those divisions. By demonstrating "the beauty of the native land" and offering Chase citizens "a rare and nonpolluting opportunity to broaden the county's economy and share more of American prosperity," the prairie park will "ease that Kansas defensiveness deriving from outsiders' ignorance of the place" and "show people how all lives here sooner or later depend upon natural diversity."[38] This prairie, in short, will unify and sustain the human community.

It is a dream that I hope will be fulfilled, but from where we were standing that morning—on a broken sidewalk, separated from the prairie itself—it seemed as daunting and elusive as any inspired by the land.

"Yeah, the Z Bar is an extraordinary place, it really is," Whitt Laughridge said to me while we sat in his main street insurance and real estate office in Cottonwood Falls. "You can't go in there yet, because of the liability. It's still being leased. But when the place finally opens up, why, people will see something truly beautiful, they surely will." Whitt was sitting in his desk chair, legs crossed and looking toward the door. Slender and bald, he appeared to be in his sixties, but his angular, handsome face had an almost boyish quality. On top of running his business, Whitt was the president of the local historical society and had been Heat-Moon's principal guide during his eight years in the county. I hoped he might provide some insight into the local response to the book and how the county had changed, if at all, since it was published. The preservation of the Z Bar seemed a good place to start, so I asked him what had changed people's minds about the project.

"They haven't changed their minds," he replied. "We're pretty independent people here. A lot of these old ranchers 'don't want no damned government interference.' Most of us, though, think it's a real jewel out there and needs to be preserved, always have. But if that land was taken off our tax rolls it would hurt us, it truly would. Now that the tax issue has been settled, I think even some of those older ranchers are feeling better about it. Still, some of them will never change their minds."

I asked if he thought *PrairyErth* had had any impact on local attitudes toward the park.

"I don't think so; I don't think so, other than it might have brought it to the politicians' attention. But around here, like I said, opinions are pretty much the same, just softened a little by the tax compromise and by the possibility of some local control. That's all."

"Do you feel the book impacted the county at all?"

"Well, we've had more visitors, I'll put it that way. In fact, Emporia State is sponsoring a *PrairyErth* elderhostel. About thirty senior citizens are coming out here to look at the places in the book."

He said that he couldn't really attribute any other changes to the book, including the restoration of the downtown, nor did Cottonwood really advertise its association with *PrairyErth*.

"We just let people find us, like you have," he said. Just then an older gentleman in a sun hat walked in, his crinkled khakis tucked into the top of worn cowboy boots.

"Hiya, Dick," Whitt exclaimed. "This is Dick Iliff. He used to run the newspaper. Dick, I want you to meet John Price from Iowa. He wants to know about Bill Trogdon."

"Whattaya want to know?" he asked, pulling up a chair. Dick's face was long and gullied, his low voice barely audible.

"He wants to know how the book impacted the county," Whitt answered for me.

"Well, have you talked about the book signing yet?" Dick asked. "I guess you'd call that an impact."

"You certainly would," Whitt said. Whitt went on to tell about the "mass confusion" surrounding the book-signing ceremonies in October 1991. The publishers had promised them that *PrairyErth* would first go on sale during the ceremony in Cottonwood Falls, before being released nationally. Local organizers had even designed a commemorative book stamp to make the event more attractive to collectors. However, on the day of the celebration several thousand showed up—way more than expected—and most were already carrying copies of the book. Despite the publisher's promises, they had already released the book. Whitt said they still sold a lot of copies, but the author had to sign more of them than he had planned.

"That nearly killed Bill," Whitt laughed.

"How did local readers respond to the book?" I asked.

"Far as I know, they thought it was great. He found so much stuff to write about out here he could hardly shut it off, and I think that surprised a few people. After all, if you're born and raised here, why, you're used to it. It's interesting to see it through the eyes of a person like Bill."

"And what did most people see through his eyes?"

"Well, not always pleasant stuff," he replied. "Bill made no bones about it when he first came here — he was going to write about us warts and all, and he certainly did. But for the most part, I think everyone was interested in the book. Like I said, he told a lot of interesting history."

"He didn't tell everything," Dick said, leaning his forearms on his knees. "He left out parts, like in that story about Gurley." Dick went on to tell the story about Floyd Gurley, a twenty-four-year-old motorman for a San Francisco streetcar company who was sent to prison for burning down the house of his ex-fiancée and her new husband in 1932, just north of Cottonwood Falls. Heat-Moon had included part of Gurley's story in PrairyErth (340–42).

The part Dick said Heat-Moon left out involved the "interrogation" of Gurley. Cy Wadsworth, the local sheriff, traveled out to San Francisco to arrest Gurley and bring him back for trial. "Cy was real good to Gurley on the way back from California," Dick said, "treated him decently, but Cy told me that once back, Harry O'Riley, our county attorney at the time, and the state fire marshal stuck Gurley's head in the toilet stool and flushed it. That's how they got the confession out of him."

I was amazed at how easily I was invited into this exchange of local stories, these competing narratives. I was eager to join in, the book granting me a kind of local memory from which to draw — a belonging made all the more pleasurable because it didn't ask anything of me in return.

"Didn't that lead to something about the White Thunder God?" I asked.

"Yes," Whitt replied. "A while after Gurley's conviction, these signs would mysteriously appear up on Osage Hills that said things like 'The White Thunder God Is Here.' Then this book mysteriously showed up on Dick's desk. It was titled *White Thunder God*, and it was supposedly about how this Gurley was a god to some lost tribe of Indians. No one knows who wrote it, but it was probably Gurley, still mad about that conviction."

"That's a great story," I said.

"True," Whitt replied, "but I'm sure you have a few stories to tell yourself."

"Well, I'm gonna have to get back to work," Dick said, standing and winking at Whitt. "I don't want to miss any meetings out on top of old Osage Hill."

"You going to commune with the White Thunder God?" Whitt asked.

"Oh, one of these days, I suppose." Dick turned toward me. "I had bypass surgery about two years ago, a collapsed lung, and some other things. Almost seems like I'm in the tomb at different times."

"But you're still here," Whitt said affectionately.

"I suppose I am. Well, good to meet ya." Dick shuffled back into the day, holding the screen door open for a few seconds before letting it slam shut behind him.

Whitt shook his head: "When those people die you lose a piece of history. I've got people who, if I ever want to know something about the county at the turn of the century, they'll have the answer. When those old timers die, it's gone. Of course, then people like me become the old timers."

I asked Whitt to tell me about his own history in the county. He said he had been born and raised in the west corner of Chase but then was drafted during the war. He returned to Chase County from the Philippines in 1946 and has resided there ever since.

"Why did you come back?"

"Mostly, I came back because this is home. This is home. Now I'm the oldest merchant here—not in age, but in tenure. Everybody that was in business when I came back from the war is now gone. Of course, the county has changed since then. There are a lot fewer people, for one. There's three thousand in the county now, but at one time there were, I think, over eight thousand, back when they were still farming with horses."

I asked him if the 1980s farm crisis had significantly hurt the county.

"Sure did. A lot of farmers and ranchers went out of business, took bankruptcy—that's a little different than during the twenties and thirties. Nowadays, they don't think nothing of filing bankruptcy, but in those days they killed themselves. I did some research one time and I came up with eighteen farmers and ranchers that—in fact, I'm living in a house right now where a fella went down in the basement and blew his head off. I said I could account for eighteen, but I'm sure I didn't get them all. My folks knew a lot who did that."

The phone rang, startling us. After Whitt hung up, he seemed ready to change the subject.

"So, you want to see some prairie, do ya?" he asked. "I'll tell you where I'd go—let's take a look at ol' Methuselah." At the front of his office, attached to the wall, was a large yellowed map of Chase County. "This is the most accurate map of Chase County that exists. We call it Methuselah because no one knows how old it is." He pointed to a road running west out of Matfield Green that led, he claimed, to a pristine prairie that looked "just like it did five hundred years ago."

Across from the map was a large board with prairie plants displayed and labeled, everything from rice grass to sideoats to bluestem.

"This is one of my many hobbies," Whitt said. "I collected most of these at the county lake. I've studied prairie plants for a long time, just love 'em, but it's still hard for me to tell the difference between some. Look at those two grasses there—one is hairy grama and the other is blue grama. The only way you can tell the difference is that one head is shaped like an eyebrow while the other is this straight sort of thing. It takes a while to train your eye to see those distinctions."

Whitt wanted me to take a look at the county courthouse, one of the more famous Chase landmarks, so we stepped outside. Built in 1873, the three-story limestone building stands at the end of Broadway, the bricked main street, its impressive bell tower rising above ornate cornices and grillwork. It's the oldest operating courthouse west of the Mississippi, and Heat-Moon spent an entire chapter in PrairyErth telling some of its stories: its famous visitors, its marriages, its jailbreaks. Whitt told me a few more, including how the limestone was mined locally and was the same kind used in the Eisen-hower Presidential Library.

"This place really does have a lot of unique stories," I said.

"Probably not more than any other place," he replied. "I'm sure there're towns in Iowa just as interesting, if you stay long enough to find out."

"That's the problem," I said. "Staying."

I told him about my impending graduation, the vagaries of the job market, how Steph and I could end up anywhere. Whitt took his hand out of his pocket to wave at someone, then turned back toward the courthouse.

"Let me tell you another story about this courthouse," he said. "There was a time way back when the justice of the peace, while marrying a couple, would make them solemnly swear to uphold the U.S. Constitution and all that. But then he'd also make them swear to settle down and make their home right here in Chase County, Kansas."

Whitt looked at me and smiled: "Maybe we should take up doing that again."

I joined Steph at the Chase County Historical Society Museum and Library. Inside were various artifacts from the past, school desks and Oliver typewriters and branding irons and flint arrowheads. To many of them I could attach stories from *PrairyErth*, such as the fragments from the plane in which Knute Rockne died.

But the big story in the museum was Heat-Moon himself. There were several newspaper and magazine pieces on display, from reviews of *PrairyErth* to more personal articles. One revealed that Heat-Moon had recently bequeathed one-third of his estate to the University of Missouri Libraries, while another announced the death of his father, Ralph, from cancer. Near the front of the museum was a glass case holding Heat-Moon's walking shoes and his cottonwood staff along-side an enlarged check for a thousand dollars from William Trogdon to the Chase County Historical Society.

"That kept the electricity on," the volunteer curator told us.

Nearby there was another display that included a photo of Judy Mackey, a local artist whose painting had been used for the paperback cover of *PrairyErth*. There were *PrairyErth* t-shirts for sale, as well as books. But the most interesting item for me was the "PrairyErth Map of Chase County," available for a dollar. It showed the location of forty-eight sites highlighted in the book. It seems that while writing his "deep map" of Chase County, Heat-Moon had also left behind a new literary geography of the place.

While Steph and I explored Broadway, I decided to ask a few more people about *PrairyErth*. A local businesswoman who did not want to be identified said that she disliked the book for several reasons. She said that some people in the county felt it made them appear un-educated, adding that her son attended university and achieved a 3.2 grade point average.

"That's not dumb if you ask me," she said.

When I asked her which part of the book she thought presented them as uneducated, she mentioned the interviews with the high schoolers.

"All they talked about was racism, and I've never seen any racism here," she said. "There's been a Mexican and black student at the high school, and both boys could date anybody they wanted to. Well, the Mexican could anyway. And there was a Mexican cheerleader. Bill made us look like a bunch of racist hicks."

She also felt he hadn't written enough about ranching in the county—"That's our history, after all."

I asked her if she felt the success of *PrairyErth* had done anything good for the community.

"Not really," she said. "All the restoration going on downtown was started by some people from Kansas City long before the book came out. They're the central investors."

She did admit, however, that after the book was published her business increased by three or four people per week. We made sure we bought something as well.

Further down the street at the ice cream and soda shop, I talked to a retired rancher who said he "kinda missed seeing Bill around, asking all those questions." His wife nodded and said that they had sent autographed copies of *PrairyErth* to their kids in California and Oregon. "They just loved 'em," she said. We talked to several other people that morning, receiving responses that varied from "Didn't think much of it" to "He sure made a lot of money, didn't he?" to "I think it's great; glad he wrote about us." It wasn't until we talked to the owner of the barbecue joint that we found someone who hadn't read the book at all. He was more interested in talking about his new honey-mustard sauce, which Steph ordered with her bull fries. When the cook delivered them, round and sizzling, and Steph took a bite, I couldn't believe what I was seeing—I had thought bull fries were some kind of large, barbecued french fry. I had no idea they were testicles.

"And you call yourself a native?" Steph said, laughing.

After lunch Steph and I visited the Mainstreet Association office where we were greeted by a very friendly Shari Sidler. She was the director of the local association, part of a statewide program designed to help counties promote business and tourism. Her perspective on Heat-Moon and PrairyErth was more enthusiastic than any we had yet encountered.

"He was a godsend to us," she said, "he really was. His book provided millions of dollars in free national publicity for this county, and it has definitely paid off. I have a whole catalog of magazine and newspaper articles over there mentioning Chase County, and I've talked to hundreds of people who have dropped by the office here and mentioned the book as the reason they came—that just blows me away. And not just midwesterners. We have two large elderhostel groups out of Boston coming here in October. They'll spend a week in the area, taking classes at Emporia State on Kansas history, and then they'll take a tour of the sites mentioned in PrairyErth. A German film crew also visited here, and—now this is amazing—about a month ago Sassy Magazine out of New York called and told me they wanted to do a fashion photo layout with the Flint Hills as the backdrop. I've been meaning to write Mr. Heat-Moon a letter and let him know how much we appreciate what he's done for this county."

Shari went on to say, as Whitt had, that the book offered Chase residents a new perspective on their home:

"Those of us who live here, we're just so used to it that we sometimes can't figure out why people are so interested in us. Mr. Heat-Moon wrote about our beautiful courthouse and, you know, it's just ordinary to us. And he wrote beautifully about our prairies. Have you heard about the Z Bar? It's not open to the public yet, but can you imagine what it will be like to walk through that tallgrass? It's a miracle that any of it still remains. It's a national treasure and we need to protect that."

I asked her if she'd include the prairie preserve on the list of things Heat-Moon has done for the county.

"Well, that discussion had been going on for about twenty years — whether PrairyErth helped or not, I can't say. I think it mostly had to do with the fact that the land will remain on the tax rolls. This county desperately needs those tax dollars. So it was a compromise. You'll still find those who are greatly opposed to it and always will be, but the feeling I get from most is, okay, it's going to happen, we'd better benefit from it. They're estimating one hundred eighty thousand tourists that first year, tapering off to sixty to eighty thousand each year after that. We've got to make sure those visitors meander down here and spend some money. I know that Council Grove and Emporia are already planning to compete for those tourist dollars."

"Have you gotten any help at the state level?"

"Some, but not enough. You know, it amazes me, but I found some people dealing with tourism for the state of Kansas who have never read PrairyErth. I was like, excuse me, here's this best-selling book about our county, about Kansas, and you haven't even read it? That was just two months ago. I've worked for the federal government, so I know that they don't understand small-town America, but I thought it would be different at the state level. It's not. So what you see in this state and others is a big push for the small towns to band together to promote themselves. We have to survive."

I asked her if she felt competition for those limited tourist dollars might change the way Chase residents interact with each other, causing more divisions. As an example, I mentioned a Wall Street Journal article describing the PrairyErth book-signing ceremony, during which members of the local Mainstreet Association were charged with stealing the signs of a competing tourist organization and even threatened with jail sentences.[39] I read her this quote from the article: "Ironically, despite Mr. Heat-Moon's romantic view of Chase County, local folks say they've never gotten along. 'I don't know if it didn't fit into his theme or what, but this has never been a Norman Rockwell kind of place,' says Mr. O'Neal [Mike O'Neal, editor of the Chase County *Leader News*]."

Shari rolled her eyes. "It was so petty. I wasn't involved with Mainstreet at the time, but from talking to people I learned that though that squabble lasted only a few months, it hurt Mainstreet terribly. One of the reasons for that was Mike O'Neil. He was one of the founders of Mainstreet in this county, but during the disagreement he didn't hesitate to slam the organization in the paper. We had to deal with the consequences of that for two years—it hurt our membership and everything. But when I was hired, Mike did a very nice front-page article on me, said nicer things about me than my mother would say. He was very positive and continued to be positive, and I thanked him for that. Unfortunately, he died just a few weeks ago."

Shari paused to look out the large picture window.

"I find it interesting that Mike said that about the community, since he really hadn't lived here for very long. He had no previous connection to Chase until he moved from North Carolina and bought the newspaper. When he first arrived people loved it because he was very aggressive in reporting some of the private agendas influencing county commissioners. But he also made a lot of enemies, and, unfortunately, some of those people did some checking into his background and found that he had had some serious legal troubles in another state. Chase County offered him a new beginning. But when it came out that he had ... well ... I guess that's all behind us now."

"So, why did you move to Chase County?" I asked.

"It was the death of my father-in-law that prompted us to move back to the area. But also the school system where we were was getting out of control. So we came back and even though I've lived here only five years, my children are fourth-generation Chase Countians. That means a lot to me. Even if they weren't, people here are real open and pretty welcoming to newcomers. I have a vested interest in this community; it's not like I'm going to leave tomorrow. No, in working for this community, I'm interested in how my actions will affect not only me when I'm a senior citizen but also my children as they grow up. How about you, do you have children?"

"Not yet," Steph replied, "but we hope to after we settle in one place."

"Are you looking for a place to live?" Shari's eyebrows shot up. "There's lots of opportunity around here, businesses that need people to run them. And it amazes me how many artists live here, people with incredible talent. About a month ago someone bought one of our buildings and is going to put in a weaving factory. They plan to have a big storefront window where people can watch the artist weaving at the loom. That's perfect for downtown Cottonwood. As a writer, as teachers, I think you'd love it here."

"I'm sure we would," I said.

More visitors walked in, a family with two restless kids who were waiting to talk to Shari. We thanked her and she followed us to the door.

"If you need to know anything more, just let me know," she said, smiling. "We could always use another young couple living here. You already know so much about us, you'd feel right at home."

The next time I saw a copy of PrairyErth was an hour later, sitting in the Old Lumberyard Café in Matfield Green. The café, which I'd heard about from friends in Iowa, was managed by volunteers from Wes Jackson's Land Institute, part of the institute's nationally publicized efforts to help restore that dying Chase County community. I'd first read about those efforts in PrairyErth, during Heat-Moon's interview with Jackson, and had been interested in seeing the results in person. The café seemed a good place to start, but despite its growing reputation Steph and I had difficulty finding it. In fact on our way down, we missed Matfield Green entirely. Driving back, more slowly, we discovered why—the town was small and overgrown, like an old wooden bucket accidentally left in the bushes. From the road we could see a few abandoned four squares, their windows punched out, and some rusty mobile homes sinking into tall, unmowed lawns. The only sign of human activity was the Hitchin' Post tavern, itself not much bigger than a mobile home. We decided to stop there to use the restrooms. When we entered the dark interior, several men slouching at the bar turned to stare. The waitress informed us that they didn't have any running water and we'd have to use the outhouse in back—which we did, reluctantly. Afterward we both agreed that Matfield Green seemed an unlikely place from which to change the world.

Yet that's exactly what Wes Jackson was trying to do. In his book *Becoming Native to This Place* (1994), Jackson writes that Matfield Green, population fifty, "is typical of countless towns throughout the Midwest and Great Plains. People have left, people are leaving, buildings are falling down or burning down." During the last few years, however, Jackson and other members of his Land Institute have been buying local houses and buildings, restoring them, and trying to answer the question of "how . . . this human community, like a natural ecosystem community, . . . [can] be built back and also protected."[40]

The café was part of that effort. Scribbled at the top of the chalkboard menu in bold capital letters was one of the Land Institute's ruling philosophies: "Ecological Accounting." It is a phrase often used by Jackson, by which he means, in part, a new approach to agricultural science: creating perennial crops, employing a combination of modern farm machinery and animal labor, and, by necessity, returning more people to live and work in rural areas, repopulating endangered towns like Matfield Green.

Ecological accounting, however, is cultural as well as agricultural, as the café illustrated. On the chalkboard was written the "account" of "Today's Pizza":

Crust:	Organically grown flour—western Kansas
	Yeast—California
	Salt—from spring water, Perkins Spring, 2 miles from here
	Firewood—10 miles southeast of Matfield Green on Jan Coover's land
Toppings:	Onions—the garden of Betty and Charlie Swift
	Tomato and Banana Peppers—our garden patch
	Zucchini—Ellie Mae's garden
	Garlic—Wes and Joan's garden
	Cheese—Emporia
Tea:	Lead Plant, local
Coffee:	Beans—South America
	Cream—Charlie and Betty Swift

Sugar — Hawaii
Sweet and Low — New York

What appeared to be happening inside the café was a kind of eating — a kind of living — that balances individual desires with the needs of the local community and ecosystems, making customers aware of both the cost and origin of what they consume. We were made further aware of the surrounding community by the numerous black-and-white photographs hanging on the walls. Each portrayed local residents: some Hispanic, some white; some young, muscular, and tan, some aged, their faces and hands textured by the elements. There was humor, wisdom, and grief in the eyes looking at us from those frames, revealing a physical and emotional diversity — a human ecology — as remarkable as the prairie itself.

The café was full of books as well, with such titles as *Ozone or Earth Worm: Who Cares?*; *Prairie Images*; *Ground and Sky*; *The History of Greenwood County, Kansas*. There, too, was a worn copy of *PrairyErth*. The mix coincided with Jackson's belief in the positive contribution offered by all creative thinkers and the need for them to return to the communities many of them left behind. "Countless writers and artists have been vulnerable to the 'official' culture," writes Jackson, "as vulnerable as the people of Matfield Green." As examples he cites Paul Gruchow and Wallace Stegner, who both confess feeling inadequate while growing up in the rural grasslands, and Willa Cather, about whom he quotes Stegner: " 'Eventually, when education had won and nurture had conquered nature and she had recognized Red Cloud as a vulgar little hold, she embraced the foreign tradition totally and ended by being neither quite a good American nor quite a true European nor quite a whole artist.' "[41]

Becoming a whole artist for Jackson means seeing art not in abstract terms but in terms of its "utility," its usefulness in validating and promoting "cultural information in the making, keyed to place." In other words getting local people, despite their differences, to talk to one another. Though no one was inside the Old Lumberyard Café, half-full coffee cups, scattered newspapers, and chairs pulled back from tables suggested a place where stories and ideas were indeed being exchanged. Restoring conversation and art to the center of community life is part of the Land Institute's cultural work, a way of restoring an atmosphere of cooperation and interdependence in a television society where, as Jackson says, "[e]ntire neighborhoods are more accessible to the world than their members are to one another."[42] For me, the evidence of these kinds of connections represented a unique celebration of place, one that stood in contrast to some of the contentious divisions I'd encountered during my travels in the region.

But how, I wondered, was PrairyErth being used in those conversations (and the worn condition of the cover suggested that it was definitely being used)? In the café Heat-Moon's fame and personality were not the issue; his face was not one of those hanging on the wall. You could find only maps of local watersheds and landforms, of communities, and not of a superimposed literary landscape distributed to tourists like myself. Nevertheless, I hoped PrairyErth was doing the kind of work for which I thought it was intended — creating connections and honoring, in Jackson's words, a "balance of emotion and technique, people and land, individual and community, plant and animal." I also hoped that Heat-Moon's account of his struggle to reimagine his identity, to remember a positive native connection to the prairies, was useful there as well. Jackson himself says that solving many of our problems begins with the "mindscape," by "looking at that old prairie, by remembering who we are as mammals, as primates, as humanoids, as animals struggling to become human by controlling the destructive and unlovely side of our animal nature while we set out to change parts of our still unlovely human mind."[43] It is poets, he claims, as well as scientists, who guide us in doing so.

Back in the car, driving into the grasslands west of Matfield Green, Steph and I began to sing "Home on the Range," the gravel beating an artificial vibrato across our voices. The verses, taken from a poem written by Kansan Brewster Higley in 1873, held before my eyes — and Stephanie's, I hoped — an idealistic, unifying vision of the land and its people, a vision I wanted to believe had been true and could be true again:

> A home, a home, where the deer and the antelope play,
> Where never is heard a discouraging word
> And the sky is not clouded all day.

Oh, give me the gale of the Solomon vale
Where life streams with buoyancy flow,
On the banks of the Beaver, where seldom if ever
Any poisonous herbage doth grow.

Oh, give me the land where the bright diamond sand
Throws light from the glittering stream,
Where glideth along the graceful white swan,
Like a maid in her heavenly dream.

I love the wild flower in this bright land of ours,
I love, too, the curlew's wild scream,
The bluffs of white rocks and the antelope flocks
That graze on our hillsides so green.

How often at night, when the heavens are bright
By the light of the glittering stars,
Have I stood there amazed and asked as I gazed,
If their beauty exceeds this of ours.

The air is so pure, the breezes so light,
The zephyrs so balmy at night,
I would not exchange my home here to range
Forever in azure so bright.

The home described in these largely forgotten stanzas is a wild prairie place of "air so pure," where antelope and deer and buffalo graze and swans glide, where you can hear the "curlew's wild scream," admire wildflowers, and find streams where "no poisonous herbage doth grow." Inside this legendary range, the native ecosystem appears alive and intact — no invasive plants, no hazardous stockyards, no amber waves of genetically enhanced grain. Perhaps because of this the range is a place where "never is heard a discouraging word." A place where the power of the land itself, its vast beauty, forces the narrator into commitment, into exclaiming: "I would not exchange my home here to range / Forever in azure so bright." This land, even before heaven.

The view from the car window suffered by comparison — short, ragged grasses and plants interspersed with patches of dry, exposed earth — reminding me, once again, how far the pendulum had swung for the bright and beautiful prairies described in the poem. Yet despite my desires, it is unclear whether such an ideal place actually existed in 1873 Kansas. If it did, it was quickly disappearing. The bison, for instance—though a small group would be reported two years later in the northwest corner of the county,[44] the demise of the great wild herds must have been evident to anyone living there at the time. The wild swans would also soon vanish from the state, as would the Eskimo curlew, to whom the "wild scream" likely belongs. At one time the Eskimo curlew migrated through Kansas in flocks rivaling the passenger pigeon. It is now probably extinct from the earth, the slaughter well underway by the time Higley put his pen to paper. And as for the human community—where never is heard a discouraging word—the "bloody Kansas" of the Civil War era was less than two decades gone, and the scourge of Indian removal and massacre, the damning haunt of racism, was ongoing. What Higley observed may have been less about local optimism and generosity than about a growing space of enforced silence.

That Higley's ways of imagining the Kansas prairies tended toward the ideal is not surprising. Like the story of so many Euro-Americans who have sought out the grasslands, his is one of new beginnings, of longing. At the time he composed his famous poem in the early 1870s, Higley was a country doctor living in a cabin near Smith Center, Kansas, just north of Chase County. He came from Ohio and Michigan where, according to some, his heavy drinking had earned him several broken marriages and a ruinous reputation. As Margaret A. Nelson puts it in her 1947 account, *Home on the Range*, Dr. Higley's move to Kansas was predicated on the hope that "[o]ut in the open country he would forget and build anew, build anew where the country was fresh and new. He looked up into the night sky, full of clean, shining stars. There was quiet, peace upon the world, God's benediction. Out in the open God's hand could almost be seen, and often felt close."[45]

Whether Higley's desires were ever satisfied by the Kansas prairies I don't know (he moved to Arkansas in 1886), but my experiences in Chase County illustrated that over a century later, those expanses remained a place to seek and hope for a new beginning: for William Trogdon to seek and test his native identity; for a newspaper editor with a troubled past to seek anonymity; for parents to seek better schools; and for park advocates and ecologists like Wes Jackson to seek and build a new agriculture—a new culture—from the ground up. And just as thirsty pioneers saw mirages of water on the arid plains, it was still a place of illusions, a place where at least one of its residents believed, despite the testimony of others, that her county was free of racial hatred. Even Wes Jackson's dream appeared, in retrospect, to be tenuous. During our visit to Matfield Green, there had been more people slumped over the bar at the Hitchin' Post than sitting at the tables in his café.

I didn't share these thoughts with Stephanie. Instead I kept singing "Home on the Range," kept her singing, the words and melody sustaining the dreams I, too, had carried with me to Kansas. As the story goes, Brewster Higley was a family friend, and Cal Harlan, my great-great-grandfather and fellow Smith County resident, helped brother-in-law Dan Kelley put the doctor's poem to music and craft its famous refrain. Over a century later one of my most treasured family heirlooms is an original copy of Margaret Nelson's book about the creation of that song. My great-grandmother Lottie Harlan-Wagner, Cal's daughter and another lifelong resident of Smith County, has hand-written in the margins the names of people she knows in the book and to whom she's related. That scribbled-on text has become my family tree, one of the ways I remember my deep past in the grasslands. Singing the song with Steph, teaching her the words, was my way of becoming, for a moment, the native storyteller. The authority. The pure man with the white feather, free of any other, more troubling ancestral past.

Impatient to experience some prairie, I finally pulled over. We slid under a barbed-wire fence and began our walk across the land. I immediately wondered if we were in the right spot. It was, as I have already mentioned, far different from the place I had hoped it would be, the place Whitt had said looked the same as it did five hundred years ago. Steph didn't say anything, but I could tell she was disappointed. She made an effort of it, hiding her feelings behind the camera lens, though they eventually emerged during the snow-on-the-mountain episode. The spitting, the sarcastic *Why are we here?* led me to wonder if I had lost an important chance to convince her to care about the prairies as deeply as I did, to keep alive the faint hope that she could live happily in this region, that she could make it our home, our future children's home. As she continued walking in search of the glorious land I had promised her, I lingered along the trampled edges of a cow pond, contemplating the fact that I was married to someone who didn't want or need to become native to this place.

Of course, Stephanie's relationship to the land wasn't really the point. I was reminded of this when, on a nearby hillside, I discovered several tall thistles similar to those I'd seen on top of the Imperial Mine in Corder. Suddenly the question of "why here" struck deeper veins. Why had I brought Stephanie to Kansas and not to Missouri? In response I might have pointed to the place itself—despite the disappointment of the immediate landscape, the Kansas Flint Hills still had more tallgrass to show off than northern Missouri. William Least Heat-Moon had given a similar response when I asked him why he'd chosen Kansas as his literary subject. Now I wished I'd pressed him further. In *PrairyErth* Heat-Moon expresses a deep appreciation for what is native to place: native limestone, native grasses, native weather, native cultures, as well as his Native American self. Given this wouldn't Missouri—the place where he had lived most of his life and another ancestral home to the Osage tribe—have been the more appropriate location for his experiment in regional identity and memory? Had he discovered, as I had, something there—or not there—in the personal landscape that had turned his deep-mapping eyes toward Kansas? Was his choice a return to a site of ancestral memory or an unconscious escape from another?

And what about his relationship to Kansas? Whatever native ties Heat-Moon had forged to the Flint Hills, they apparently hadn't been enough to keep him there. He did not own a house in Matfield Green or anywhere else in the county, was not volunteering time at the Z Bar, was not actively restoring the prairies. Instead he was off writing about rivers, a restless traveler once again. What was left of the tether that connected him to that place? The bones and spirits of his ancestors, he might say. And, of course, his best-selling book, sitting worn and used on a table in Wes Jackson's café and in living rooms and libraries across the nation. It was doing, as I had discovered, important work for the county. But where was the living body that connected to those bones, those words, that resurrected them inside the daily struggle to settle responsibly in place? Chase County, it was clear to me, was many things to Heat-Moon—a home of sorts —but it was not where he lived. That distinction was very important to me at the time.

Then again, the Flint Hills weren't where I lived either, and between the two of us Heat-Moon had spent a lot more time in Kansas, walking its prairies, telling its stories. Yet like Heat-Moon's journey, my journey was one of origins, of memory—and of "shadows." The following day Steph and I would visit a windmill near Harlan, Kansas, which marks the location of the long-gone family homestead, the birthplace of my grandmother Mildred Wagner Price and her siblings. The windmill stands in a milo field, useless, a gap between its legs, skeletal joints joining horizontal beams to vertical, a few loose blades chiming in the gusts. Standing there, I could have claimed that those blades, like cuneiform, drew an image of continuation, that it was a site of memory "linking," as Heat-Moon says, "seens with unseens, heres with theres, nows with thens."[46] But if it was such a place, it was no more so than that mound of disturbed earth in Corder, Missouri. I had traveled to Kansas—I finally acknowledged —in the hopes of choosing one ancestral past over another, one regional identity over another. What was becoming increasingly clear, however, is that no such choice exists. We cannot choose the past or the places that create us any more than we can choose our biological grandparents, our genetic heritage. We must simply do the best with what we are given.

But how?

Instinctively, beside that broken windmill, I reached for Steph's hand. It was such an ordinary gesture—I didn't think twice about it at the time—but now I wonder if it didn't offer some kind of answer, even reassurance. Wendell Berry, while defining a responsible relationship between writer and place, offers a metaphoric connection to marriage. By living in the place one writes about, Berry claims, the "relation to one's subject ceases to be merely emotional or esthetical, or even merely critical, and becomes problematical, practical, and responsible as well. Because it must. It is like marrying your sweet-

heart." Back then I had thought of my marriage, in part, as a conversation, even conflict, between places, but now I see it as the thing
that taught me—well before the Iowa floods, that first longing for
the prairies—how to care responsibly about home. Inside marriage,
I am held accountable to the past, am confronted with my failures
and inconsistencies, my sins. But there, as well, is the daily possibility of grace, the encouragement to reach for a better self. Marriage has, as predicted, complicated my relationship to home, but
it has also helped alleviate what Berry calls "the nearly insupport-
able burden" of a destructive history by affirming my life "as a thing
decent in possibility."[47] Whatever my past holds—personal, familial,
racial, ecological—I have the power to respond by being vigilant in
the present, by educating myself and others, including my children.
Learning from that past, while striving to improve the present and
the future. In this endeavor my marriage will play a substantial role.
Steph and I, no matter where we live, will hopefully be striving together, inside our marriage, inside our place. Inside the promise that
defines all committed love: to be there, to try.

Back in Chase County, however, the decent possibilities were not
at all evident to me. Especially while sitting alone by the cow pond,
contemplating that degraded corner of the Flint Hills prairies. The
isolated thistles, as they had in Missouri, seemed to draw close the
land's calamitous history, against which our best efforts appeared fu-
tile. Dust, wind, sky—the surrounding prairie looked to be moving, inevitably, toward this more elemental, more brutal identity. If
that process becomes complete, what will there be left to choose in
our relationship to the land, in our relationship to our selves and to
each other? Nothing, perhaps, but the "azure so bright" mentioned
in Dr. Higley's poem, a reminder not so much of the glories of heaven
as of its inescapable judgment.

"Hey, look," Steph said, sitting down next to me at the cow pond,
"we should probably get going. We can always return here and find
the prairies you're looking for. We must just be in the wrong place."

"You're right," I said as I stood up. We brushed the dirt off our
shorts, took one more look around, and then, as so many had before
us, we left.

CHAPTER 5

A Healing Home *Mary Swander's Recovery among the Iowa Amish*

"It's been eleven years, this weekend," Mary Swander said to me while sitting at her kitchen table, Labor Day weekend 1994. "Eleven years of healing. And here I am." *Here* was Mary's home, a converted one-room schoolhouse set in the rural, eastern Iowa landscape of corn- and bean fields, grassy ditches, and rolling timbered hills. *Here* was her garden plot, green and leafy, and the adjacent pens sheltering geese, turkeys, sheep, and pygmy goats. *Here* also was the surrounding Old Order Amish community of Kalona, the horse-drawn buggies clip-clopping along the asphalt, their dairy cows grazing in alfalfa pastures. But most important, *here* was Mary's forty-year-old body sitting straight-backed in the chair, face and arms flush from the September sun. Alive.

"I should be dead," she said, eyebrows lifting. "I keep reminding myself of that. I've talked to quite a few people who have had traumatic illnesses or near-death experiences and we've often mentioned the preciousness of life. But you can lose that sense so fast, once the crisis is over. I have to remind myself of what that suffering was like. Tomorrow, for instance, I'll probably fast, then the next day throw a one-person picnic, just to remind myself how far I've come."

Mary, an Iowa-born poet and nonfiction writer, had indeed come a long way from Labor Day weekend 1983 when she received a vaccine overdose that destroyed her immune system, nearly killed her, and left her hyper-allergic to almost everything—a contemporary and largely unrecognized condition called "environmental illness" (EI). Before that weekend Swander had lived on the fly—moving from western Iowa, where she spent her childhood, to Georgetown University in Washington DC, back to Iowa to attend the University of Iowa's Writers Workshop, then on to Europe and various "hippie artist colonies"—giving little thought to her surroundings, her food, her body.

That all changed in 1983 when a doctor prepared a vaccine for her allergies and sent her home to inject what turned out to be "a mismixed, overdosed vial of nearly fifty antigens." For six weeks Swander lay in a Chicago hospital bed with an IV needle stuck in her arm, unable to eat. Her doctors, after desperately searching for safe foods, insisted that she eat only organic produce grown without pesticides or herbicides. In 1989 after years of suffering and seeking cures, Swander moved to rural Kalona, Iowa, a place of "sanctuary"[1] where she could garden and forage for food without physical fear of the air, water, soil, and people around her. A place where, with the help of her Amish neighbors, she could truly begin to heal.

Out of This World: A Woman's Life among the Amish (1995)[2] is Swander's story of physical recovery from environmental illness. But it is also a story of bioregional recovery, of reclaiming a healing connection to the surrounding human and natural communities of home. As such, Swander's life and literature offer a unique imperative for becoming native to this damaged place, one that out of necessity makes no distinction among body, community, nature, and the creative spirit. It asks us to not only imaginatively recover the deep past of the grasslands but recognize—at the most intimate, physical levels—how that mostly destructive history is alive in the present. Swander's life and work offer a grim warning. But for me, disheartened as I'd become that summer from a new awareness of the region's destructive past, her work also offered a much-needed sense of hope.

I first met Mary Swander in 1990 at an Iowa City bookstore where she and her coauthor, Jane Staw, were reading from their recently published nonfiction book, *Parsnips in the Snow: Talks with Midwestern Gardeners* (1990). At the time Mary was well-known in the region for her poetry and was beginning to gain a national reputation, particularly for *Driving the Body Back* (1986), a lyrical account of transporting her mother's body across Iowa for burial. It was a book I had read and admired, and it left me wanting to know more about this writer from my home state.

At the beginning of their reading, Mary and Jane explained how they had traveled throughout the Midwest together, visiting with organic gardeners. The resulting book featured a number of different places, urban and rural, and portrayed the geographical and cultural diversity of a region often perceived as uniform. Mary took her turn reading about the myriad of fresh vegetables they sampled and the equally diverse lives and life philosophies of the gardeners who nurtured them. Some gardened as a way to remember lost family, some to alleviate physical and emotional pain, and some to fulfill a sense of communal and spiritual responsibility.

As they read I was surprised by memories of my own grandfather, Roy Price. Roy was the son of Tom Price, the Missouri coal miner, and though I knew very little about that side of my family—I had not yet traveled to Corder—I did know that Tom had been an enthusiastic gardener. Whatever else the Price legacy held, it also included the need for a patch of black earth and some seed. During the afternoons of my adolescence, I would often spot Grandpa Roy in our yard, carrying a hoe or a hand cultivator to his large plot out back. Usually I would avoid him, afraid that I would be asked to run seed lines or pick beans, getting my hands dirty and itchy or, even worse, becoming bored. Unlike my ancestors, I hated that kind of work.

After Mary finished reading, she asked that the lights be dimmed. She slipped a Greg Brown tape into the player, a song about his grandma canning vegetables, and the slides began to roll: juicy watermelon halves, succulent tomatoes, young grapes on the vine.

Interspersed were photos of the gardeners, many of them aging, their faces tan and wrinkled. In the moments between slides, when the room was thrown into darkness, I could almost see before me the figure of Grandpa Roy in his gray Kansas City Royals t-shirt, standing alone and proud among the vibrant, leafy rows. It is the view I often had of him from behind our family room window, full of curiosity about his life and his hobby but rarely venturing out to lend a hand. It seems I had barely begun to wonder about his obvious love for the soil when he passed away in the fall of my junior year of high school. Now, nothing but a maverick clump of rhubarb marks that there was ever a garden in our backyard at all.

The song ended and the lights came back on. Mary introduced several people in the front row, gardeners who had been featured in the book. During the reception audience members approached them to talk about canning squash or the best time to pick eggplant. Or, like me, they talked about people in their lives, now gone, who had given them a glimpse of their passion for gardening. Mary was joyous, almost giddy, laughing in a high, contagious cackle as she signed books. People lingered for over an hour, celebrating, perhaps, what one gardener called the "beauty and bounty" of the midwestern places and people we shared.

The generosity of that evening left little clue as to the severity of Swander's life at the time. She never mentioned EI, but I had heard from friends who had been her students that she made all kinds of strange requests of them in class, like that they not wear perfume or deodorant because she might "faint" or "go weird." These friends recalled how uncomfortable it was, in the abstract world of the writing workshop, to be made self-conscious of their bodies. It wasn't until I picked up a copy of her latest poetry collection, *Heaven-and-Earth House* (1994), that I was introduced to Swander's private experience of illness. The three sections of her book blend the world of the Amish, its social and spiritual bindings, with the bindings of her body and the land. Hers is a world of the Amish phone booth and buggy — of community — and also the world of the hospital, of horrifying, even fatal loneliness. In one poem she describes preparing a meal of okra, while in another, she describes an L.P.N. preparing the dead body of a suicide victim, a woman who, like Swander, suffered from toxic poisoning. Several other poems focus on poisoned people: a hairstylist, a copper miner, a farmer. Unifying it all is a narrator, raging against her own poisoned flesh, slaughtering ducks and pithing frogs and picking vegetables and wild edibles, articulating a world where body, spirit, community, and land irresistibly fall into one another, a world where "underneath, we are all / flesh, all grass, the weed, the blade, the word."[3]

Yet *Heaven-and-Earth House* just skimmed the surface of Swander's world, leaving me with many questions about the implications — cultural, personal, ecological — of her peculiar existence. Though her poems did not directly mention the prairies, Swander's relationship to the midwestern environment appeared to be so different from any other I had read about, so fraught with physical urgency and risk and renewal, I felt my literary journey into the grasslands would be incomplete without talking to her. In the spring of 1994 I called Mary and asked if the poems in *Heaven-and-Earth House* were autobiographical. She said yes, for the most part, and added that she was working on a memoir further exploring her life among the Amish, her illness, and her relationship to the land. I asked if she would mind sharing a copy of the manuscript with me, and a few days later *Out of This World: A Woman's Life among the Amish* arrived in the mail.

I found *Out of This World* to be a surprising and important narrative, one in which Swander's bioregional sensibilities are clear from the start. In the opening segment, "To Start a Cold Motor," Swander does not mention her EI but instead chooses to locate herself, and the reader, inside a series of local human and environmental relationships. The narrative begins just after Christmas with Swander riding a horse-drawn cart, singing "Jingle Bells" and delivering Mason jars full of preserves from her garden as gifts to her Amish neighbors. Swander explains that she and her immediate neighbors are considered outsiders — "English" — within Amish society: "As simply as we live, as much as we try to preserve the environmental integrity and blend in with the spirit of the landscape here, we also know that we, with our cars and telephones, are worldly. Yet, because the Amish are freed from competitiveness and striving, because they maintain a real sense of community and live a life I wish I could, I'm drawn to them and feel honored whenever they include me in their gatherings and customs."[4]

Though Swander is an outsider, the rituals of gardening and the natural forces of weather create opportunities for connection. As she delivers her preserves, she explains that after several dry winters the recent snowfall will provide the necessary moisture for a bountiful spring garden, and a bountiful garden ensures more opportunities for her to give gifts of food to her Amish neighbors, to repay them for the "honor" of living among them. In Swander's Kalona the cycles of local ecology, the interrelationship among snow, soil, and plant life, allow her to contribute to local community: "My fingers warming and thawing, I felt reassured that nature had settled some of its debts and that I had settled some of my own."[5]

Swander's weave of ecology and community complicates what might seem at first glance to be a stereotypical treatment of Amish culture. At one point Swander refers to herself as a "voyeur" peering into a world of the past, full of horse-drawn buggies, quilt frames, and homemade pickles, a world free from the "competitiveness and striving" of modern society. This initially reminded me of other literary treatments of the Amish, such as Sue Bender's Plain and Simple: A Woman's Journey to the Amish (1989). Bender, an artist and family therapist from California, visits Kalona for only a few months, seeking in Amish culture an alternative to the stresses of modern urban life, a "plain and simple" life to help her recover from a "starving" soul.[6]

Swander, however, dramatically departs from Bender's spiritual abstractions when, shortly into her narrative, she serves us a bowl of bear meat stew. The bear meat is a gift from Amish neighbors who had heard she had a "medical condition" that made her intolerant of most foods. At this point she introduces her EI and its history, from the initial overdose to her move to Kalona—a move motivated not by a starving soul but by a starving body. Though I had heard of Mary's illness and read about it in her poetry, I was not prepared for the description in Out of This World of its full severity, especially the isolation. Most of her friends, though they tried to understand, found her illness "just too weird" and became "offended" when she didn't offer them the expected meal or even a cup of coffee. Dating became difficult. Because she had lost so much weight her offers increased, but once these men discovered she couldn't go to restaurants or even cook them a "normal" meal, they lost interest. She also stopped going to mass, in part because she could no longer ingest the wine and wheat of communion.[7] She found herself almost totally cut off from the social, romantic, and spiritual communities that had previously supported and defined her.

While separating her from some people, the forces at work within her body, like the forces of weather described in the opening segment, allowed her a unique connection to the Amish: "I may have been one of the first English [the Amish had] met who, on at least one level, lived a simpler and more difficult life than they did." Recognizing in Swander someone similarly "out of this world," Amish neighbors helped her in small but significant ways, giving her gardening advice and supplies of nonreactive foods. Their friendship also alleviated her loneliness. Eight years after her poisoning, her first whole meal in the company of others took place in an Amish home. As they bowed their heads over the bear roast and garden beans, "a feeling of community, of love, and of thankfulness to these people who made this effort to include me shot through my body."[8] Though the focus of that moment is on fellowship and spiritual support, the fact that Swander registered her gratitude in her body is telling—her "debts" to the Amish are also those of the flesh.

Swander's illness forces her to not only challenge popular myths about the Amish but also reevaluate many of her own deeply held beliefs—narrowing her vision, as she puts it, in order to "ultimately expand it." Her notions of female power expand when she receives herbal medicines from an Amish woman. The religious myths of her Catholic youth are given a new, more physical, more "primitive" dimension by her ritualistic consumption of a steamed yucca plant. Her faith in modern medical technology is replaced by a faith in the healing power of the soil. Her disappointment at not being able to conceive a child because of early, EI–induced menopause is softened by her maternal relationship with animals and plants. She becomes more political as well, a more vocal critic "of the whole American way of life" with its indifferent medical system, its poisoned food, and its polluted landscapes.[9]

Her notions of home are also transformed. Swander confesses that as an adolescent growing up in rural Iowa, she experienced a "shame-ridden longing" to leave, a longing "intrinsic to the small towns and moderate-size cities of the Midwest," especially its writers:

This was Willa Cather leaving Red Cloud, Nebraska. . . . This was F. Scott Fitz-gerald bidding good-bye to Saint Paul, Minnesota, Hemingway to Oak Park, Illi-nois.

"I've got to get out of this dump," I told myself when I left Iowa for college in Washington DC, and rejoiced in my good fortune to be moving away from a place where the world perceived its people to be as flat and boring as its landscape. I was never coming back.

But after becoming aware, through EI, of the deep, even mortal con-nection between her body and her geographical place, she developed a more committed relationship to home. It is a relationship, how-ever, that further separates her from friends and from contemporary American society:

My peers, fellow graduates of the baby-boom-moving-school, suggest that a sense of home has nothing to do with actual geography or physical space, that home is something internal, spiritual, what you carry around inside you.

This is certainly a mobile concept. . . . But most of my friends, especially those in academia or the corporate business world, plunk themselves down in a locale or a house for which they have no affinity. Many of them live for five to fifteen years in a spot that does not tug at their psyche or soul. They aren't interested in the history of the place, nor the evolution of its landscape and environment. Instead, they hope nearby are good restaurants and schools, and a cheap fitness club. No, as much as I like the ephemeral notion of home, I like exploring the opposite idea, that home may be an almost physiological tug toward a concrete physical place.[10]

Environmental illness not only "tugs" Swander back to Iowa, it forces her to look beyond abstract regional stereotypes and take note of her natural surroundings. What she sees, in part, is a reflection of her own illness. She notes that the native prairies that once existed in Iowa have, like her own body, been "ravaged," "destroyed," and "finished off" by modern technologies. Yet the land also contains counterbalancing images of healing and hope. Though most of the prairies and wetlands are gone, she observes frogs and other ani-mals continuing to adapt and survive in unlikely "haven[s]," such as a pond near her home. In this way the natural world offers her "reminders of pain at every turn but also such joy in the little pleasures that surround me in this environment."[11]

Though Swander uses the landscape as a metaphor for her illness and recovery, her relationship to the ecological community, like her relationship to the Amish, is founded on physical necessity rather than merely symbolic value—the health of the land directly affects the health of her body. This becomes particularly evident during Swander's account of a summer drought when grasshoppers invade her garden, threatening to wipe out her vegetables and, by extension, her health. Suddenly the entire natural history of the grasslands, the loss of its native ecosystems, converges on her life:

But a little more than a hundred years ago, when my great-grandparents settled in Iowa, before farmers tiled and drained their fields, the state was dotted with bogs and sloughs that supported dense populations of birds. Canada geese, canvas backs, and ring-necked ducks, . . . sandhill and whooping cranes darkened the sky on their fall and spring migrations, and when they circled down to land, ate their share of grasshoppers. Year round, the native prairie chickens gobbled up thousands more of the insects, but the prairie chickens went the way of the buffalo, men hunting them for sport until near extinction. So here I was dealing with one human-made ecological imbalance on top of another.

Unable to use conventional pesticides, Swander seeks help from an extension agent, an organic gardening hotline, Amish neighbors, and the diaries of pioneer women. After several failures Swander finally recalls a distinctly bioregional solution: "bug juice." She gathers hundreds of grasshoppers, throws them in a blender, liquefies them, and sprays the mixture on her plants. The living grasshoppers are repelled, "like cures like,"[12] and her garden survives.

Swander's grasshopper plague offers clear warnings about the past and future of the grasslands. It leads her, for example, to "rage at the way the prairie has been ravaged by the people who settled the Midwest, my ancestors and the pioneer women among them." It also leads her to imagine more environmentally friendly methods of agriculture, like those being developed by Wes Jackson's Land Institute. Swander's illness, however, forces her to be even more concerned about the present: "All those [larger environmental] losses affected me, but I was waging my own, even more immediate, environmental battle. The drought meant the destruction of my garden, and without my garden I couldn't eat." Though Swander seems at this moment to be isolated within the needs of her own body, she later demonstrates how this narrowing of vision leads, once again, to a larger—yet still practical, still immediate—sense of responsibility. While walking through a small Iowa prairie preserve, she reflects:

I try to imagine what this plot would be like if its waist-high grasses and wildflowers extended to the horizon, if it were unscarred by power lines and the constant din of passing traffic. In Doolittle Prairie, I began to wonder if gardening, this activity that I thought had been keeping me in touch with nature, was only, in a weird paradoxical way, destroying it. Perhaps I should give up gardening altogether, restore my plot to prairie, and just forage; then I truly would be in balance with my native environment. For wasn't my small garden a part of the larger farming problem that had so changed the landscape? . . . As tense as it was, my locust plague got me to thinking beyond my own rake and hoe to a new perception of food. In a small way, this new vision may begin to heal me and my landscape."[13]

Acting on her concerns, Swander allows some of the wild plants, such as dandelions and plantain, to remain in her garden plot, welcoming them into her spring salads. She also becomes protective of the native grasses and legumes growing in nearby ditches, harvesting them for food. Soon there are positive aesthetic changes, including the presence of more butterflies. Healing, for Swander, becomes more of a reciprocal process, linking the physical needs of her body to those of the surrounding ecosystem.

"And what of the larger population and landscape?" Swander asks.[14] Given the environmental challenges facing Iowa, this question takes on added significance—especially for those of us living here. Iowa is the most ecologically disturbed state in the union, with less than one-half of 1 percent of its native habitats remaining, and only around 20 percent of its land potentially capable of ever supporting native plant communities.[15] Iowans continue to pay for this environmental disaster with their health. The Des Moines Register reported in 1996 that nearly 760,000 Iowans drink tap water contaminated with cancer-causing weed killers, and 120,000 drink from private wells with excessive nitrate levels.[16] Another study found that residents who live in Iowa counties where large amounts of pesticides are used were 60 percent more likely to die of leukemia.[17] These statistics appear to prove that what Utah writer Terry Tempest Williams has said is true, that "[i]t is through the body we feel the world, both its pain and its beauty." Likewise, Swander suggests action that arises from a new respect for the continuum between body and place:

Big changes start with small decisions. What if, for starters, more of us returned to gardening, then each midwesterner nurtured his or her own prairie patch? Not just a "meadow in a can," but a real selection of indigenous plants that could be used for breakfast, lunch, or dinner. What if, deep down in our own tissues, we began to feel the changes these native foods brought? The return of a portion of control over our food sources, our physical and mental health, and balance of our natural environment. As long as the prairie is populated mostly by Euro-Americans, it will probably never return to this natural state, but a network of native gardens might be enough to keep its identity before us, reminding us how much we've lost and, with careful living, how much we might gain.[18]

Given the scope of prairie destruction in the Midwest, Swander's gardening approach to restoration might seem naive — it did to me. The term "gardening" itself veered perilously close to a national myth that, as Richard Manning puts it, leads many of us to believe "that it is our God-given mission to line it up in rows and make it grow." Yet upon further reflection, the type of gardening Swander advocates appeared to move beyond traditional notions of control and beauty, embodying instead what Manning argues is the antithesis of the gardening myth: an awareness "that all of life is a complex of checks and balances, driven by both growing and dying, and that anything we do to tilt the system will spin through a place in waves of catastrophe for whole generations."[19] Similarly — Swander seemed to ask — might our smaller, "careful" efforts at restoration spin out in waves of positive change?

Shortly after returning from Chase County, I reread Aldo Leopold's *Sand County Almanac* and stumbled upon a quote that resonated with not only my experiences in Kansas and Missouri but my understanding of Swander's work. "We shall never achieve harmony with land," Leopold writes, "any more than we shall achieve absolute justice or liberty for people. In these higher aspirations the important thing is not to achieve, but to strive." The problem, as Leopold points out, is "how to bring about a striving for harmony with land among a people many of whom have forgotten there is any such thing as land." For me, Swander's life offered a potential response to this problem, a striving that not only grows, as Leopold says it must, "from within" but also one that is imposed from without by the degraded, poisoned environment through which most of us walk, unaware. Swander's illness proves that there is no distinction among ecology, self, and community; between poison and poisoned, healer and healed. At the molecular level, becoming native to place is not a choice — we are, literally, the place where we live. *Out of This World* calls on those still residing on what's left of the prairies — a landscape where for centuries "wind became water became earth became flame" — to acknowledge and act on this elemental, "physiological tug" to place.[20]

But as I prepared to interview Mary Swander at her home in Kalona, the question once again became, "How?" Her life still seemed in key ways out of this world, an impossible accomplishment for most of us living in the "real" world of rental apartments, commuter jobs, and technological convenience. My world. Still, the positive possibilities that Swander's life represented — for turning a "life sentence around into a life passion,"[21] for recuperating what might appear to be an already dead place — filled me with anticipation for our visit.

*   *   *

Finding Mary Swander's home was relatively easy — Kalona was just twenty miles south of Iowa City, where I had lived for nearly ten years before moving with Steph to the small town of Belle Plaine. It was Labor Day weekend 1994, and my car was zipping along the country curves, past ditches full of emerald grasses and blue chicory and fiery lilies, past farmhouses and machine sheds. The closer I got to Kalona, the more those farms were joined by craft shops and handmade furniture stores and cozy bed-and-breakfasts. It began to remind me of every other quaint rural tourist town I'd seen while traveling across the Midwest, towns that sold sentimentalized versions of the past in the hopes of a more lucrative future.

Flashing lights erupted in my rearview mirror.

"Didn't you see that buggy sign back there?" the police officer scolded as he wrote me a warning. "You've got to be careful around here. It's a different world." Sure enough, just over the hill there was another officer stopping traffic to allow an Amish buggy to cross the intersection. It was the typical black, single-horse, four-wheel carriage with open front and enclosed back. The reins were in the hands of a teenage boy in dark pants and suspenders, and in the rear were four or five younger girls wearing bonnets who stared out the windows at me. I stared back, trying to recall what I knew about these "peculiar people," as they call themselves. The Old Order Amish trace their origins to the Swiss Anabaptists, a sect that developed during the Protestant Reformation and in different forms spread to Germany, Moravia, and Holland. Because they denounced infant baptism, believing that membership in the spiritual community was one of informed choice, they were persecuted and many immigrated to America in the early 1700s. Most members, now called Mennonites or Amish, initially settled in Pennsylvania but quickly spread to other areas, including Iowa in the early 1840s.

In Kalona that communal past was more than sentiment. Watching the carriage of children cross in front of me, listening to the clip-clop of the horses' hooves, it seemed clear that the Old Order Amish had maintained their ancestral commandment to live apart from secular society, to resist its encroachments, and to experience daily, in the words of one historian, a "conscious change (rebirth) of life and intent."[22]

I turned onto a gravel road and eventually spotted Mary Swander's white one-room schoolhouse sitting on a rise, an American flag snapping in the breeze at the top of its pole. Mary was outside, bent over her garden. She waved as I got out of the car and gestured for me to join her in surveying the vegetables.

"Look at that," she said, pointing to the ragged edges of the Russian kale. "We had a goat invasion the other day. Scalawag and Mac got out and had a field day in here—Didn't you, Mac!"

Mac, a pygmy goat with a salt-and-pepper coat, stared back across the fence through his one good eye. The other was glossy, rolled down in its socket. Mary walked over to him, crouched, held his face between her hands, and kissed his forehead.

"You didn't do that much damage, did you, boy? N0000." Mary turned to me. "You know Mac's story, don't you?"

I did. In *Out of This World* Swander describes how, shortly after Mac was born to Scalawag, an inexperienced vet misapplied a debudding chemical, burning one of Mac's eyes. Despite another vet's claim that Mac would die, Swander fought his infection, rocking him in his pen, feeding him antibiotics, nudging him into activity, praying for his life. By "rail[ing]" against his death, she claims to have broken with the unsentimental, "rural emotional ethic" of her childhood that accepted death and disfigurement, never balking at the inevitable. As a girl she had decapitated chickens, castrated pigs, and watched as dogs were shot for attacking sheep. Yet in the struggle to survive EI, she had learned to fight against death and physical disability, including her own bout with near blindness. Thanks to her efforts, Mac survived with one bad eye and has become part of Swander's sustaining community. "Disability connects us," she writes, "creates a stronger spiritual glue for all earthly creatures."[23]

Inside the schoolhouse Mary and I sat down at the oak kitchen table. It was large and sturdy, with four blue placemats set neatly at the edges. In the center she had placed a few stems of sweet everlasting in a small glass vase. At first I thought she might be expecting a group of friends to drop by, but Mary made it clear that there would be very few visitors that weekend. It was the eleventh anniversary of her illness, a time for solitary ritual and reflection, a time to remember that she "should be dead." Her own personal holiday.

"That's an old midwestern thing," she said. "When I was growing up in rural Iowa, we always celebrated birthdays and anniversaries and death days. There's wisdom in that. It's a way to personalize time."

All around us in the kitchen was evidence of that rural past spilling into the present. Big iron skillets hung just below shelves of canning jars, while in the large living room there was a wood-burning stove, an Amish quilt hanging on the wall, and a crocheted afghan draped across the back of a wooden rocking chair. With the exception of her electric steamer, her air conditioner, and her computer, this could have been her grandmother's farmhouse in Manning, underscoring one of Mary's fundamental beliefs: the past can heal you. She didn't realize that possibility, she told me, until her struggles with EI drew her to the well-known psychotherapist Lawrence LeShan.

"LeShan's whole thing was to take these terminally ill people, put them on a healthy diet with exercise, and help them rejuvenate their own spiritual beliefs. He'd also get them to recollect the happiest moment in their lives and then reactivate the conditions of that moment in the present. For many of us that happy moment had to do with being a part of a supportive community. The example LeShan used was this Puerto Rican guy from New York who was dying of liver cancer. When LeShan asked this guy to recall the happiest time in his life, he recalled being a teenager in a street gang. So they went about trying to find a job that would bring that past happiness into the present. He ended up as a fireman. Perfect! He was once again with a gang of guys, enjoying the same support and solidarity, the same sense of excitement, the life-and-death situations, but this time he was working for good instead of evil. A month later he was still alive, a year later, then two years later. *Still alive.* That inspired me, and I began to think back through my own life. I discovered that I was happiest when I was a little kid living with my grandmother in Manning, hanging out on her farm, running around outdoors and riding horses. In a way, I've reactivated that past happiness right here. My Amish neighbors have given me an extended family to be a part of, once again. And whaddayaknow, I'm still alive, too."

Mary cited other examples of how her Amish neighbors had "saved" her, which included helping her locate, among other necessities, organic foods. As she told me this, I considered how different her perspective was from most popular portrayals of these "peculiar people." The reputation of the Old Order Amish for being shy and reclusive around "English" was a standard part of most literary and sociological portraits. Amish are encouraged from a very young age to limit their interactions with outsiders in order to protect social cohesion and spiritual integrity. Outsiders are viewed, at an elemental level within the community, as poison. I asked Mary how she had managed to become so close to them.

"Well, first of all, I'm an outsider and always will be. Acknowledging that is part of respecting them. Still, because of my illness, I live in many ways a more restricted life than the Amish do. They have structured rules regarding dress and transportation and work and community relationships that I don't have, but I have a lot more restrictions regarding food and dust and other things. Having lived that restricted life, I think I can understand their restrictions. In return, they're really good about understanding what my life's about."

Mary wanted me to know, however, that the Amish weren't the only religious sect living in the area; there were also Mennonites. When I asked her to define the difference, she revealed the surprising diversity of Kalona.

"There are eighteen different sects living here, ranging from Old Order Amish, who use horses, all the way to Mennonites, who drive in cars and dress like you and me. There's also the Beachy Amish who live like the Old Order Amish except they can have cars and telephones. It's all the same belief system, but there are nuances in how they practice those beliefs, usually concerning dress codes or rules of social conduct. And within those major sects, there are all kinds of splinter groups. It's hard to keep it straight—no outsider really can. Some individuals break off from one family and start their own group, and some shunning goes on."

I had been wondering if Mary would mention shunning—a severe, psychological punishment that complicated any portrait of the Amish as giving and tolerant. In accordance with Old Order customs, if a member of an Amish community is deemed to have violated the tenets of the faith—including infidelity and marriage to a non-Amish but also mistreatment of the soil—that person may be "shunned," totally deprived of any interaction with family or other community members.[24] I asked Mary if she had ever witnessed this practice and what she thought about it.

"Yeah, I've seen it. And I've seen what it can do to people—it does terrible, terrible things to them. I mean they're totally cut off from their support network. It used to really bother me—well, it still bothers me—but what are they supposed to do? Without rules for behavior, how would they keep themselves from vanishing into the mass culture around them? The threat of shunning encourages responsibility, accountability."

I still had my doubts, and the hard realities of Mary's own exclusion from contemporary society made the Amish practice seem even more cruel. Nevertheless, the issue resurrected questions I had about our individual accountability to community and place—questions that had, from the beginning, informed my journey into the grasslands. I asked Mary if she felt that if not shunning then some kind of accountability might be useful in midwestern society, including among its writers and artists.

"Well, I can only speak for myself," she replied, "but I think we could definitely use a dose of responsibility. I know some writers who've moved here and don't even know about the farm crisis. If you're writing about a place, you should try to understand the historical, economic, and social factors at work in that place. That should be a requirement for inclusion. For me it's been a matter of going to the library but also a matter of getting out and talking to people. One way I accomplished this as a writer was to work for the Iowa Arts Council. Because most of the writers here are clumped on the eastern side of the state, the council used to send us to these rural western towns for days at a time to run performances and workshops. It was just a riot! Sometimes I'd visit a town a little early looking for local myths or stories, like a town murder or whatever. I'd walk into a café and start a conversation with a person, and then over comes someone else, maybe an elderly person with grandchildren—grandparents still provide most of the daycare in small towns—and they'd start telling me more stories. Later on we'd write those stories into some little play or long funky poem and perform it in fire stations or vfw halls or barns—we had a ball! That's when I really started to get back in touch with my home state. It helped me rediscover just how bright the people really are here and how much they have to offer."

Mary claimed that what had made those visits so valuable was that they provided artists with some income while allowing them to become, however briefly, part of the social fabric of a rural community. In return their talents helped many rural citizens reaffirm just how unique and interesting their lives are—something important for Iowans in general.

"In some ways Iowans live a pretty privileged life," she continued, "a life relatively light on crime and violence. But they also suffer from a kind of psychological and cultural oppression that comes from being told by other Americans, either directly or indirectly, that you're a dumbshit. At Iowa State I feel it's part of my mission as a teacher to encourage my writing students to shed that negative sense of themselves, to rediscover a respect for their intellectual and artistic abilities and a respect for the beauty and integrity of the land around them."

As an example, Mary recalled a recent nonfiction writing course.

"I tried, whenever possible, to integrate regional and local examples. For instance, I assigned parts of Linda Hasselstrom's *Windbreak*, then asked them to keep their own journals for a week and to bring in the best entry to share with the class. They resisted at first, claiming that the daily events described in Linda's book were more interesting than anything in their own lives. So I asked them, 'What's so interesting about this woman's life?' And one of them responded, 'Well, like, she lives on this really neat ranch.' 'And where did you grow up?' 'Well, I just grew up on a farm.' 'Wait a second, wait a second! Growing up on a farm is not about being boring or stupid!' I tried to get them to realize that they each have an area of expertise that's interesting to outside readers."

I asked her if she had wrestled with a similar sense of inadequacy as a student. She claimed her undergraduate experience had been even worse at Georgetown, where she suffered the "double whammy" of being both a midwesterner and a woman.

"When I was majoring in English at Georgetown—and this was the sixties and early seventies—not one book by a woman author was assigned and certainly not a woman midwestern writer. Oh yeah, I read one short story by Willa Cather, but all the rest of the required literature was by males—all of it. So it was difficult for me as a young writer to find any female role models. While searching the library I discovered a bunch of southern women writers: Flannery O'Connor, Eudora Welty, Carson McCullers, Katherine Anne Porter. I became totally enthralled with them, probably because unlike most of the male writers I was reading, these women had a sense of humor. I especially connected with Flannery O'Connor, all that Catholic and rural stuff. She really has become my soul sister; we've shared so many experiences, including illness. She had lupus, which carries many of the same symptoms as EI."

Since Flannery O'Connor had attended the University of Iowa's

Writers Workshop, I wondered if that program had been more open to Mary's interests as a regional woman writer.

"Well, there were a couple women instructors there, but they tended to be overshadowed by the men—John Irving, Ray Carver, John Cheever. Those men were great writers, and I learned a lot from them, but something was still missing, someone who truly understood where I was coming from. I think it's terrible that universities here don't hire more midwesterners to teach writing students. Students need examples of people who have grown up in the same places they have and who have learned to transform that experience into art. People who come from other places to teach here may have good intentions, but they ultimately lack the sensibilities necessary to fully understand what it means to come-of-age in this place. That kind of knowledge serves an important, practical purpose in helping students develop as artists and intellectuals. Not hiring professors here because they are midwestern is like racism or sexism—you can't appreciate how cruel it is until you've experienced it personally."

"Do you think the lack of those kinds of teachers has contributed to the flight of midwestern writers from the region?"

"Yes, for sure. Writing about your home is hard work, if you want to do it well, and we need all the guidance we can get from our teachers. It's very difficult, even painful, to step back from your own culture and realize the problems with its mythological structures. For instance, the land—it unites all midwestern writers, all midwesterners. Our entire social structure and economy has literally emerged from the soil beneath our feet. Agriculture has been the basis of almost everything out here. Even if you live in a place like Minneapolis—that city was built on grain. Still, many midwesterners believe that the land here is uniform, boring. Not so. That's what I tried to show in *Parsnips in the Snow*. If you travel from northern Minnesota down to southern Missouri, you're traveling through five horticultural zones, not to mention the different ethnic populations, from northern European to Italian to African American. It's linguistically diverse as well. People in Wisconsin call water fountains 'bubblers,' and they call money machines 'time machines.' Don't ask me why. The point is it takes effort to appreciate that diversity. And it takes even more effort to acknowledge how misguided the settlement of the prairie was, especially when you've grown up here with farmers and have close economic ties to the land."

It seemed to me that southern writers or writers from any region would face the same difficulties. Yet as someone once observed, midwestern writers tend to move to other regions, while southern writers just move to their attics. "Why is that?" I asked her.

"Well, I think in general the work of regionalism is underappreciated by writers here in the Midwest in a way it hasn't been in the South. I think it's a consequence of the cultural oppression I mentioned earlier, the self-denigration. I consider myself a midwestern regionalist in the Grant Wood sense. As a young painter he went off to Paris because he thought all good painters had to be French Impressionists. Well, he wasn't French and wasn't an Impressionist. He was an Iowan. So he came back home and rediscovered his art in the land and people he grew up with. The result wasn't something petty and provincial but work that reverberated with audiences throughout the country and the world. That's what I'm trying to do."

I asked if she had experienced any anti-midwestern bias when applying for academic jobs in the region. She said she had but emphasized that the more important point was that despite those prejudices, local writers and teachers were trying to find ways to stay and were willing to sacrifice to do so. At Iowa State Mary has an arrangement where she teaches a full load in the fall, then takes the spring and summer off. Though she accepted a pay cut and works her "butt off" teaching in the fall, the arrangement allows her time to tend her garden, to write, and to continue connecting with her various healing communities.

It also didn't hurt that her books were published by major houses in New York, I thought. Out of my own tenuous hope, I asked if she believed the opportunities to publish books with midwestern settings and characters and themes were increasing.

"Yeah, for a long time it was neglected. But what became evident to me after I wrote *Driving the Body Back* is that readers here are hungry. They are saying: 'Hey, give me something about my own home place and people I understand and can plug into.' New York is just stupid not to understand that and take notice. But I think they're beginning to. It's pretty hard to ignore the success of Ian Frazier's

Great Plains or William Least Heat-Moon's *PrairyErth* or Jane Smiley's *A Thousand Acres*. All those good, successful books. What really made me happy recently, though, was an Iowa woman who approached me after a reading and praised me for giving something back to the state as a writer. That's nice to hear, especially when you know there are people here who don't care about my writing because I'm local."

"How have your neighbors in Kalona responded?"

"They've never made me feel unwelcome as a writer," she said. "In fact, I've used my writing to barter with them for goods and services. One example is this guy who lives around the corner. He runs this small engine repair shop where I take my lawnmower every fall to be serviced. I was talking to him one day and it turns out he used to teach in a one-room schoolhouse and likes to write, especially about his garden. So he asked me if he could have a copy of my gardening book, and I said, 'How about if I trade you a copy of the book for the maintenance on my lawnmower?' He said, 'Okay.' After we talked some more about gardening, he said, 'You know, with all the advice I'm giving out, a fella could write it up for the newspaper.' I said, 'That's great, why don't you do that?' Next thing I know, he's got a regular gardening column in the Kalona newspaper."

"When it came to your Amish neighbors, did you feel an obligation to write against other representations of them?"

"Not really. To begin with, there aren't that many personal narratives about living with the Amish, and most of them are about coming here from the outside looking for something spiritual or whatever. I didn't come here looking for that kind of thing and I certainly didn't come here looking for a book. That came later, but initially my motives were more urgent, more about physical survival—I was dying. Now, Kalona is not a community of sick people, but it is certainly a community of survivors, and that spoke to my situation. I wouldn't be here if it weren't for the illness, and it continues to shape my relationship with this community and landscape."

The kettle on the stove began to whistle, and Mary got up from the table.

"Tea?" she asked.

"Sure," I said, and she poured me a cup. She returned the kettle and glanced out the window, perhaps checking for wayward goats.

"Why don't we go outside," she said.

From the front steps I noticed how carefully tended her garden was, with each vegetable in its own place and no weeds. Tall stalks of sweet corn graced the northern borders, while much shorter, leafier plants enjoyed an uninterrupted southern exposure. Colorful marigolds were interspersed to discourage insect invasions. The garden's orderliness was, in some ways, a reflection of the immense rows of corn and beans on nearby corporate farms. But Mary's hand-cultivated plot was much smaller, its contents and borders determined by individual necessity, not by greed or convenience or, as the Amish might say, the sin of pride. Her agricultural success was the result of humbling herself to the past, to the organic techniques used by Native Americans and pioneers and the Amish, instead of pursuing modern chemical and technological shortcuts. Mary's careful preservation of what was once Fairview School provided further evidence of her respect for local history. In the yard the tall frame of the school's old swing set could be seen, as well as the remnants of a baseball diamond—reminders that the place had once been filled with children. Now, however, it was Mac the goat who stood on the pitcher's mound, staring us down with his one good eye.

"I think he's feeling a little guilty," she said. "But he and Scalawag really didn't do that much damage. They're like children to me; they do some of the same funny stuff. Of course, my vegetables are like my children as well. I love them all."

I asked her if she considered some of the wild plants to be members of that family.

"Oh sure," she said. "I've tried to restore the ditch over here. It's got big bluestem and other natives, and there are some places down by the river that are special to me, full of wildflowers."

Mary picked some okra—"a real survivor," she said—and handed it to me to take home to Steph. I thanked her and asked how she was doing in her battle with EI.

"I'm doing great, really. I have everything that I could want now. I'll never eat sugar or anything like that again, you know, but now I can actually look at a recipe and say, 'Oh, I can make that.' I don't really have any complaints. I am going to get a chicken coop, though, and put it up by the baseball diamond next spring. I'm going to get about fifty birds: ducks, turkeys, guinea, and geese."

She started laughing: "It's going to be *crazy* around here! I'm going into *fowl*!"

Mary raised her arms in the air, her voice carrying over the garden and the ball diamond as if she were the home plate umpire calling a game. As I pulled out of the driveway — looking forward, I confess, to something other than okra for lunch — I saw her standing over her garden. Perhaps she was choosing which vegetables to eat on her one-person picnic, her personal anniversary. Or maybe just envisioning another hard-earned, bountiful harvest.

The next time I saw Mary she was stooped over a cane, slowly limping into an Iowa City auditorium to attend Terry Tempest Williams's reading. It was April 1996, almost two years after our initial interview. I couldn't believe how sick she looked — her face was very pale, and the hair hanging out from under her beret seemed as dry and brittle as straw.

"What happened?" I asked, slowing to walk at her pace.

"Didn't you hear? Some drunk hit me." She kept her eyes on the auditorium stairs, careful of where she put her cane. "It's been a nightmare; I can't even begin to describe it. I'll tell you later."

The fact that I saw Mary at a Terry Tempest Williams reading was appropriate. In *Refuge: An Unnatural History of Family and Place* (1991), Williams had written about the connection between nuclear testing in the deserts near her Utah home and her mother's cancer — another intimate connection between body and place. That evening Williams read various selections from her work, but what I found most interesting was the recent political use of her writing. She recounted that during the summer of 1995, conservative representatives from Utah placed the Utah Public Lands Management Act before Congress. If passed the act would have undermined the integrity of the 1964 Wilderness Act and open designated wilderness areas in southern Utah for development and mining. In response Williams and Stephen Trimble asked nineteen authors, including Barry Lopez, Rick Bass, and John McPhee, to write short personal pieces in defense of preservation. The result was *Testimony: Writers of the West Speak on Behalf of*

Utah Wilderness, which was distributed to every member of Congress. Senator Bill Bradley wrote this about the collection: "Good writing can make a place come alive. *Testimony* gives voice to the magnificence and quiet majesty of southern Utah's wilderness lands. I found its essays and poems useful in setting a tone for what is at stake in the battle over Utah wilderness, particularly for those who had never experienced the lands of the Basin and Range or Colorado Plateau. If writing itself can be an act of public service, then this collection is it." In the end the land remained protected, demonstrating the need — as Williams has said elsewhere — for writers to "bear witness": "[T]he story that is told can provide a healing ground. Through the art of language, the art of story, alchemy can occur. And if we choose to turn our backs, we've walked away from what it means to be human."[25]

I looked at Mary, sitting just a few rows in front of me, her back uncomfortably straight, her neck stiff and immobile, and wondered how the reading was resonating with her. *Out of This World* had been published by Viking about a year before, and I was curious how readers had responded to her narrative of body and earth in the grasslands — a landscape far less dramatic, less wild than the red rock canyons of Utah. But when I met up with her on the way out, her small, deliberate steps made my literary questions seem inappropriate. I just asked if she needed any help.

"No thanks," she replied, "I got my bull dong cane."

"Your what?" I asked. Mary smiled.

"Don't you know the story of my cane? It was my uncle's and it's made out of a bull's cut-off, uh, 'member.' It's a pretty big one isn't it?" She let out a short burst of laughter.

"Yes," I said, staring at the golden, almost translucent shaft. "It sure is."

It was amazing to see her humor coming through in such a situation. We continued walking to the top of the auditorium, visiting briefly about the Williams reading, which she had enjoyed.

"Give me a call sometime," she said. "A lot has happened since we last talked."

Mary and I didn't hook up again until a few months later, in June. The ditches were speckled with the soft pink of native wild rose, as well as the lavender of invasive prairie clover—an ongoing battle for survival, seldom noticed. When I pulled into Mary's driveway and got out of the car, I spotted a few changes. Near the baseball diamond was a new chicken coop with a giant peacock painted on the side. The biggest change, however, was the dog that came bounding toward me from behind the house, barking. It was huge and yellow and drooling—I prepared myself for pain.

"Bear! No! Leave him alone!" Mary shouted from the screen door. The dog stopped and turned to look at her as she opened the door and stepped into the sun. Soon he was at her side, wagging his tail. Mary reached down to scratch his head.

"Don't mind him," she said. "C'mon in."

I followed Mary through the house and onto her new screened-in back porch—she was still limping, but no longer in need of the bull dong cane. Bear was on the other side of the screen, staring at Mary with concerned, protective eyes.

"Can you tell me about the accident?" I asked.

"I was driving home from a Christmas party in Ames last December when this drunk ran a stop sign, bolted out in front of me, and I hit him. I suffered a severe head injury and was ordered on bed rest for the entire month of January. I asked the doctors if I should do anything more and they said not unless I woke up one morning paralyzed. And that's exactly what happened—I woke up one morning and couldn't move. Well, I could, thank God, move my hand enough to dial the phone. But I wasn't sure I'd ever be able to walk again. And it may have caused other problems related to the EI. The doctors think the car accident suppressed my immune system again, which is already severely suppressed, and I ended up with transverse myelitis, an infection of the spinal cord that's similar to polio. That's what I was fighting all winter. But anyway."

Mary changed the subject to *Out of This World*. It had sold out three printings in hardcover and the paperback would be released that week. She had also won the national Whiting Prize for Nonfiction and the Ruth Suckow Award given by the Iowa Center for the Book in Des Moines. Clearly general readers were responding positively, but I was curious about the local response, especially from her Amish neighbors.

"Last summer," she replied, "just after the book came out, I held a cast party in Kalona and invited everybody who was in the book. It was *so* much fun! All the names were changed, of course, so they sat right down with their copies, looking for themselves. I got a little good-natured grief—one person said, 'Hey, she claims I'm bow-legged!'—but a lot of people around here bought the book, even some Amish. Donna, my neighbor, was talking to Moses one day and asked him if he'd read the book. He said, 'Yep.' And then she asked him if he saw the first page where I'd dedicated the book to him and his wife, Miriam. He said, 'Yep.' 'Well,' Donna said, 'how'd you like it?' 'Well,' Moses said, 'I don't believe I'd pay twenty dollars for it.'"

Mary burst into laughter.

"Actually," she continued, catching her breath, "the Moses and Miriam characters came to my reading in Iowa City last summer. Donna and Stu took them. Donna said that they didn't say a word after the reading. Then, when they were almost out of town, Moses asked, 'Is she going to do that again sometime?' That made me feel great."

Mary said that Viking had sent her on a fifteen-city reading tour last summer: all over the Midwest, then to New York, Denver, and the Pacific coast. She would be touring again in July. I asked if she had received different responses in different regions.

"I got a tremendous response in the West, especially Denver and Seattle. Both places sold out the book before I even got there, and then almost a hundred people showed up for each reading. It was great. I think the book's popularity was related to the great numbers of environmentalists and environmental organizations in those areas. I also think that West Coast readers see the Midwest as exotic, so it was a real culture study for them. In the Midwest readers were more enthusiastic about the natural history material, the information on the prairie."

"Really?" I said. "Why do you think there was so much interest in that aspect of your book?"

"Well, it's a part of our natural history that not many of us living here truly understand. I mean, there's not that much prairie left to see and appreciate. So I think even though many of my readers live in this region, they found the idea of the prairie to be exotic, just like the readers on the West Coast thought the Amish were exotic. It's a matter of distance."

Mary's book had also received attention from the national media, placing her in the unexpected position of having to protect local Amish from unwanted intrusion.

"The *Today Show* said they wanted to come down here to talk about the book, but they just wanted to use me to film the Amish in their kitchens. I told them to take a hike. Several other television shows wanted to do the same thing, but I told them it was against Amish religious principles. The Amish believe that having your picture taken violates the commandment, 'Thou shalt have no graven images.' So hauling cameras into their homes would not only violate their privacy, it would also violate their religion. As soon as I told that to the TV people they said, 'Oh, okay' — click."

In contrast to her unwillingness to be a spokesperson for the Amish, Mary had become a public advocate for EI victims. She was interviewed by several journalists in the medical field and was the keynote speaker at both the Women's Health Conference and the Vocational Rehabilitation Conference in Des Moines. They had all been receptive audiences, sincerely interested in becoming informed about EI. Even so, there had been few advances in treatment — Mary claimed that conditions had, in fact, "gone downhill." The only two medical centers in America to treat EI, in Chicago and Dallas, had closed — insurance companies had rejected their claims, citing the treatment as "experimental."

"So there's no longer any place for EI victims to go," she continued. "I don't know what I would have done if I had gotten sick today — I probably would have died. Insurance companies still think EI is psychological. Even if it were psychological — and it's not — people would deserve the same compassion and care. But it's worse than that — most insurance companies don't think it exists at all. And there are, oh my God, all these people who are suffering. I ran into someone at every reading. There was a guy in Denver who could only eat five foods, and I just get letter after letter from people who can't eat anything, can't live anywhere. It makes me very, very angry."

"Have you acted on that anger?" I asked, thinking of Terry Tempest Williams. "Have you done any political work outside of writing the book?"

"Not much," she said. "I'd like to do more, but so much of my energy has been spent just trying to survive. But I hope my book does some good—that is my central political work. Just writing about something can create changes. Language and metaphor have the power to join people together and to educate. For instance, people with environmental illness often call themselves 'canaries,' as in 'canaries in the mine.' In the old days they used to lower a canary into a mineshaft to determine if it was filled with poisonous gas. The poisoned bodies of EI victims are literally a sign that we are all living in a poisoned world. That's a powerful metaphor, and yet it's more than a metaphor. It's reality. Chemical poisoning should be particularly scary for people in the Midwest. I once taught a class on environmental literature—this was before my book came out, so my students knew very little about my illness—and I divided them into groups and asked them to do presentations on how environmental poisoning affects human health. It was amazing how many students claimed to have been poisoned in one way or another by farm chemicals. They reported on their own nervous disorders and skin diseases and about how much hell they went through trying to figure out what was causing it all. Everyone around them was in denial."

"What are the sources of that denial, do you think?"

"One is that the economy here is controlled, to a large extent, by big chemical companies, and they have a lot of influence with our politicians and with agricultural educators. The other day, for example, on the front page of the Des Moines Register, I read an article in which some turf management expert with the ISU extension office claimed that there were no toxic effects from lawn chemicals. I couldn't believe it."

The wind picked up, becoming so loud it was difficult for us to hear each other.

"Hey, hey!" Mary exclaimed over the noise. "We're having ourselves a big blow here—yeehaw! Better get the birds inside before it starts raining!"

We walked out to the new chicken coop. As the wind tossed her short blond hair, Mary explained that she had bought the coop with the money she'd received from the Whiting Foundation:

"When they phoned to tell me I'd won the money, the first thing I said was, 'Oh goody, I can get my chicken coop.' They must have thought I was nuts!"

Bear was tearing through the small herd of goats, barking and chasing one-eyed Mac, even nipping him in the haunch. Meanwhile Mary and I were trying to herd the young ducks and turkeys. The ducks went directly into the coop, but the turkeys were less cooperative. One ran off and tried to blend in with a group of geese.

"You know," Mary said, "these turkeys think they're geese because that's all they've been around. This spring a couple of geese went into the pond, and one of these turkeys just followed them right in and actually swam across the pond. I couldn't believe it!"

Between Mary's limp and my poor "round-up" skills — not much improved since nearly getting killed on Dan O'Brien's ranch — it took us a while to corral the turkey. He kept ducking behind the coop, escaping, getting cornered, then escaping again. I was soon out of breath. Finally, Mary shooed him into the coop. As she shut the door, she reminded me that the turkeys were more than entertainment and exercise.

"That little bugger we just caught is a blankety-blank amino acid. And that one over there is a different blankety-blank amino acid. I got cute little amino acids running all over this place."

Mary explained that each turkey was fed a different kind of food, producing a particular kind of amino acid in their meat — a vital source of nourishment for her. The ducks provided fat. Some of Mary's friends and visitors, while admiring her almost familial relationship with her animals, became uncomfortable when they realized she actually ate some of them.

"People can't believe that I kill and eat these critters," she said. "It's not exactly my favorite thing to do either, but I have very little choice in the matter. I was actually a vegetarian for a while but that made me even sicker. I have to eat a lot of protein to stay healthy and meat still is the best source for that. But I don't regard eating these birds as being unnatural. Human beings are carnivores, predators, and predators play an important role within the big ecological scheme of things. To remove ourselves from that is artificial. I try to raise these birds the best way I can—not only feeding them but showing them respect. I guess that's one of my political statements. It's really something to raise a bird from the time it's a chick and then slaughter it. It's given me a completely different point of view than when I was just picking stuff up at the grocery. I feel like I'm closer to the cycle."

I was reminded of Dan O'Brien's desire to reconnect to wildness through his falcons and what he believes is a cultural resistance to accepting our role as predators. For Dan, however—as for most of us—this reconnection is a choice; for Mary it is a physical necessity. The Amish, Mary continued, unlike many Americans, had no trouble understanding her predatory yet respectful relationship to animals. She claimed that despite their reputation for being austere, they are actually "closer to their bodies than most because they still use folk remedies and still care for their dying and deliver babies at home." It is also the nature of their work, which requires daily physical contact with the land. Here was another link between Mary's rural childhood and her present life among the Amish.

"I grew up chopping up chickens and pulling their guts out," she said. "That was *real* work, as were most of the chores on the farm."

Walking back across the yard, I noticed Mary's spring garden. The plants were smaller than when I'd last visited and still carried a bright, newborn sheen. I wondered how Mary's recent accident had affected her ability to work in the garden, as well as other aspects of her life. When we sat back down inside, she said she was in the middle of writing an essay about her recent struggles for an anthology on illness that she was coediting with Patricia Foster, a professor at the University of Iowa who had struggled with anorexia.[26] The fact that they had sold the anthology was for her a sign of how the culture had changed from just five years ago when it was nearly impossible to find such books. As she talked about those days, her voice began to waver, gradually increasing in volume.

"I remember how angry I was when I first became ill, that I couldn't find any personal narratives that spoke to my situation. Even before the EI, I was angry. I was in a car accident when I was fifteen and ever since have had really severe pain in my neck and back. I had no models for how to express the experience of that pain.

Then, in 1980 or '81, I picked up an edition of the Iowa Review that had 'pain' as its theme. It was filled with all these important writers, and I remember thinking, 'Oh great, finally some top-notch people are going to write about physical pain.' Well, it turned out they all wrote about *psychic* pain. I was furious. If they'd asked me, I could have told them about *real* [she slapped her hand on the table], *tangible* [slap], *pain* [slap]! I don't want to hear about their angst! To make matters worse, they included one of those charts that doctors give patients to determine the nature of their pain—you know, whether it's 'shooting' or 'darting' or whatever—and where it's located. I had used that chart so many times during treatment, *so many times.* But these people had used the chart to make a supposedly ironic, clever statement about physical versus psychic pain. I was like, 'This is not funny! Pain is real! The body is real!'"

She turned away and looked at Bear, lying on his side in the sun, and was silent for a while.

"So anyway, in regards to this anthology, it's probably good that Patricia is in charge of editing all the mentals and I'm in charge of all the gimps."

She was trying to be funny, but her outburst still seemed to be echoing across the room. I'd never known, until then, how close her rage lived to the surface. It appeared to have surprised Mary, as well, and perhaps as an explanation she pointed to a chair in her living room.

"Right after the accident, when I couldn't move, I was stuck in that wingback over there. Then I moved to the kitchen chair. Friends had to come out here in the morning, put me in that chair, and then come back out here later to put me to bed. One time a person got me up, but I forgot to ask her to put me back down, so I had to wait all those hours until the next scheduled person came along. It was torture. I'm writing an essay about it right now, called 'The Fourth Chair.' The third chair was that wheelchair, which was so incredibly frustrating. Those were the first three chairs, and I'll tell you, it was a dark night of the soul. I didn't know if I'd ever walk again. The fourth chair was at my desk where I sat when I finally recovered enough movement to start writing again. That's when I really began to transcend, to heal. So on the one hand there was this terrible loneliness, this inner anxiety and fright. And on the other was this solitude, that moment when I could finally use my time and space for contemplation and creative work. In this essay I'm trying to figure out where loneliness fits into solitude, where one slips into the other, how they communicate with each other, and finally, how they both work to create a space in which you can give to others, connect to others."

"What do you mean by 'connect'?" I asked.

"I'm thinking here of Thomas Merton," she replied, her gaze returning to the wingback chair. "I first read his books just after I got sick with EI. Merton started out as this rich wild guy living the high life, a real mess. Then he had this kind of Saint Paul conversion and joined the Trappists. As a monk he continued to move farther and farther away from human company until he was living alone in a little hermitage in the woods. Out there he not only continued to meditate but also became more observant of the world around him — the flow of the leaves, the birds — until the physical moved freely into the spiritual and back again. Isolating himself within the natural landscape allowed him to explore his own inner landscape, to find the shadowy self he'd been grappling with and turn it into something positive. He also struggled with physical pain. He was extremely allergic, his skin so sensitive he could barely tolerate clothes. Most of the time he was sitting out there naked. To save himself he had to bring all those things into balance: the body, the land, and the spirit. But the next step — maybe the most important one — was that he had to give it all back to humanity through his writing. That was his gift to the world. Although my circumstances weren't voluntary like Merton's, our journeys have been very similar. And like him I've tried to make my writing a gift to others."

"What is the nature of that gift?"

"Part of what I'm giving back, I think, is a model of childlike abandonment of self and body to the landscape around me and letting that become my connection to God in the larger sense. That quality of self that allows the physical to flow into the spiritual is something I've also noticed in many of the Amish. In addition I've tried to offer readers an example of how to accept mortality in spiritually productive ways. Too often our religious teachers instruct us in the immortality of the soul and ignore the connection between the soul and the daily experiences of the body. Most mystics understood that connection. I read quite a few of them this winter—Merton, Hildegaard, Aldous Huxley, Buddha—anything anyone gave me. I was so desperate. A lot of these spiritual leaders were sick or made themselves sick, like Clare of Assisi, Saint Francis's companion. Clare believed in complete deprivation and poverty, so she starved herself to death. Francis had to force her to eat. And look at the suffering, bleeding Christ. I became particularly interested in Mary Baker Eddy—she was cool, I'll tell ya. She believed in the healing power of homeopathic medicine in combination with prayer and positive thinking, all goodness and love. This stuff about denying kids medication, that crazy stuff, she never said anything like that. In fact she writes in her book that no one should fail to turn to modern medicine if needed. She never denied the needs of the body. It seems that the original founders of all these spiritual traditions were amazingly enlightened, and then their followers screwed everything up."

"How do we avoid screwing things up?" I asked, thinking of the long, troublesome relationship between Judeo-Christianity—the tradition in which I had been raised—and the environment.

"We need to keep searching for balance, for a life that brings together our spiritual, physical, and ecological experiences. When we deny one or more of these experiences, we put ourselves and others in jeopardy. For example, a lot of environmental problems can be traced to the denial of death—we think that because our souls are eternal, we don't need to take care of the earth. That is an example of imbalance, and it is literally killing us all. To correct this we need to appreciate our own mortality, our physical connection to the cycles of nature, and remind ourselves of our responsibility for the physical well-being of others in this world. Catastrophic illness can lead to such an appreciation, but I wouldn't wish that on anybody. I think it can also be achieved by seeking solitude in nature, meditating and participating in the cycles of the land. On my book tour last year, one of the most frequently asked questions was, 'Do you think we should all live like the Amish?' I said, 'Of course not—that's impossible.' But I do think you can take an hour a day, a weekend a month, or a week a year to live apart from the madding crowd and contemplate your relationship to your body and spirit and to your fellow creatures on this planet. Just take time to get back in balance. That's what the Amish can teach us."

"Have you found that balance in your life?"

"Well, I don't think anyone is ever completely balanced, but I continue to strive for that point. Here again the garden provides a great example. As a metaphor it's pretty great. Gardeners are always pulling stuff out, but in recent years I've tried to invite stuff back in, indigenous grasses and flowers. At one point, things got a little out of hand and the grasses started to take over. Of course, I couldn't let the broccoli die for the sake of the grasses—I need the broccoli for my health. So now I've limited the native plants to the fence area and the ditch. In that way I've created a comfortable balance between my vegetables and the native species, between harvesting and foraging, between the needs of my body and the needs of the land. But the process is always incomplete, as it is in my life. I'm continually striving to reach a more perfect balance."

A heavy rain was now falling. I commented on how dry it had been that year and how much we needed the moisture.

"Yeah, isn't it great," she replied. "This place can be so lush and giving. So often we're looking for the spectacle in nature, the mountain or forest or ocean—that's why it's harder to inspire people to defend the land here. This place isn't about spectacle. This place is about less obvious dramas, like a good rain after a long dry spell."

As we silently admired the downpour, I wondered how long Mary would continue to reside in her schoolhouse, seeking balance.

"Do you plan to stay here the rest of your life?" I finally asked.

"That wouldn't be too bad," she replied. "I've already got my funeral planned. When the Amish die, their friends and family wrap them in sod before burial: of dust you are made and to dust you shall return. I think it would be wonderful to be wrapped in the earth, this earth right here. In a way this land and I have been intimate companions—we've both struggled so hard to heal. So after they lower me down right over there by home plate, they can just let it grow wild. I'd like to see all this go back to wild prairie. Wouldn't that be great, to be able to get lost again in prairie grasses, like all those pioneers? Hear the wolves howl again? That would be wonderful."

Bear grunted, as if we had been talking about him, and raised his soaked yellow head.

"Hey, Bear!" Mary said. "Just look at him out there getting wet. You know he has a perfectly good doghouse, but he never uses it. During the blizzards this winter he'd just lie down outside the porch here and let the snow drift over him. You'd just see his nose sticking out. Then he'd wake up and go 'Oh!'"

Mary leaned her head back and laughed. A short while later, as I got in my car, she invited me to her living crèche in December, a re-enactment of the nativity scene she holds every winter. I joked that I'd come as the little drummer boy, the local artist with low self-esteem.

"Great," she said, waving. "We need a little rumpuh-pum-pum going at that party."

As I pulled out of the drive, I saw her walking slowly toward her garden. For both Mary and the land, the cycle was once again moving forward, from death to life. In the east a thundercloud clapped like the hands of the faith healer she'd written about in a poem, calling out the common prayer: "Lord, God, let this illness, all those old sorrows inside me, out. / Oh, Sweet Jesus, out, out, out!"[27]

* * *

Six months later, Steph and I were standing at Mary's door in a brisk December wind. I had my decorative drum slung over my shoulder and two honey drippers for sticks. Steph came as a shepherdess, cradling a toy sheep under one arm and a toy buffalo under the other.

"Glad you could make it!" Mary exclaimed.

Inside there were around forty people talking in small groups, filling the place to capacity. Children, some wearing elf caps, chased each other around the furniture. Colorful lights were strung along the edges of the ceiling, and her kitchen table was heavy with dishes brought by the guests—sweet potato pie, organic meatloaf, garlic potatoes, pecan pie, red bean salad, herb bread. One of Mary's turkeys, perhaps the one I had chased around the coop, lay hot and steaming on its tray. Steph and I added our own plate of pickled herring and crackers, an old Swedish Christmas tradition on my mother's side.

Mary introduced us to her neighbors Stu and Donna, the ones who helped Mary deliver Christmas preserves to Amish friends in the opening of her book. Gradually we mingled with the other guests as well, some of whom I recognized from the university, authors and botanists and even a British lord. Others were from the local community or surrounding farmsteads, but, predictably, none of them were Amish. Though the Amish had played a significant role in Mary's recovery, this group of "worldly" individuals had also been essential. I looked around, wondering who had moved her from chair to chair during her recent recovery. Who had provided her with necessary foods and books and conversation? Who, now and through the years, had helped restore her?

Eventually my eyes rested on Mary herself, standing near the kitchen table, surrounded by friends. Seeing her in the company of others, without the more practical excuse of a literary reading, felt strange. While reading her books and visiting her, I had become used to the image of Mary alone in her schoolhouse. I had questioned whether such a disciplined life on the land could succeed without withdrawing from modern society, as the Amish had. The presence of these people, however, suggested that Mary's version of careful living, her personal and environmental convictions, didn't necessarily require isolation. Those convictions appeared, in the warmth of our gathering, to have created a community around her.

After we ate, Mary introduced Osha Gray Davidson, a nationally known journalist and author from Iowa City, who lit the menorah and explained the meaning of Hanukkah, the rededication of the temple in Jerusalem. Next a musician friend played her dulcimer and sang the carol in which the manger animals recount the gifts they gave the baby Jesus, their wool and warmth. Then Mary's living crèche began, with Lord Acton playing Caesar Augustus and announcing the census that drove Joseph and Mary back to his birthplace to be counted. In *Out of This World* Mary recalls friends who've asked how she can celebrate such a patriarchal holiday. She responds:

[T]his is the myth I grew up with. It's as simple as that. I've examined it now from every angle. I've found its cracks. I've figured out its evolutionary roots, and acknowledged my anger over its faults. Yet I've also discovered that I like the celebratory nature of the holiday, as well as the sense of sacredness that it forces me to *contemplate. And there is something very dangerous in completely rejecting your heritage. It's good to step back, even move away for a while from one's childhood assumptions and indoctrinations. . . . But if not a return or reconciliation, then at least a reconnoitering of one's original mythical structure seems a key to the health of the human—for both body and soul."*[28]

That evening no one seemed to be questioning Mary's motives.

After Caesar's proclamation we all stepped into the crystalline winter night. Swander, wrapped in a blue bed sheet, played the Virgin Mary and walked alongside a real donkey. Our procession included kings and goddesses and angels and minstrels—Jews, Christians, Wiccans, Agnostics—all making their way slowly across the hard ground, beneath the belt of Orion, and singing "O Little Town of Bethlehem." Mary knocked on the door of the "inn," otherwise known as Stu's mudroom, and was gruffly refused by its keeper. Finally we all crowded into the stable with the horse and the donkeys. We gathered in a rough circle, with Mary near the center, and sang more songs—"Hark, the Herald Angels Sing" and "Joy to the World." Inside that barn, with the support of her friends, Mary was "reconnoitering" one of the myths that had shaped her identity from childhood, but one which, through this communal ritual, had grown more inclusive of different life experiences and beliefs. More inclusive of the earth itself. In *Out of This World* Mary recalls a past crèche enacted in that same barn:

All the Christmases of my past flashed before me, from those of great joy and festivity of my youth, to those rather barren ones of the past few years. Trees and stockings, wrapping paper and bows, even the great beauty of the choirs during Midnight Mass, all fell away at this moment. Another beauty took over. One of simplicity and starkness. Of living your life on the animal level, of going through the miracle of birth on the basest plane, finding your god, finding your place, your connection to all life in a wooden shelter with the smell of droppings around you. In that instant, the Christmas myth became wilder, more feral, more full of energy and raw female power, closer to the primitive spirit world, closer to me.[29]

After we sang "Silent Night," Mary asked us to bow our heads in prayer or meditation. I recalled, in that moment, the snowy streets of my own Iowa childhood, the familial faces around the Christmas table, their windy talk and laughter flickering the candlelight.

There, once again, was Grandpa Roy. At Christmas Grandpa would already be talking about what new things he would grow in the frozen plot out back. I marveled, in memory, at the obvious joy he experienced while contemplating the soil, especially given what I now knew about the disturbed earth on which he'd been raised. Whatever else my grandfather had carried with him from Corder, Missouri — memories of a decimated landscape, of racist violence, of familiar bodies covered with coal dust and ice — he had also carried memories of his father, Tom, carefully tending a garden. That, too, was the legacy of Corder: a gentler relationship among body, spirit, and earth. A legacy that perhaps allowed my grandfather to reconnoiter the past in his own ways.

It was this gentler legacy Roy had tried to pass on to me, along with dedication to family, community, and education. And something else, a larger lesson he might not have anticipated. Though I could hardly express it at the time of Mary's crèche, recovering my grandfather's life, from Missouri to Iowa, had taught me that if the relationship to home is to become truly responsible, the full history of the land — human and natural, legendary and real, destructive and restorative — must become personal history. During that often painful journey of recognition, we are directed not only by the body of the earth but also by the bodies of the people we love, ancestors alive now and in memory. We have much to learn from the ways those people carry themselves in the world, however diminished, the ways they abide both its injury and forbearance. We have much to learn, as well, from the ways they refuse to abide.

I am still not a gardener, and inside that cold barn I was unsure if I would ever experience the transformative relationship to the soil that Mary — and possibly my grandfather — had achieved. Then again, our celebration that night was about redemption — "rebaptism," as the Amish might call it, the conscious rebirth of life's intent. Mary's presence there embodied that possibility, reminding me that the fundamental choice we face in our relationship to the land is perhaps not to be native to place but to embrace nativity, the already connectedness of body, spirit, and earth. Commitment then becomes not just a matter of knowledge and memory and resolve but of faith. Inside that faith, who's to say where nativity might lead us in the grasslands, to what actions, alone and in communion with others? Who's to predict the healing distance we might cross?

"I want to thank you all for everything you've done for me during the last year," Mary said. "May you have a wonderful Christmas and a great New Year."

We started walking back toward the schoolhouse. As children ran by us, Steph and I paused to look out across the western fields, barely visible beneath a light crust of snow. She rested her chin on my shoulder and pointed to the sky, tracing the constellations of Aries the ram and Pegasus the horse and Taurus the bull.

"A winter barnyard," she said. "And look over there—the Northern Cross, stuck in the prairie."

Sure enough, there it was. We pondered it, silently, then continued walking beneath Polaris, the North Star. The light that guides us, in every season, toward the landscapes of home.

CHAPTER 6

What This Prairie Will Awaken *Walnut Creek National Wildlife Refuge*

Dawn on the Iowa tallgrass prairie. As the autumn sun draws amber from the big bluestem and a light breeze shivers the cottonwoods, we wait. It is October 9, 1996, and about twenty of us have gathered here at the Walnut Creek National Wildlife Refuge[1] to witness the return, after more than a century's absence, of wild bison to native Iowa prairie. Eight young bison stand in a nearby stock truck ready to be released into the small corral. I can see their shadowy hulks shifting behind the perforated, metal sides. There is the occasional snort, the steam of breath. They are edgy, I assume, from the all-night journey from Fort Niobrara Wildlife Refuge in Nebraska. I try to imagine that journey, the highway noises, the headlights — how ordinary this truck must have seemed to interstate travelers on their way to jobs or distant family. None could know what we know: that after a few days, these eight bison will move from the corral into the surrounding 40 acres, then into 750 acres, and finally, when the herd has swelled to 150, they will roam, along with elk and white-tailed deer, the thousands of prairie acres here. None could know what we know: that these animals will return to our home a semblance of its indigenous spirit.

Just two hundred years ago, here in central Iowa, lush tallgrass prairies and oak savannahs supported a myriad of wildlife—bison, elk, cougar, wolf, and bear—engaged in delicate cycles of interdependency. The bison, though, with their great size and number, became the symbolic heart of the grasslands. In North America before European settlement, there were an estimated fifty to sixty million of them. In western Iowa as late as 1839, pioneer convoys passing through the state reported being stopped for days by bison herds.[2] By the turn of the century they were extinguished from Iowa and only three hundred remained on the continent. It was one of the most dramatic wildlife losses in history, perpetuated by men like Buffalo Bill Cody, born on the eastern side of Iowa in Le Claire. Cody claimed to have killed over four thousand buffalo during his stint as a meat supplier for railroad workers in the 1860s, and he carted around his own personal herd to ride and stampede in front of nostalgic crowds at his Wild West show. Yet miraculously, the bison did not cross the thin wire into extinction. They were saved in part by a few farsighted conservationists, including Cody's fellow Iowans Congressman John Lacey and the zoologist William T. Hornaday. Hornaday, who once shot bison to provide specimens for an eastern museum, eventually became the first president of the American Bison Society (1905) and was instrumental in the creation of several national bison preserves, including Fort Niobrara. Since then bison have experienced a modest rebound and now number around 150,000, mostly in private herds.[3]

Few of those herds reside in my corner of the grasslands. I grew up a couple of hours from here, in west-central Iowa, and didn't see a wild bison until I was nine during a family vacation to the Black Hills of South Dakota. It was the summer of 1975 and we were staying at the Game Lodge in Custer State Park. One evening we all piled into a tourist jeep to go see the resident bison herd, African-safari style. They were grazing in a secluded valley over which the evening shade was slowly folding. Calves huddled near cows while the bulls grazed in distant solitude. As our jeep moved slowly through the herd, my younger sister Susan became spooked by the dark hulks and started to cry. Mom asked our guide, with his baseball cap and cowboy boots, if there was any danger of being gored. He said no, it wasn't quite mating season, and even if it were you could tell a bison was agitated by looking at its tail — it would be raised in the air. That image, along with the big animals themselves, became part of what made South Dakota exotic and wild in my imagination. I didn't want to leave. Iowa, in comparison, seemed boring, empty. Indeed, the last free roaming bison in the state had been shot in 1870 in Pocahontas County, just a few miles from where I was born.

As a child I knew nothing of this sad history, and yet in that moment among the Black Hills herd, I felt strongly the emptiness, the lack it had already carved into my life. I wanted to keep their wildness near me forever. At a trinket shop in Wall, I bought for a quarter a small foam bison with plastic horns and eyes and a little tuft of fuzz glued to the top of its head. Back home in Fort Dodge, I played with the tiny bull during the day, charging it into my toy race cars, then kept it on my bed stand at night, to watch over me. After a few weeks, though, it lost its horns and one of its legs, and after six months it vanished altogether. My own little extinction.

Back at Walnut Creek, Fish and Wildlife officials are hanging off the sides of the stock truck, poking broom handles through the vents to try to coax the bison, those reluctant Iowans, through the narrow opening and down the shoot. They refuse to move. There is a loud bang as a yearling kicks a metal divider, and one of the men falls off the side and into the grass. He gets up, brushes off his jeans, and walks away in frustration. Earlier Dave Aplin, a public use specialist for the refuge, explained that the Fort Niobrara herd in Nebraska is famous for its wildness, and he recounted the difficult challenge of rounding up and selecting these few bison.

"You cannot believe the power of these animals," he warned us. "We have no idea how they'll respond once they're released, so we ask that you keep noise and movement to a minimum, including cameras. Remember, these creatures are wild."

Wild. It is hard for me to explain how foreign this word still is to me. As a child what little I knew about nature I mostly learned from tacking dead butterflies to Styrofoam, popping the plastic lids off marigold kits, walking the well-marked trails at Dolliver State Park, and traveling to distant places like the Black Hills and Yellowstone. In contrast, Steph spent much of her Idaho childhood among the white pines of the Sawtooth Mountains and the black lava buttes of the high desert. Visiting Idaho with her has helped me understand that wilderness is not so much about the known as the unknown; it is immense, unpredictable, dangerous — a place where you can get lost, be found, gain faith. I have never known such a place in Iowa, nor have my parents, nor my grandparents. Tallgrass prairie, prior to European settlement, covered 85 percent of Iowa, close to thirty million acres. After the introduction of the steel moldboard plow in 1850, it took just eighty years to convert nearly all of those acres to farmland. Now, only around thirty thousand acres of tallgrass remain.[4] Across the Midwest the destruction of the prairie wilderness was so quick and so complete that it moved Aldo Leopold in the 1940s to comment: "What a thousand acres of Silphiums [native compass plants] looked like when they tickled the bellies of the buffalo is a question never again to be answered, and perhaps not even asked."[5]

Here at Walnut Creek the question lingers. I first read about the refuge in the Des Moines Register where the lead editorial proclaimed that Walnut Creek, an eight-thousand-acre, thirteen-and-one-half-square-mile area near the capital city, would someday be full of six-foot bluestem, shooting stars, compass plants, showy orchids, prairie chickens, bluebirds, plovers, and rare butterflies.[6] I read this just prior to the great floods, months before my reawakening to the land, so although the article caught my attention, it didn't particularly move me. For some reason, however, I kept it stashed in the top drawer of my desk. Just over a year later, when I heard on the radio that Walnut Creek would be holding a groundbreaking ceremony for its new learning center, I had changed enough to retrieve the article and make plans to attend.

In September 1994 I turned my car for the first time onto the gravel road that led to Walnut Creek National Wildlife Refuge. This visit occurred shortly after my initial interview with Mary Swander and was the last stop on that first summer's journey into the grasslands. My car became lodged in a slow, surprisingly long line of cars and trucks, all headed for the groundbreaking ceremonies. In the Black Hills I would have expected to fight tourist traffic but not here in Iowa. At the site a large canopy was set over the podium and chairs, but most of the people — maybe three or four hundred — were milling around in the sun, looking out over the rolling acres of mostly scrub grass soon to become tallgrass prairie. A group of schoolchildren were sitting in a circle around a refuge official as he showed them a collection of wildflowers about to be planted, and a bus full of senior citizens was unloading its passengers. There, too, was an English professor I knew from the University of Iowa, wearing a sun hat and walking his dog. We waved to each other.

After we took our seats, the first speaker related some of the history of the refuge. Officially created through an act of Congress in the spring of 1990, the land was originally earmarked as the site of a nuclear power plant. When that fell through, Iowa Democratic Congressman Neal Smith approached the U.S. Department of the Interior's Fish and Wildlife Service about developing a new wildlife area at Walnut Creek. When federal scientists arrived to investigate, they discovered unique potential for ecosystem restoration, with numerous unbroken patches of tallgrass prairie and oak savannah remaining on the property. In the early half of 1991, biologists made plans to restore and reconstruct the native ecosystem at Walnut Creek and to build an environmental education center, seed storage and process facility, and miles of trails for visitors.

What makes Walnut Creek unique, however, is that it is the first and largest federal prairie restoration to emulate historic ecotypes on farmland and to return displaced plant and animal communities to their biotic homes. Early prairie restorations — like what took place at Buffalo Gap and other national grasslands — have been more indiscriminate, introducing grass seed with little regard for local ecotypes. At Walnut Creek the process is informed by the unique personality of local soil and plant types — only those seeds collected within a ninety-mile radius are planted here. What grows at Walnut Creek will belong there.

Perhaps because Walnut Creek is about being native to place, about biological belonging, there was a touch of Iowa patriotism informing all the ceremonial speeches. But it was patriotism unlike anything

I had experienced during my years in the state. The speeches were not filled with the usual Iowa abstractions — family values, heartland pride, small-town friendliness, and the rest of the lingering Arcadian ideal. Instead it was an awakened pride in our all-but-vanished natural heritage. Congressman Smith, whose lobbying helped establish the refuge, talked about the process of restoring a "lost vision" of the Iowa prairies where future generations — perhaps those schoolchildren sitting right over there — will spend days and nights following the life-giving trails of native animals, seeing where elk have eaten back invasive saplings, where a water-filled hoof print of a bison has allowed a dormant plant to spring forward, where long-gone songbirds have built nests and raised young. These children, Congressman Smith said, will know better the chain of life, the powerful force of the land to which they belong.

Molly Beattie, director of the Fish and Wildlife Service, also described a vision of the restored grasslands and said that she could think of no place more appropriate than Iowa for that vision to be realized, a state that had given America two of its pioneers in wildlife conservation: Ding Darling and Aldo Leopold. Darling, a one-time cartoonist for the *Des Moines Register*, served under Franklin Roosevelt as the director of the U.S. Biological Survey, the forerunner of the U.S. Fish and Wildlife Service. Darling was largely responsible for the creation of the Federal Duck Stamp that fowl hunters buy every year, providing money to purchase more than four million acres of vital habitat in the National Wildlife Refuge system. A staunch defender of environmental education, Darling also funded, mostly out of his own pocket, the first cooperative wildlife research unit at Iowa State University. There are now forty-three such units nationwide.

"Aldo Leopold," Beattie continued, "who was born in Burlington, Iowa, called me and many other people into natural resources management with his writing, particularly *Sand County Almanac*, which precipitated the science of wildlife management. In fact when I was sworn in as director of the Fish and Wildlife Service, I held a copy of *Sand County Almanac* under the Bible."

Beattie went on to describe the unique "ecosystem approach to conservation" taking place at Walnut Creek and to praise the active partnership among environmental groups, corporations, educators, and private citizens that has made the restoration possible. Walnut Creek, she said, is an example of local alleviation of what Leopold called "biotic pain." All over the country, Leopold claimed, "land doctoring" is taking place, but "land health" is yet to be born. Walnut Creek is, according to Beattie, a giant step forward in land health, restoring not just individual wildlife or plant species but also the health and wholeness of their habitat. She claimed this was particularly important with the prairie, which "is not majestic like a mountain range or awesome like the ocean" but rather holds, as Leopold said, a "sublime beauty" that must be observed up close, discerned in "the thousands of little parts that fit together in the magnificent interdependency of life."

"And perhaps of all the teaching that goes on here," she continued, "the most important will be to impart the faith that even with just a few threads left, people can weave back together the natural ecosystem if they just work together."

There is a rumble from within the stock truck, men shout warning — "Here we go!" — and the first bison charges down the shoot. Despite Dave's orders, the sound of our snapping cameras erupts like applause, and the animal suddenly stops in the middle of the corral. It is a young shaggy bull, heavy-headed, with a prominent hump. His tail is erect and the thick muscles of his haunch are twitching as he glares at one of us, then another, then another. We lower our cameras. There is more rumbling, more shouting, and a young female emerges from the truck. She is smaller, darker, with longer horns. She nudges the bull with her head and they slowly wander to the far side of the fence, pause, then graze on bluestem.

"That's a good sign," says Pauline Drobney, who is standing next to me, holding her infant son. "They like the food here."

Pauline, a native Iowan, is one of the federal botanists charged with restoring native plant communities to the refuge, these thousands of acres of overcultivated, eroded land. The fact that bison have made it back here is a tribute to the hard work of Pauline and many others. Bison not only require vast amounts of land, they also need a suitable diversity of native species to graze on throughout the year. That initial diversity has been established, and the bison can now fulfill their proper role within the biotic community. Pauline believes these bison will graze off invasive, cool-season grasses like timothy, providing opportunities for native, warm-season grasses like bluestem. And because bison prefer grass, she hopes they will clear the way for more wildflowers and thus more butterflies and bees and songbirds. They will, in short, help heal the land.

I, in contrast, have not been very much help at all. Before going to Walnut Creek, I had never been an environmental activist, never been a member of the Iowa Prairie Network or the Nature Conservancy or any other group working to preserve and restore the native ecosystems of the state. For one, I had never seen a wild Iowa prairie while growing up, and it is difficult to care about what you've never seen. As Leopold wrote, "We can be ethical only in relation to something we can see, feel, understand, love, or otherwise have faith in."[7] All too often the natural places I did see and love proved to be not as good at garnering faith as disappointing it.

Brushy Creek, for example. It was a forty-two-hundred-acre wooded area where as a teenager I walked for hours along streams, admiring wildflowers and exploring limestone caves, or sat to read beside aboriginal mounds, shaded by ancient bur oaks. Less developed than nearby Dolliver State Park, it was a place where a restless adolescent might hide for a while. I eventually left for college and did not return to Brushy Creek for many years. In unconscious ways, though, I depended on its existence in the world, on the fact that it was still out there, waiting for me. A few years ago I read in the paper that Brushy Creek valley was in the process of being flooded for a recreational lake. I try to understand the other side — perhaps it will give a needed boost to the local economy — but for me the destruction of Brushy Creek is one of the reasons I have been reluctant to commit to natural areas and environmental causes in this state. Why learn to care about something that will inevitably leave you broken by grief?

Through the rituals of restoration, however, Walnut Creek has helped reconnect me to the natural and human communities of home. Collecting and planting enough local seed to restore an eight-thousand-acre prairie has required a lot of local labor, and many have volunteered. Steph and I harvested seed at what refuge officials call a "feed-and-seed" potluck held about twenty miles from Walnut Creek. After breaking bread with other volunteers at a small park, we walked to a nearby patch of undisturbed prairie. I was assigned to purple prairie coneflower (one of the first native plants I'd learned to identify) and Steph to black-eyed Susans. As I moved through the tall amber grasses of this twenty-acre remnant, snipping off the round, prickly seed heads and placing them in my paper bag, I thought back to the first time I saw a field of wild coneflower, in June at Buffalo Gap. I had been alone in the landscape then, bewildered and frightened inside my pup tent. Now, Steph was working alongside me, occasionally chucking a decapitated Susan at my head. She was reveling in her mission. Afterward she would claim that it was the first time the midwestern landscape had truly given something to her and that she'd given something in return. The beginning, she'd say, of learning to feel at home.

There were others, too—around twenty-five of us. Nearby, a retired farmer in khakis and suspenders was collecting lead plant and telling an elderly woman how he loves everything about the prairie except the ticks: "I'm a tick beacon, lady; a tick beacon!" Also within sight, a teenage boy, pimply and sullen, meandered in one of the far corners of the preserve—he was responsible for gathering rattlesnake master. Weaving her way around all of us was a young girl, around seven, skipping and singing a song of her own creation: "Thimbleweed, thimbleweed, where're you hiding, thimbleweed?" The tiny prairie was alive with people.

As we worked side by side, I was struck by how different my experience of this community was from my experience during the 1980s farm crisis in Fort Dodge. I was an adolescent then, a time when, for me, the sense of community was often defined by confusion, violence, and exile. Friends' families moved away from town, following factory jobs or seeking new beginnings. I heard and knew about suicides; the unemployed father of one of my schoolmates hung himself from an extension cord in the garage. During that time economic, racial, and religious strife trickled into the hallways of my public high school, erupting into violence. Walking through those hallways was an exhausting act of evasion, of avoiding eye contact with the kids whose desperation and instability shone through the pores of their skin like oil. They might explode at any second, and some did —there were weekly fistfights, it seemed, and occasionally a knife was drawn. Sometimes at my locker I'd pray that I might just crawl inside and hide there until God's wrath had passed from my home. But there was no escape. Fear permeated everything, like gymnasium sweat.

In school we were given nothing to help make sense of our experience, no statistics or demographics. We were not told that poverty levels approached 30 percent in some Iowa counties,[8] or that between 1980 and 1987 our state's population declined 6.6 percent—over 10 percent in some rural counties.[9] I didn't hear the word "farm crisis" until I went to college, not until 1985 when farmer Dale Burr made national news by shooting his banker, his wife, and himself in Hills, Iowa. Even then I didn't make the connection. Fort Dodge was a relatively large industrial town of twenty-five thousand, an intermediary landscape, not quite city and not quite rural small town. We had no easy myths against which we could measure and interpret the severity of our situation—no pastoral idealism, no inner-city claim on real poverty. No identity at all, really.

Literature offered some perspective. In senior English class the teacher assigned *My Ántonia*. I found it long and foreign, except for Jim's desire—like my own—to escape the "curious depression" of life in his town, to leave it forever in the "incommunicable past." But this was a narrative of exile, not about my time or my place or my people, and so it taught me little about commitment and everything about the away-from world of my mind: I'll be a success, I'll be a whole person, I'll survive, if only I can get away from this town, this land where the fields are seeded with nothing but despair. Years later just after the floods of 1993, when I began to awaken to what remained of the prairies, my first impulse—not so surprising—was to travel to other places like South Dakota and Kansas. Natural beauty and its most articulate advocates, I thought, are elsewhere. The communities of home, both natural and human, are elsewhere. Not here. Not in this constricted, strangled place.

As I stood in the Iowa prairie during the feed-and-seed, looking out over the rolling hills of fire-like color, I wondered what Douglas Bauer would have to say about the view. A one-time editor at *Playboy*,

Bauer grew up in Prairie City, just a few miles from Walnut Creek. In his autobiography, *Prairie City, Iowa: Three Seasons at Home*, Bauer describes experiencing a similar sense of exile when he was an adolescent, "a growing certainty" that he would leave "the mute, hard-bitten impulses of central Iowa." In his book Bauer returns to Prairie City in 1975 after his marriage and editing job fall apart to help his dad on the farm and to reorient himself within the cycles of the land. Then he once again leaves for the East Coast. In a later essay Bauer recounts another trip to Prairie City during the 1980s farm crisis. This time, instead of talking with farmers at the grain elevator he's talking to a farm crisis hot-line director who is trying to keep those same farmers from killing themselves. Inside that tragic context, Bauer proclaims that life in his hometown "has never seemed spacious and easy to move about in, but just the opposite—densely cluttered with the reduplicating presence of one's past and with the awful claustrophobia of knowing your particularly specific end. No one likes to feel crowded, I've replied to local people who ask me how I can possibly live in cities; that's why I can't live here." That psychological, economic, and cultural constriction is embodied, for Bauer, by the cultivated landscape his father peruses from his front porch: "It's neither a place nor a view that I would—that I could—choose, since I know I couldn't live with the congestion of the fields."[10]

Sometimes I feel a similar congestion, living here in Iowa. But standing on that tiny prairie, I felt only alleviation, a suspension of the weight I had carried with me for all those years, unacknowledged. There was within me not a heavy reduplication of my past in the grasslands but an easy breathing in of that past, of the history that had shaped me. There with me, once again, was my grandfather Roy —and perhaps his father, Tom—harvesting seeds from their gardens. There, too, were the distant generations of farmers in my family, swinging their sickles beneath the autumn zephyrs. The ends had changed, but the gestures of our bodies were, by degrees, the same— the hand, my hand, reaching out for the seed, snapping it off, feeling its rough promise in the cracks of my palm.

And as a people, a community, the work of restoring the prairie may yet prove that our hands do not have to be, as Hamlin Garland once claimed, "all desolating." While the October sun set beneath the grasses, I gathered seeds alongside people from the city and from the farm, young and old, a spontaneous community helping to recover a native landscape we'd never really seen or known. It was a gathering of faith. Not the "hard-bitten" faith described in Bauer's version of Prairie City, or the immature, easily disappointed faith of my adolescence. It seemed, instead, closer to the more elusive yet more sustaining faith described in the Book of Hebrews: "the substance of things hoped for, the evidence of things not seen." It was a faith made all the more significant by taking place in a state where, less than a decade ago during the farm crisis, so many communities had been divided and damaged by economic battles over the land. Iowa is still recovering from those difficult years, much has been lost, but the prairie we are building here, together, is perhaps evidence that as the land can heal so, too, can we.

I am distracted for a moment by the sight of a reporter carefully lowering a microphone near the head of the bison bull—what does he think it has to say? Dave barks at him from across the corral, and the noise seems to jar loose the rest of the bison who rumble down the shoot. Four are calves, and one of them wanders over near the fence where I am standing. I am amazed at how soft his coat appears, hardly enough, I think, to protect him from the winter. It will protect him, of course, as it has his kind for centuries; he belongs here. And what his body doesn't know about this land, he will learn. "That's the benefit of these younger animals," Dave said earlier. "They're willing to adapt." Pauline, however, is more interested in what we will learn from the calf.

"There are mysteries about Iowa tallgrass only buffalo can solve," she says to me. "As they graze this land, what kinds of plant will flourish, what kinds will fall away? What kinds of animal will move in? What kinds of fire—how hot, how fast—will burn here? All of this is a big riddle, an experiment in the unknown."

Though the future of the refuge is bright—the Fish and Wildlife Service is promoting Walnut Creek as a departmental success story —Pauline wonders if we'll find the collective wisdom to fully heal this broken land. I wonder as well. Congressman Neal Smith lost his

1994 reelection campaign, and Molly Beattie, Fish and Wildlife Service chief—the woman who, just two years earlier, had talked about alleviating the biotic pain of this lost prairie—died from brain cancer in July. She was forty-nine. How do we measure the loss of such a voice for the land? How do we call forth that same voice from inside ourselves?

During the last few years I have come to know one possible answer to that question. As I ventured out of literature and into the landscape, I did not know what I would find: what kind of place, what kind of writers? Dan, Linda, William, and Mary—authors who invited me into their lives, who shared with me their ideas, their hopes, their inner conflicts and convictions—have come to mean a lot to me as individuals, but together, as a community, they've become something even more significant. They've become an example of not only the struggle to find self-recognition in this endangered, threadbare place but also the struggle to articulate for others what it is that the land demands of us in our daily lives: the nature of responsibility. This struggle is something that language alone cannot easily summarize. It is something that also needs to be lived.

What's more, by seeking out these writers and their home places —by following the many side trails along the way—I've been led back to my own home, back to a rediscovery of what Wendell Berry calls the "beloved community." Too often, Berry argues, American writers have been concerned only with "the individual who is misunderstood or mistreated by a community that is in no sense beloved," and the writers I visited certainly had complex, sometimes antagonistic relationships with their communities and regions. Yet in distinct ways each offers the hope that a writer might, as Berry says, get beyond the role of "pariah or gadfly or exile" and seek instead

the tragic imagination that, through communal form or ceremony, permits great loss to be recognized, suffered, and borne, and that makes possible some sort of consolation and renewal. . . . [A return to the beloved community] would return us to a renewed and corrected awareness of our partiality and mortality, but also to healing and to joy in a renewed awareness of our love and hope for one another. Without that return we may know innocence and horror and grief, but not tragedy and joy, not consolation or forgiveness or redemption.

212 Why This Prairie Will Awaken

The ceremonies that draw us nearer to that community, at once natural and human, are the ceremonies of the body as well as the mind and spirit. That is part of what I have come home to find here at Walnut Creek, a "common experience and common effort on a common ground to which one willingly belongs."[11] At this stage of my journey, it is more than enough.

Pauline's baby squeaks, so she rocks and sings softly to him. I look at the sun on his pink forehead, his left fist reaching free from the blankets. He, too, may be part of the mystery of Walnut Creek, this experiment in the unknown. If Pauline stays with the refuge, her son will grow up with the bluestem and the buffalo and the elk — a wild Iowa I never knew as a child. He will wander among the tallgrass, perhaps become lost in it a time or two. He will gather prairie seeds and plant them and eat them. He will witness, again and again, the gathering of Iowans and others on this healing land to celebrate, at last, its native beauty. This prairie may also come to inhabit his dreams, transforming his identity. If so, how will it shape him? It will, I hope, make him alert with joy and wonder and freedom. But will it also teach him humility, commitment, and a deep, unshakable love for life outside himself?

There is no way to tell right now and perhaps, like Molly Beattie, we will not be here to see the story unfold. If so, if I am not here to see it, I hold to the writer's naive hope that my words will remain, that some account of this moment will be available for Pauline's child — for my own future children — to pick up and read. But that may not be the case. So I hold to another, more enduring hope: that at Walnut Creek, in hillsides full of purple coneflowers and black-eyed Susans, in the vast expanses of native grass, there will remain the evidence of how we touched, briefly, the land here. That the bison and elk — the whole wild, beloved community — might be here as well, to awaken the land in their own ways, to call us all back, year after year after year, to bloom again in the prairie sun.

Notes

1. THE FIRST MIRACLE OF THE PRAIRIE

1. The term "grassland," as it is used throughout the book, will refer to places — both urban and rural — that were dominated by a native ecology of grass at the time of European settlement. "Prairie" is also used, though many scientists today apply this term only to native tallgrass prairies. I apply the term more liberally because at the time the distinction meant very little to me. Also, though many of the grasslands I visited were severely degraded or consisted mainly of "secondary" and invasive growth (such as Buffalo Gap), elements of the native grasslands ecosystems remained. By still referring to these places as grasslands or prairies, I hope to call attention to that larger ecological heritage, no matter how diminished.

2. These lists of tribes and their activities were gathered from Manning, *Grassland*, 69.

3. The statistical data listed here and elsewhere, unless otherwise noted, represents a compilation of different sources collected between 1994 and 1997. I am especially indebted to the research conducted by Richard Manning, John Madson, Osha Gray Davidson, Elliott West, Janette Thompson, Tom McHugh, and James Dinsmore. Their books are cited in the bibliography.

4. Thompson, *Prairies, Forests, and Wetlands*, 5.

5. Nancy S. Foster and Scott E. Hygnstrom, eds., *Prairie Dogs and Their Ecosystem*. Brochure distributed at National Grasslands Visitor Center, Wall SD, in June 1994.

6. West, *The Way West*, 86.

7. West, *The Way West*, 86–87.

8. Cooper, *The Prairie*, 11.

9. Irving, *A Tour on the Prairies*, 145–46, 271; Parkman, *The Oregon Trail*, 208.

10. Pike quoted in Flores, "A Long Love Affair with an Uncommon Country," 3; Butler quoted in Gayton, *Landscapes of the Interior*, 97; Dickens, *American Notes and Pictures from Italy*, 182–83; Cooper, *The Prairie*, 24.

11. Leopold, *Sand County Almanac*, 54.

12. Stegner, *Bluebird*, 203; Thacker, *The Great Prairie Fact and Literary Imagination*, 188; Sanders, *Writing from the Center*, 40; Manning, *Grassland*, 195–96.

13. Stegner, *Bluebird*, 206; Worster, *Under Western Skies*, 18; Berry, *A Continuous Harmony*, 67.

14. Kittredge, *Who Owns the West?* 98; Garland, *Crumbling Idols*, 12–13, 53–54, 30.

15. Garland, *Son*, 400, 414, 440.

16. Garland, *Son*, 416; McCullough, *Hamlin Garland*, 26.

17. "change the"–"live away": Garland quoted in Johnson, introduction, xxvii; "pen had": Garland, *Son*, 464.

18. "an intellectual"–"democratic art": Garland quoted in McCullough, *Hamlin Garland*, 28; Fuller quoted in McCullough, *Hamlin Garland*, 29.

19. "the warm sun": Garland, *Son*, 78; "something sweet": Garland, *Son*, 188; "The prairies": Garland, *Prairie Songs*, 3; "[T]he garden": Garland, *Son*, 105; "had vanished"–"all gone!": Garland, *Boy Life*, 388.

20. "till the coulee": Garland, *Son*, 67; Castañeda quoted in Jordan, "Playing God on the Lawns of the Lord," 115–16; "We'll meet": Garland, *Boy Life*, 389.

21. "[w]ithout a complex": Berry, *A Continuous Harmony*, 68–69; "[o]ne's relationship": Berry, *Recollected Essays*, 337.

22. Worster, *Under Western Skies*, 253.

23. Jackson, *Becoming Native to This Place*.

24. Kroetsch quoted in Thacker, *The Great Prairie Fact and Literary Imagination*, 188.

2. REACHING YARAK

1. O'Brien, *Rites*, 3, 4.

2. Dan O'Brien, "Notes," *Western American Literature* 30 (May 1995): 91.

3. O'Brien has since published two nonfiction books on the subject: *Equinox* and *Buffalo for the Broken Heart*.

4. O'Brien, *Rites*, 9–10, 21.

5. O'Brien, *Rites*, 170.

6. "affection": O'Brien, *Rites*, 55; "Peregrines and men": O'Brien, *Rites*, 30; "the same" and "[Peregrines] nest": O'Brien, *Rites*, 31.

7. "affinity and": Wilson paraphrased in Carpenter, "Living with Nature," 62; "open, grassy": Holmes, "Beyond Beauty," 67; "an enormous": Wilson quoted in Carpenter, "Living with Nature," 62; Orr, "Love It or Lose It," 12.

8. O'Brien, *Rites*, 18, 32–33.

9. Manning, *Grassland*, 73; "last of": O'Brien, *Rites*, 115; "John Colter": O'Brien, *Rites*, 21; "What made": O'Brien, *Rites*, 116; "[Kris] had": O'Brien, *Rites*, 181.

10. "We had begun" and "is not": O'Brien, *Rites*, 61; "very much like": O'Brien, *Rites*, 116.

11. "she was": O'Brien, *Rites*, 169; "her migration": O'Brien, *Rites*, 184.
12. O'Brien, *Rites*, 185, 191–92.
13. Flores, "A Long Love Affair with an Uncommon Country," 15.
14. O'Brien now raises bison on the ranch, an experience he writes about in *Buffalo for the Broken Heart*.
15. O'Brien, *Equinox*.
16. Manning, *Grassland*, 136.
17. Russell, *Kill the Cowboy*, 79–80.
18. Audubon, *The Birds of America*, 36.
19. Dickey, "The Heaven of Animals," 32.

3. NOT JUST ANY LAND

1. Hasselstrom, *Going Over East*, 36.
2. Berry, *Recollected Essays*, 338; Ehrlich, *The Solace of Open Spaces*, 5.
3. Suckow quoted in Burns, *Kinship with the Land*, 142; Garland, *Son*, 154–55; Stegner, *Wolf Willow*, 24–25.
4. "Broad generalities": Hasselstrom, *Going Over East*, 105; "Merely traveling": Linda Hasselstrom, letter to John Price, January 10, 1995.
5. Hasselstrom, *Going Over East*, 4, 3.
6. "rancher's daughter": Hasselstrom, *Windbreak*, 10; "mow as much": Hasselstrom, "Broken-In Writer," 147.
7. Hasselstrom, *Going Over East*, 199.
8. "When I was divorced": Hasselstrom, *Land Circle*, 246; "need to": Hasselstrom, "Broken-In Writer," 150.
9. Hasselstrom, "Broken-In Writer," 155.
10. Hasselstrom, "Broken-In Writer," 155, 156, 157.
11. Hasselstrom, "Broken-In Writer," 156.
12. Hasselstrom, *Windbreak*, 160.
13. Hasselstrom, *Windbreak*, 29.
14. Hasselstrom, *Going Over East*, 8.
15. "try to explain": Hasselstrom, *Going Over East*, 10; "I love": Hasselstrom, *Going Over East*, 189–90; "When wind": Hasselstrom, *Going Over East*, 193; "What will I": Hasselstrom, *Going Over East*, 199.
16. "Suddenly": Hasselstrom, *Land Circle*, 158; "look beyond"–"around me": Hasselstrom, *Land Circle*, xiii; "I must learn": Hasselstrom, *Land Circle*, 132; "And what does": Hasselstrom, *Land Circle*, 156.
17. Hasselstrom, *Land Circle*, 218, 132, 177.
18. "The land": Hasselstrom, *Land Circle*, 89; "The female": Hasselstrom, *Land*

Circle, 226; "as to a sister": Hasselstrom, *Land Circle*, 244; "I wasn't born": Hasselstrom, *Land Circle*, 240–41.

19. Sandoz, *Old Jules*, viii; Kittredge, *Owning It All*, 173.
20. The revised version of Hasselstrom's manuscript has since been published as *Feels Like Far*. Page numbers and quotes are from this published edition.
21. Hasselstrom, "Broken-In Writer," 158, 162.
22. Hasselstrom, *Feels Like Far*, 226.
23. "Tears pour": Hasselstrom, *Feels Like Far*, 188; "its life": Hasselstrom, *Feels Like Far*, 186.
24. Thacker, *The Great Prairie Fact and Literary Imagination*, 2.
25. Hasselstrom, *Windbreak*, xiii.
26. Ryden, *Mapping the Invisible Landscape*, 222, 241.
27. Hasselstrom, *Going Over East*, 145.
28. Worster, *Under Western Skies*, 48.
29. Hasselstrom is referring to Frank and Deborah Popper, scholars of land-use geography at Rutgers University. For a more thorough discussion of their "buffalo commons" idea, see Matthews, *Where the Buffalo Roam*.
30. Berry, *What Are People For?* 84.
31. Hasselstrom, *Land Circle*, 89.
32. "The Only Place" can be found in Hasselstrom, *Land Circle*, 223–24.
33. Hasselstrom, *Land Circle*, 261.
34. Since our conversation, Linda has continued to live in Cheyenne. She has also continued to spend part of the year on the ranch, where she now hosts writing retreats for women at her home, Windbreak House.

4. NATIVE DREAMS

1. "For years": Heat-Moon, *PrairyErth*, 11 (hereafter, Heat-Moon, *PrairyErth*, will be cited as PE); "The Roniger": PE, 14.
2. Diamond, *Fertile Ground*, 9; Hasselstrom, *Land Circle*, 89; Holm, *Prairie Days*, 17.
3. PE, 27, 28.
4. Hogan quoted in Jensen, *Listening to the Land*, 128; PE, 118.
5. Most of this information was taken from an obituary of Ralph Trogdon on display at the Chase County Historical Society Museum in August 1994. The article has since been removed and I have been unable to locate publishing information. The hyphen in "Heat-Moon" was added after the publication of Heat-Moon's first book.
6. Heat-Moon, *Blue Highways*, 5.

7. Nuwer, "William Least Heat Moon," 83.

8. Plummer, "William Trogdon," 74.

9. "idea of"–"entered upon": Momaday, *The Names*, 97; "That dim": Momaday, *The Names*, 25.

10. PE, 14, 16.

11. PE, 74.

12. "[I]t was": PE, 282; "Tom's grand": PE, 287; "vassalage": PE, 428; "Christian farmers": PE, 585.

13. Padfield, "The Expendable Rural Community," 159; "morality, independence": Shortridge, *The Middle West*, 8; "America's technological"–"freedom": Shortridge, *The Middle West*, 11.

14. PE, 427.

15. "togetherness": PE, 323; "hellhole": PE, 319; "Podunk[s]": PE, 323; "If you're": PE, 320.

16. Lloyd Soyez: PE, 375; "I'm afraid": PE, 39; Fidel Ybarra: PE, 235.

17. "odious methods": PE, 56; "Except for": PE, 588; "We were": PE, 591.

18. "ruinous tension" and "blood quantums": PE, 587; "When the": PE, 40; "Some goddamn": PE, 239; "the mystic": PE, 240; "To [aboriginal people]": PE, 160.

19. "[p]eople connect": PE, 84; "[e]very major": PE, 109; "After the": PE, 110.

20. PE, 159.

21. "[g]ood people": PE, 112; "a rare" and "to put": PE, 111; "show people": PE, 112.

22. "experience still": Nora, "Between Memory and History," 7; "The American": PE, 266; "created by": Nora, "Between Memory and History," 19; "I carried": PE, 336.

23. "assess technology"–"naming them": PE, 499; "new Chase": PE, 500; "a new sense": PE, 502; "We've probably": PE, 503.

24. PE, 504.

25. "the Venerable"–"Native American name": PE, 608; "participatory"–"on history": PE, 610.

26. "Maybe this": PE, 616; "How do": PE, 612; "A circled": PE, 621–22.

27. PE, 118.

28. PE, 442.

29. I would find out later that in 1860 Lafayette contained the most slaves (6,374) of any county in the state. Source: "A Timeline of Lafayette County, Missouri: Before 1900," *Lafayette County Legacy: A Sourcebook of Lafayette County, Missouri History*, ed. Susan A. Echelmeier, 2000, 2001, 2002, http://www.geocities.com/susanresearcher/early.htm.

30. "This silent": Madson, *Where the Sky Began*, 38; "discovery of": Madson, *Where the Sky Began*, 37; "the net gain": Madson, *Where the Sky Began*, 50.
31. His name has been changed.
32. See Davidson, *Broken Heartland*, 101–23.
33. I have yet to find historical evidence of that particular murder, though I did find confirmation that in 1911 a group of Corder citizens "intimidated" a black family to leave town by "shooting shots into the air and setting off explosives." Source: "A Timeline of Lafayette County, Missouri: 1900–ON," *Lafayette County Legacy: A Sourcebook of Lafayette County, Missouri History*, ed. Susan A. Echelmeier, 2000, 2001, 2002, http://www.geocities .com/susanresearcher/later.htm.
34. Heat-Moon, *River-Horse*.
35. "William Trogdon" has since been removed from the title page of both *Blue Highways* and *PrairyErth*, though it is still mentioned in the author's biographical note for PE.
36. *Wichita Eagle*, August 19, 1994, p. 1.
37. PE, 162.
38. "Farm houses": PE, 55; "If you": PE, 110; Davidson, *Broken Heartland*, 109; "the beauty"–"natural diversity": PE, 111–12.
39. Helliker, "At One Time."
40. Jackson, *Becoming Native*, 54, 55.
41. "Countless writers": Jackson, *Becoming Native*, 96; Stegner quoted in Jackson, *Becoming Native*, 96–97.
42. Jackson, *Becoming Native*, 97, 98, 89.
43. Jackson, *Becoming Native*, 102, 60.
44. Mechem, "Home on the Range," 328.
45. Nelson, *Home on the Range*, 84–85.
46. PE, 363.
47. Berry, *Recollected Essays*, 337, 335–36.

5. A HEALING HOME

1. Swander, *Out of This World*, 16, 270. Hereafter, *Out of This World* will be cited as OTW.
2. This subtitle belongs to the original hardcover edition. The paperback title is *Out of This World: A Journey of Healing*. Page numbers are the same.
3. Swander, *Heaven-and-Earth House*, 24.
4. OTW, 6.
5. OTW, 12.
6. "voyeur": OTW, 7; Bender, *Plain and Simple*, xii.

7. "just too," "offended," and "normal": OTW, 22; She also stopped: OTW, 24.

8. OTW, 28–29.

9. "ultimately expand": OTW, 30; "primitive": OTW, 26; "of the whole": OTW, 107.

10. "shame ridden"–"coming back": OTW, 258; "My peers": OTW, 262–63.

11. "ravaged"–"finished off": OTW, 168–69; "haven[s]": OTW, 95; "reminders of": OTW, 208.

12. OTW, 163, 165–66.

13. "rage at": OTW, 168; Wes Jackson mentioned in OTW, 169; "All those [larger]": OTW, 158; "I try": OTW, 169–70.

14. OTW, 170.

15. Manning, Grassland, 249, 188.

16. Des Moines Register, April 23, 1996, p. 2A.

17. Leon Burmeister et al., "Selected Cancer Mortality and Farm Practices in Iowa," American Journal of Epidemiology 118 (1983): 1. Quoted in Davidson, Broken Heartland, 43.

18. Williams quoted in Jensen, Listening to the Land, 313; "Big changes": OTW, 170–71.

19. "that it is" and "that all of life": Manning, Grassland, 185.

20. "We shall never," "how to bring," and "from within": Leopold, Sand County Almanac, 210; "wind became": OTW, 274.

21. OTW, 105.

22. Quoted in Schwieder and Schwieder, A Peculiar People, 11.

23. "rail[ing]" and "rural emotional": OTW, 184; "Disability connects": OTW, 192.

24. Schwieder and Schwieder, A Peculiar People, 66–67.

25. Bradley quoted in Trimble and Williams, Testimony; "bear witness"–"be human": Williams quoted in Jensen, Listening to the Land, 320–21.

26. Foster and Swander, The Healing Circle.

27. Swander, Heaven-and-Earth House, 28.

28. OTW, 253–54.

29. OTW, 255.

6. WHAT THIS PRAIRIE WILL AWAKEN

1. The name has since been changed to Neal Smith National Wildlife Refuge.

2. Dinsmore, A Country So Full of Game, 14.

3. Manning, Grassland, 239.

4. Thompson, Prairies, Forests, and Wetlands, 7, 9.

5. Leopold, *Sand County Almanac*, 49.

6. *Des Moines Register*, May 16, 1993.

7. Leopold, *Sand County Almanac*, 251.

8. Christine Ross and Sheldon Danzinger, "Poverty Rates by State, 1979 and 1985: A Research Note," *Focus*, University of Wisconsin — Madison, Institute for Research on Poverty (fall 1987): 1–5. Quoted in Davidson, *Broken Heartland*, 9.

9. Davidson, *Broken Heartland*, 59, 190.

10. "a growing"–"central Iowa": Bauer, *Prairie City, Iowa*, 18–19; "has never seemed": Bauer, "The Way the Country Lies," 57; "It's neither": Bauer, "The Way the Country Lies," 65.

11. "beloved community": Berry, *What Are People For?* 78; "the individual": Berry, *What Are People For?* 85; "pariah or": Berry, *What Are People For?* 86; "the tragic imagination": Berry, *What Are People For?* 78; "common experience": Berry, *What Are People For?* 85.

Bibliography

Audubon, John James. *The Birds of America.* With a Foreword and Descriptive Captions by William Vogt. 1827–30. New York: Macmillan, 1941.

Bauer, Douglas. *Prairie City, Iowa: Three Seasons at Home.* Ames: Iowa State University Press, 1979.

———. "The Way the Country Lies." In *A Place of Sense: Essays in Search of the Midwest,* ed. Michael Martone. Iowa City: University of Iowa Press, 1988.

Bender, Sue. *Plain and Simple: A Woman's Journey to the Amish.* San Francisco: Harper Collins, 1989.

Berry, Wendell. *A Continuous Harmony: Essays Cultural and Agricultural.* New York: Harcourt Brace Jovanovich, 1972.

———. *Recollected Essays: 1965–1980.* San Francisco: North Point Press, 1981.

———. *What Are People For?* San Francisco: North Point Press, 1990.

Brown, Dee. *Bury My Heart at Wounded Knee: An Indian History of the American West.* New York: Holt, Rinehart, and Winston, 1971.

Burns, E. Bradford. *Kinship with the Land: Regionalist Thought in Iowa, 1894–1942.* Iowa City: University of Iowa Press, 1996.

Carpenter, Betsy. "Living with Nature: E. O. Wilson Argues That Species Extinction Threatens the Human Spirit." *U.S. News & World Report,* November 30, 1992, pp. 61–67.

Cather, Willa. *My Ántonia.* 1918. Boston: Houghton-Mifflin, 1995.

———. *O Pioneers!* 1913. New York: Penguin, 1989.

Cooper, James Fenimore. *The Prairie.* 1827. New York: Penguin, 1964.

Davidson, Osha Gray. *Broken Heartland: The Rise of America's Rural Ghetto.* 1990. Iowa City: University of Iowa Press, 1996.

Diamond, Irene. *Fertile Ground: Women, Earth, and the Limits of Control.* Boston: Beacon, 1994.

Dickens, Charles. *American Notes and Pictures from Italy.* 1842, 1846. Oxford: Oxford University Press, 1987.

Dickey, James. "The Heaven of Animals." In *James Dickey: The Selected Poems,* ed. Robert Kirschten. Hanover NH: Wesleyan University Press, 1998.

Dinsmore, James J. *A Country So Full of Game: The Story of Wildlife in Iowa.* Iowa City: University of Iowa Press, 1994.

Ehrlich, Gretel. *The Solace of Open Spaces.* New York: Penguin, 1985.

Flores, Dan. "A Long Love Affair with an Uncommon Country: Environmental History and the Great Plains." In *Prairie Conservation: Preserving North*

America's Most Endangered Ecosystem, ed. Fred B. Samson and Fritz L. Knopf. Washington DC: Island Press, 1996.

Ford, Richard. *Rock Springs.* New York: Vintage, 1988.

Foster, Patricia, and Mary Swander, eds. *The Healing Circle: Authors Writing of Recovery.* New York: Plume, 1998.

Frazier, Ian. *Great Plains.* New York: Farrar, Straus, Giroux, 1989.

Garland, Hamlin. *Boy Life on the Prairie.* New York: Harper and Brothers, 1899.

————. *Crumbling Idols.* 1894. Cambridge MA: Harvard University Press, 1960.

————. *Main-Travelled Roads.* 1891. New York: Signet, 1962.

————. *Prairie Songs.* Chicago: Stone and Kimball, 1893.

————. *A Son of the Middle Border.* New York: Macmillan, 1917.

Gayton, Don. *Landscapes of the Interior: Re-Explorations of Nature and the Human Spirit.* Gabriola Island BC: New Society, 1996.

Gruchow, Paul. *Journal of a Prairie Year.* Minneapolis: University of Minnesota Press, 1985.

Hasselstrom, Linda. *Between Grass and Sky: Where I Live and Work.* Reno: University of Nevada Press, 2002.

————. *Feels Like Far: A Rancher's Life on the Great Plains.* 1999. New York: Mariner, 2001.

————. *Going Over East: Reflections of a Woman Rancher.* Golden CO: Fulcrum, 1987.

————. "How I Became a Broken-In Writer." In *Imagining Home: Writing from the Midwest,* ed. Mark Vinz and Thom Tammaro. Minneapolis: University of Minnesota Press, 1995.

————. *Land Circle: Writings Collected from the Land.* Golden CO: Fulcrum, 1991.

————. *Windbreak: A Woman Rancher on the Northern Plains.* Berkeley: Barn Owl Books, 1987.

Heat-Moon, William Least. *Blue Highways: A Journey into America.* Boston: Houghton Mifflin, 1982.

————. *PrairyErth (a deep map).* Boston: Houghton Mifflin, 1991.

————. *River-Horse: The Logbook of a Boat across America.* New York: Penguin, 2001.

Helliker, Kevin. "At One Time, Homes on the Range Never Heard Discouraging Words." *Wall Street Journal,* March 20, 1992, p. 1.

Holm, Bill. *Prairie Days.* San Francisco: Saybrook, 1987.

Holmes, Bob. "Beyond Beauty: Nature Soothes Body and Soul." *U.S. News & World Report,* November 30, 1992, p. 67.

Irving, Washington. *A Tour on the Prairies.* 1835. Alexandria VA: Time-Life, 1983.

Jackson, Wes. *Becoming Native to This Place.* Lexington: University of Kentucky Press, 1994.

Jensen, Derrick. *Listening to the Land: Conversations about Nature, Culture, and Eros.* San Francisco: Sierra Club, 1995.

Johnson, Jane. Introduction to *Crumbling Idols*, by Hamlin Garland. Cambridge MA: Harvard University Press, 1960.

Jordan, Teresa. "Playing God on the Lawns of the Lord (Osage County, Oklahoma)." In *Heart of the Land: Essays on Last Great Places*, ed. Joseph Barbato and Lisa Weinerman. New York: Vintage, 1994.

———. *Riding the White Horse Home: A Western Family Album.* New York: Vintage, 1993.

Kittredge, William. *Owning It All.* Saint Paul MN: Graywolf Press, 1987.

———. *Who Owns the West?* San Francisco: Mercury House, 1996.

Leopold, Aldo. *A Sand County Almanac.* 1949. New York: Ballantine, 1984.

Madson, John. *Where the Sky Began: Land of the Tallgrass Prairie.* San Francisco: Sierra Club, 1982.

Manfred, Frederick. *Lord Grizzly.* New York: Penguin, 1954.

Manning, Richard. *Grassland: The History, Biology, Politics, and Promise of the American Prairie.* New York: Viking, 1995.

Matthews, Anne. *Where the Buffalo Roam: The Storm Over the Revolutionary Plan to Restore America's Great Plains.* New York: Grove Weidenfeld, 1992.

McCullough, Joseph B. *Hamlin Garland.* Boston: Twayne, 1978.

McHugh, Tom. *The Time of the Buffalo.* Lincoln: University of Nebraska Press, 1972.

Mechem, Kirke. "Home on the Range." *Kansas Historical Quarterly* 17 (1949): 313–39.

Momaday, N. Scott. *The Names.* Tucson: University of Arizona Press, 1976.

Nelson, Margaret A. *Home on the Range.* Boston: Chapman and Grimes, 1947.

Nora, Pierre. "Between Memory and History: Les Lieux de Mémoire." *Representations* 26 (1989): 7–25.

Norris, Kathleen. *Dakota: A Spiritual Geography.* New York: Ticknor and Fields, 1993.

Nuwer, Hank. "William Least Heat Moon: The Road to Serendipity." *Rendezvous: Journal of Arts and Letters* 21, no 1 (1985): 79–91.

O'Brien, Dan. *Brendan Prairie: A Novel.* New York: Scribner, 1996.

———. *Buffalo for the Broken Heart: Restoring Life to a Black Hills Ranch.* New York: Random House, 2001.

———. *The Contract Surgeon.* New York: Lyons Press, 1999.

———. *Eminent Domain.* New York: Crown, 1987.

———. *Equinox: Life, Love, and Birds of Prey.* New York: Lyons and Buford, 1997.

———. *In the Center of the Nation.* New York: Atlantic Monthly Press, 1991.

———. *The Rites of Autumn: A Falconer's Journey across the American West.* 1988. New York: Anchor Books, 1989.

———. *Spirit of the Hills.* New York: Crown, 1988.

Orr, David. "Love It or Lose It: The Coming Biophilia Revolution." *Orion* 13 (winter 1994): 8–15.

Padfield, Harland. "The Expendable Rural Community and the Denial of Powerlessness." In *The Dying Community,* ed. Art Gallaher, Jr. and Harland Padfield. Albuquerque: University of New Mexico Press, 1980.

Parkman, Francis, Jr. *The Oregon Trail.* 1849. New York: Penguin, 1982.

Plummer, William. "William Trogdon Takes to America's Back Roads and Returns a New Man—William Least Heat Moon." *People Weekly* 18 (April 1983): 72–73.

Russell, Sharman Apt. *Kill the Cowboy: A Battle of Mythology in the New West.* New York: Addison-Wesley, 1993.

Ryden, Kent C. *Mapping the Invisible Landscape: Folklore, Writing, and the Sense of Place.* Iowa City: University of Iowa Press, 1993.

Sanders, Scott Russell. *Writing from the Center.* Bloomington: Indiana University Press, 1995.

Sandoz, Mari. *Old Jules.* 1935. Lincoln: University of Nebraska Press, 1985.

Schwieder, Elmer, and Dorothy Schwieder. *A Peculiar People: Iowa's Old Order Amish.* Ames: Iowa State University Press, 1975.

Shortridge, James. *The Middle West: Its Meaning in American Culture.* Lawrence: University Press of Kansas, 1989.

Smiley, Jane. *A Thousand Acres.* New York: Knopf, 1992.

Stegner, Wallace. *Beyond the Hundredth Meridian.* 1954. New York: Penguin, 1992.

———. *Where the Bluebird Sings to the Lemonade Springs: Living and Writing in the West.* New York: Penguin, 1992.

———. *Wolf Willow: A History, a Story, and a Memory of the Last Plains Frontier.* 1962. Lincoln: University of Nebraska Press, 1980.

Swander, Mary. *Driving the Body Back.* New York: Knopf, 1986.

———. *Heaven-and-Earth House.* New York: Knopf, 1994.

———. *Out of This World: A Woman's Life among the Amish.* New York: Viking, 1995.

———. *Parsnips in the Snow: Talks with Midwestern Gardeners.* Iowa City: University of Iowa Press, 1990.

Thacker, Robert. *The Great Prairie Fact and Literary Imagination.* Albuquerque: University of New Mexico Press, 1989.

Thompson, Janette R. *Prairies, Forests, and Wetlands: The Restoration of Natural Landscape Communities in Iowa.* Iowa City: University of Iowa Press, 1992.

Trimble, Stephen, and Terry Tempest Williams, eds. *Testimony: Writers of the West Speak on Behalf of Utah Wilderness.* Minneapolis: Milkweed, 1996.

West, Elliott. *The Way West: Essays on the Central Plains.* Albuquerque: University of New Mexico Press, 1995.

Williams, Terry Tempest. *Refuge: An Unnatural History of Family and Place.* New York: Pantheon, 1991.

Worster, Donald. *Under Western Skies: Nature and History in the American West.* New York: Oxford University Press, 1992.

Young Bear, Ray A. *Black Eagle Child: The Facepaint Narratives.* Iowa City: University of Iowa Press, 1992.

DATE DUE

GAYLORD			PRINTED IN U.S.A.